Spotlight
on
Transition to Teaching
Music

MENC MENC
MENC MENC
The National Association for Music Education

*MENC would like to thank the MEA state editors throughout the country,
who oversee and facilitate the distribution
of essential information to MENC members in their states.*

Production Editor: Elizabeth Pontiff
Assistant Production Editor: Andrea Keating

Contents

Appendix:

The *Spotlight* series comprises articles that have appeared in magazines of MENC affiliates over the past several years. The purpose of the series is to broaden the audience for the valuable work that is being done by music educators across the country. Were it not for the dedication of the state editors and article authors, this series would not be possible. MENC would like to thank these individuals for their contributions and to encourage others to share their expertise through MEA and MENC publications.

Introduction

Reports indicate that in many states, music positions are unfilled because no qualified applicants are available or they are filled by teachers who do not have a degree in music education. Thirty to 50 percent of new teachers who work in urban areas leave the field in their first three years of service. To assure continued quality music instruction, MENC must work within its own programs and activities and in collaboration with others to recruit more and better teachers to music education, nurture new teachers, and continue to support and energize veteran teachers.

—MENC Strategic Plan, July 2002

While the problem of retaining qualified classroom teachers continues, the music education profession is still vibrant and growing.[1] But, today's music educators face new and difficult challenges daily. What can you do to help your profession? *Spotlight on Transition to Teaching Music* contains a variety of ideas from those involved in music education at all levels. This latest addition to the Spotlight collection looks at this and related questions and offers answers culled from MENC members everywhere.

Many people are unaware that there is a teacher shortage, and that fewer teachers are entering the field and many are either retiring or leaving after only a few years. Did you know that CMENC and Tri-M can encourage students to become music educators and provide them their first opportunities to actually experience teaching?

Budding music educators are prepared for the classroom during their college years. What do they learn? What do they need to know? Can they make it through the often demanding course work and student teaching?

Once in the classroom, these new educators struggle with a host of issues never mentioned in their methods classes, from filling out paperwork to figuring out how the music library is organized. If they are lucky, they find a mentor—someone, either part of an official program or not, who guides them through their first years of teaching, providing lesson ideas, tricks, inspiration, or just a shoulder to cry on. Could this mentor be you?

Beyond this lies the realm of accomplishment and experience that makes teaching music worthwhile. Unfortunately, many teachers reach burnout in only a few years and forget that they joined this profession to share their passion for music with others (and get paid for it). Is there a way to prevent this and provide needed encouragement?

We must all work to encourage young people to join us in teaching music and be sure that those who have already begun their careers receive the support they need to keep going. *Spotlight on Transition to Teaching Music* is filled with ideas from fellow classroom teachers, preservice music educators, music supervisors, and even music education students to help recruit, retain, and encourage those involved in passing the knowledge and love of music on to the next generation.

Notes

1. American Association for Employment in Education, Educator Supply and Demand in the United States (accessed February 2004 from www.ub-careers.buffalo.edu /aaee/S_DReport2000.pdf).

Section 1

Is there a teacher shortage?

 Section 1

Is there a teacher shortage?

Teacher Shortage: Salaries and a Whole Lot More
Brian Anderson

I have recently read with great interest the newspaper articles, editorials, and letters to the editor concerning our state's newest educational crisis. We have a teacher shortage, and everyone has an opinion on how to solve the problem. Education associations believe that many factors, including time, better working conditions, and lack of respect for the profession need to be improved, but offer an increase in teacher's salaries as the primary measure to solve this complex problem. Taxpayers and legislators offer a variety of opinions on this and the other important issues facing education. Incredibly, everyone who is quoted in the media claims to have the best interests of the students of Nebraska in mind, and their method will solve the crisis we now face.

Actually, the teacher shortage in Nebraska is nothing new. Professional organizations have predicted this problem for a number of years. We have reached the point, however, where the low numbers of new teachers entering the profession combined with the high numbers of experienced teachers taking early retirement or leaving the profession altogether, has left us in dire straits. Sadly, we can no longer fill all of the music positions in Nebraska. You can find an advertisement for a music position in each and every *Sunday World-Herald*, and this past year, I have received an average of three to four phone calls per month from schools in search of a music teacher.

You may think, as I did initially, that this could possibly be good for music education in our state. If school systems cannot find enough music teachers, they will have to come up with innovative methods of recruiting new teachers including better working conditions, increased administrative and community support for music, and increased salaries. Right? Upon reflection, however, I believe school systems may choose to place music in a lower academic status or completely remove it

from the curriculum. Will school systems struggling to find a music teacher continue the good fight for their students if it is so difficult to find a qualified music teacher? I believe some may choose to hire noncertified personnel or reduce music positions to half- or part-time, a practice that is already happening in some areas of the state. Any way you look at it, this has the potential to be devastating to music education in Nebraska.

How do we solve this complex problem? It will take a combined effort of all the stakeholders: educators, administrators, parents, students, communities, legislators, and other decision makers. A salary increase is, I believe, necessary, but is not the only obstacle to recruiting and retaining quality teachers. While many people not familiar with education may believe that teachers work 8:00 a.m. to 4:00 p.m. nine months of the year, we know the real story. Teachers work long hours, and music teachers, in particular, are called upon to work nights, weekends, and in some cases, summers just to meet the performance demands of the community. When these heavy demands are combined with other frivolous duties such as cheerleading or prom sponsor, it leaves little time for family or other social activities. Making sure that music teachers are not tied down by these extra duties and are given ample time to plan will help.

Teachers went into this profession to make a difference in helping students learn and find a love for learning. This rarely happens in supervisory duties such as study halls, lunch duty, and patrolling the school parking lots. Relieving teachers of these duties will go a long way to improving working conditions. You would never ask your doctor to patrol the hospital cafeteria, yet teachers are expected to do this on a daily basis. If teaching is to receive the same professional respect it deserves, teachers must be relieved from these mundane and meaningless duties.

Increased professional respect for teachers is another step in recruiting and retaining teachers. You would not trust your health to anyone but a doctor, or your legal well being to anyone but a lawyer, yet in today's world, everyone knows how to teach better than the trained professionals. Any parent or taxpayer feels it is his or her obligation to question a teacher on classroom curriculum, methods, or assessment, while in numerous cases, teacher support from administrators in this area is eroding. Our students, the potential next generation of teachers, witness this and look for another vocation to pursue.

As music teachers, we must continue our advocacy efforts to let our communities and decision makers know how important music is in the education of our students. Advocacy is an ongoing process, but you will never know how important it is until you need it. Teaching students is the easy part; it is teaching parents, guidance counselors, administrators, and taxpayers that is the most difficult aspect of your job. Work in this area will yield a valuable network of support in times of trouble.

We must identify and recruit our best and brightest music students to become music teachers. Yes, a salary increase would help, but we cannot count on that in the present or the future. As music educators, we must instill and nurture in our students the same love we feel for music, then encourage them to spread this love and fulfillment to the next generation. Nebraska's music associations are coming up with incentives to help in student recruiting. Scholarships for high school music students and college student teachers from NMEA, NSBA, and others will hopefully help to fill this void.

Yes, Nebraska and the entire nation are in the middle of a teacher shortage, and yes, it will take a combined effort from everyone to solve this crisis. I urge you to become active to keep our profession moving forward, and to keep music a viable and crucial component of every child's education. The time is now, the next move is ours.

This article first appeared in the April 2000 issue of the Nebraska Music Educator. *Reprinted by permission.*

More Students, Fewer Teachers = Teacher Shortage
Carolynn A. Lindeman

As the coordinator of music education at a large, urban university, I receive calls weekly from music teachers who have been issued a temporary music credential and want information on how they can become permanently certified through our university's credential program. I also receive calls from school principals, music coordinators, and human resource directors asking for help in finding and hiring music teachers. The reason for this flurry of telephone activity is simple—we have a serious music teacher shortage in California! As a result, many teachers are hired without the requisite papers, and some music teaching positions are left unfilled.

California is not the only state where this teacher shortage is in full swing. States such as Alaska, Connecticut, Florida, and Oregon are experiencing the same phenomenon. The shortage is projected to become even worse in the next decade, with two million new teachers needed nationwide. More students and fewer teachers appear to be the principal reasons for the shortage. Here are some facts about the booming enrollments and the teacher shortage.

More Students
By the year 2007, schools in the United States will educate over two million more students than they do today. This booming enrollment is a result of rising birth rates in the 1990s and has been affectionately christened the baby boom echo. In a report released by the U.S. Department of Education, it is noted that K–12 school enrollments (elementary and secondary public and private schools) for the 1997–98 school year reached an all-time high of 52.2 million. The projection is that by the year 2007, that number will climb to 54.3 million.[1]

Fewer Teachers
While the student enrollments grow, more and more teachers are reaching retirement age and leaving the profession. According to The National Center for Education Statistics, as of the 1993–94 school year, one quarter of all public-school teachers were 50 or over.[2] A 1996 National Education Association survey revealed that 46.1 percent of teachers began teaching more than two decades ago.[3] With 200,000 more teachers needed per year over the next decade, this graying of the profession creates an obvious challenge.

The challenge cannot be met solely, however, by new music education graduates entering the teaching profession. According to the latest Higher

Education Arts Data Services (HEADS) summary, 3,300 music education bachelor degrees were awarded in 1995–96.[4] These data indicate clearly that there are not enough new music educators entering the teaching ranks to take the places of the retiring teachers, let alone to meet the needs of the additional students.

Attracting Teachers

Put all of these facts about students and teachers together and you can see that we have a major challenge on our hands. Attracting (and retaining) fine music teachers will be a number-one priority for our profession for the next few years. The good news is that teaching as a profession will surely get more play, and that could mean higher salaries and more benefits.

Some school districts and states are trying a variety of financial incentives to entice teachers to their geographic area. For example, Dallas offered a $1,500 signing bonus to new teachers. Baltimore paid teachers $5,000 to buy a house in the city, plus $1,200 in moving expenses.[5] Obviously, while these cash offers may be attractive, the real goal should be to entice qualified and capable teachers to the profession.

Here is where we as music educators come in. As school music teachers, we have a built-in opportunity to encourage students to study music and prepare to be teachers. We must let our middle school, high school, and college students (yes, even the performance majors!) know that music teaching is a viable and rewarding career. We have to attract our best and brightest to become professional music educators and begin as early as possible to offer them multiple opportunities to develop the needed skills.

In addition, as this crisis escalates, we must be proactive in ensuring that qualified, credentialed music teachers are in our classrooms. With a shortage as severe as this, a warm body in every classroom may become the focus. This is obviously unacceptable. Unqualified teachers can spell the end to many school music programs. Instead we must encourage school districts and licensing agencies to keep their standards high. We want music educators in our classrooms of today and tomorrow who demonstrate the best in subject matter knowledge and teaching know-how. Our students deserve no less!

Notes

1. U.S. Department of Education, National Center for Education Statistics, "The Impact of the Baby Boom Echo on U.S. Public School Enrollments" (Washington, DC: October 1997).

2. June Kronholz, "Teacher Retirements Portend Acute Shortage," *Wall Street Journal* (24 July 1997): B1, B9.

3. Jeff Archer, "NEA's Portrait of a Public School Teacher: White, Female, Aging," *Education Week*, 9 July 1997.

4. Higher Education Arts Data Services, Music, "Data Summaries 1996–97." Information available from HEADS, 11250 Roger Bacon Drive, Suite 21, Reston, VA 20191.

5. "Preparing Two Million: How Districts and States Attract and Retain Teachers," *Education Update* 41, 1, January 1999.

This article originally appeared in the Spring 1999 issue of Europe's EMEA Journal. Reprinted by permission.

There Is a Music Teacher Shortage in Arizona—I May Have Caused It!!!

Larry Mabbitt

It pains me to admit this, but I think I caused the music teacher shortage in Arizona. As I was reflecting back the other day (it seems the older I get, the more that sort of thing happens), I remembered a time or two hundred when I talked with kids about being a music teacher.

As I mulled through my memories, I seemed to faintly recall incidents when I may have been really tired (everyone who teaches music knows about that). Or, I may have been upset with my administrator(s) (everyone who teaches music knows about that). Or I might have been upset with a recent performance (everyone who teaches music knows about that). Or I may have just been in a (expletive deleted) mood (some who teach music know about that).

I faintly remember talking about long hours, low pay, lack of respect, lack of understanding, lack of financial support, and frustrations over my feeder schools. (Everyone knows about one or the other of the things on that list.)

What really bothered me was that I wasn't all that clear on what I may have said about the joys of teaching great people about music. I may not have remembered to tell them about the tremendous satisfaction of watching one of my twenty-eight ensembles really do well at the Solo and Ensemble Festival, the pride and joy I felt watching my kids perform in the All-State Festival, or the elation I felt sitting at an ASU concert, realizing that 28 percent of those kids on stage were my former students.

I am sure I failed to say that my pay carried with it health insurance, dental insurance, vision insurance, and sick leave. I probably failed to talk about the benefit of having most of my way paid to attend conferences where I came home with two thousand great ideas, some of which I actually put into practice. I'm sure I forgot to mention my professional peers who supported, challenged, and helped me grow both personally and professionally. I probably didn't mention the great camaraderie of being with other music teachers at festivals, conferences, and concerts. I'll bet I didn't mention the ever enlarging circle of people I could call close friends because of my professional association with them.

I know I never mentioned the great time I had with colleagues as I served in a variety of roles in AMEA, MENC, AAAE, etc. I probably just blabbered something about "another lost Saturday." And I for darn sure failed to say a word about the great satisfaction I felt working with my colleagues around the state as we tackled tough problems and found darn good solutions for them.

What was I thinking? Here, right in front of me, was a kid contemplating following in my professional path. This kid had an entire life to live, an entire career to fulfill, a chance to have all the great experiences I had, a chance to become my colleague. *And I blew it.*

As the vice-president of professional growth, I am disgusted with those memories; those lost-forever opportunities. I feel I owe every music teacher in Arizona, every principal still looking for a music teacher, and every kid without a music teacher an apology.

I know that none of you have ever exhibited such despicable behavior. So, I know now, it is all my fault. Geeze, I am so sorry. I will do better. Please make this promise to me if you hear me saying negative things about my life as a music educator: tap me (that's *tap*) on my shoulder and ask me, "Has it really been all that bad?"

I will be embarrassed, I will probably turn red, and I will apologize and then start to tell the truth. Thanks for your help. And, once again, I apologize for causing all this trouble.

This article originally appeared in the Winter 2000 issue of the Arizona Music News. *Reprinted by permission.*

How can we recruit and retain more music teachers?

 Section 2

How can we recruit and retain more music teachers?

What Happens to Our Beginning Teachers?

Dwayne Dunn

As was stated in this column in the Fall 1999 issue of *Arizona Music News*, I want to devote this space to issues contributing to the shortage of certified music teachers in our state. Last issue we mentioned some of the broad factors that affect music education students, university music education curricula, employment conditions, opportunities in education, and young teaching professionals. Perhaps it would be helpful to look at some specific cases in an attempt to "put a face" on the problems.

Although the names and details have been changed, the following narratives are actual accounts of what can happen to music education graduates.

"Amy" was an excellent student, making nearly straight As in her college classes. She was an excellent violinist and probably could have chosen to major in performance studies except that she had a deep desire to be a teacher.

Although she had married just after completing high school, during her college years she had worked hard to prepare herself for the demands of the teaching profession. When she excitedly announced she would be expecting a baby during her student teaching semester, her family and teachers worried that she might not finish the degree for which she had worked so hard.

But, because she was organized and prepared, Amy was able to negotiate successfully the challenges of pregnancy and student teaching. She even returned several weeks after the baby was born to make up the end of her student teaching semester. Although she graduated as one of the most promising teachers in her class, Amy chose to invest her time in her family as wife and mother rather than accept a teaching position right away. She hopes to begin her teaching career some day,

when her children are older.

"Mike" came from Michigan to study music in Arizona after choosing not to attend college right after high school. He had been influenced by a music teacher, Daniel, who had studied in Arizona a few years ago. Daniel sold Mike on the quality of music instruction available and the beauty of living in Arizona.

While studying here, Mike became involved and connected in the community through school, church, and social outlets. He met a beautiful young woman and they planned to marry after he graduated. Because he was a bit older and more mature than many of his classmates, Mike was always seen as a thoughtful and serious music student, with high prospects for success as a choral conductor.

Furthermore, he was excited to stay in Arizona, where his fiancee's family lived, when he heard of several secondary choral openings in the area. Although he had glowing recommendations and successful interviews, Mike was not offered any of the high school or middle school choral jobs in the area; these were filled by "in-district" transfers despite the objections of principals, students, and parents. The only job Mike could find was teaching elementary strings and general music, which he accepted.

Despite working outside of his primary area of training, Mike was pretty successful during his first year, but jumped at the opportunity to teach what he really wanted—middle school and high school choir—back home in Michigan. The sad thing is, many of the local choral jobs he was excited to take have changed teachers two or three times since he left the state.

Although he was a pretty fair trumpeter, "Bret" was always a better teacher than performer. He really excelled in front of students, with strong managerial and administrative skills. He was excellent at keeping students on task and motivating them to work hard in music. His life had not been an easy one. He had a rocky relationship with his parents, often not speaking to them for months at a time. He had been through several difficult, even abusive relationships, but was now stronger and wiser.

Because he received no help from home, he had to work thirty hours per week at a local hospital to support himself while in school. Despite tight finances and a schedule that allowed no personal time, Bret maintained a solid B average and was surprisingly successful as a student teacher, even though he still had to work fifteen hours per week to make ends meet.

Five weeks before student teaching ended, the hospital where he worked offered him a full-time position at $33,000 per year to begin immediately after he graduated. Although he loved teaching, the salary of a starting teacher was not much more than the money he had made working part-time during college. He decided that financially the hospital position was the best choice for him.

The point of these anecdotes is to illustrate that sometimes our best, most promising graduates do not end up becoming Arizona music teachers, despite our best efforts. Personal decisions, family situations, background, union rules, available jobs, and teacher salaries may influence graduates in ways beyond our control.

This article first appeared in the Winter 2000 issue of the Arizona Music News. *Reprinted by permission.*

Teacher Shortage
Betty Ellis

By the year 2007, our profession will need a total of 123,500 choral, band, orchestra, and general music teachers in private and public schools. Statistically 6,000 music teachers leave the profession each year. A survey of MENC state presidents in August 1999 found that twenty-three states rank the teacher shortage as a high concern. Presently there are over 63,000 music teachers in the nation. A little over 5 percent of those teachers live in the Northwest.

Some of the news is actually good. In 1988 the ratio of student to music teacher was 548:1. In 1996 that had dropped to 469:1. There has been a 49 percent increase in graduates in all teaching fields since 1983, from 134,870 to 200,545.

The American Association for Employment in Education lists the status of many teaching fields in five categories ranging from "considerable surplus" to "considerable shortage." The 1997 report for the school year 96–97 finds an overall balance of music teacher supply and demand, although different regions vary somewhat, the Northwest as a region ranks in the "some shortage" category in both instrumental and vocal areas, whereas Alaska ranks separately in the "considerable shortage" category.

All of us must take some responsibility and help with possible solutions to the teacher shortage. What can we do? This past July, your representatives to the MENC National Assembly listed several possibilities.

1. Encourage support systems for beginning teachers. Many state associations have begun a mentoring program with various complexions, some offering stipends to retired teachers, some offering grants to new teachers, and some just pairing host and new teachers. Each of us can look out for a new teacher, take them to coffee, call them on the phone, seek them out at in-services, or go visit them at their school.

2. We must build stronger relationships between K–12 schools and teacher training institutions. MENC members could volunteer to be guest speakers in education and music classes to answer questions and give information about the teaching field. Many of you have given your time and energy to work with practicum students and student teachers. Form partnerships with CMENC chapters in your area. Two-way communication between higher education and K–12 educators is imperative for the profession. Many college performance majors have an unclear message about the value of a career in education. There are many fine examples of music educators who are also excellent and sought-after performers.

3. Provide encouragement and information to high school students. MENC members can serve as a resource to guidance counselors and give information on professional opportunities in the music education field. Participate in a school-to-work program and host a music student from the high school to work with strong middle school and elementary teachers. Give them guided teaching experiences in a safe and structured setting. High school directors, watch for students who show a potential gift for teaching and promote experiences for their growth in musical leadership. How many of you first considered a career in teaching music because of the role model of your own music teacher? Arrange for

someone to speak to your All-State performers, festival participants, and school performing groups about the possibility of a teaching career in music. Start a Tri-M chapter in your high school. The November report of active Tri-M chapters in the Northwest shows only Wyoming with an active Tri-M chapter. Last February I surveyed the students in the All-Northwest honors groups. I had an ulterior motive to spark the possibility of a future in music education in case they had not already done so. Of the students responding, 66 percent have considered teaching music. How many will actually follow through? What will they need to succeed?

4. Improve the image of teaching as a profession. Be a good teacher. Nothing sells music education better than a strong music program taught by a team of dedicated, inspirational teachers. Take the opportunity to show the public the positive impact of music education. Mentally prepare and help your colleagues prepare for those crisis points in the education field. Statistically we know that most teachers who leave the profession do so at the four-to-five year mark and the nine-to-ten year mark. If

you recognize the signs, you are more likely to persevere. If you recognize the signs in a colleague, help them through it. Part of being a good teacher is being an informed teacher. Keep current by reading publications, talking with colleagues, and sharing ideas. Attend professional conferences. Stay involved in professional organizations. But also, take care of yourself personally and emotionally. Begin that running program, that yoga class, or that trip to study ancient ruins that you have been putting off.

I went into teaching because I found music to be an intellectual, emotional, and creative outlet for my musical energies, and I wanted to share the joy, the challenge, and the discovery of learning with my students. I would go into teaching again without reservation or regrets. Why did you go into teaching? Have you shared that reason lately? Have you shared that commitment with your students? You never know how far-reaching your influence may be!!

This article originally appeared in the December 1999 issue of Wyoming's Windsong. *Reprinted by permission.*

Our Dilemma: Raising Music Teacher Preparation Standards and Increasing the Number of Graduates
Iris S. Levine

I believe we are united in our goal to have high standards for our music education students and have more music teachers in the schools. The question then is how do we achieve this and whose standards are to be raised?

It is my opinion, although it may not be a popular opinion, that the standards to be investigated are of us—the educators. To that end, I have a series of questions for each of us to ponder:

Am I a good role model?
Am I well educated in my subject matter?
Am I fair and humane in my classroom and assessment process?

Do I repeat the same repertoire? Do I perform a variety of styles including large works with instrumental accompaniment as well as a cappella short pieces? Do I include world music? Am I successful in presenting quality repertoire by both genders? Do I continuously research new works and engage my students when I search for repertoire so that they understand the frustrations and

excitement of the process?

Do I promote high standards by teaching my students score study, vocal health, diction, performance practice, rehearsal technique? Do I exhibit these attributes in my own rehearsal so students learn by my example?

Do I believe that the performance is the "end all," or is the process just, if not more, important? Do I advocate solfeggio and music reading knowing that my students may then do the same in their own classrooms? Do I encourage my students to listen to and follow others by bringing in guest conductors?

Am I well organized and do I clearly communicate expectations to my students? Do I make my students pass through inane rights of passage? Does my style invite students to ask questions or should they take my word as gospel?

Am I a caring, humane person who understands that students have strengths and weaknesses that may not coincide with mine? Do I advise my students based on what is best for each of them rather than what is best for me?

Am I a good role model by demanding the very best from myself as well as my students?

Do I discuss trends in choral music and alternative methods of choral education? Do I encourage discussion in class, by e-mail, or on listserves?

Do I encourage them to be a sponge and learn from every possible source?

Do I live by and encourage professionalism? Do I question authority (in my opinion, not a bad trait)? Do I serve on committees so that my students see me as one who is dedicated to my profession? Do I maintain a rigorous public performance schedule so that my students know that I continue to have high personal performance standards?

Do I visit area high schools and work with beginning as well as advanced choirs? Do I invite high school students to visit my school? Do I offer my services to high school directors and share ideas with others in my community? Do I send my students out into the schools so that they can be of assistance as well as gain knowledge from experienced teachers?

Do I encourage advocacy of the public school music program? Do I publicly support teachers? Do I encourage the community to respect and honor teachers or do I sit in my lofty tower and hope that, magically, it all happens?

Do I try to recruit the very best students into the music education program or do I settle for those who do not want to be a performance major?

Am I fully aware of and do I communicate the attributes of a good teacher? Do I seek out those who might have those attributes or do I hope that they will change once in the classroom? Am I honest with my students? Do I encourage them to perform to their personal best?

I believe, perhaps naively, that if our individual standards are high and consistent, our program standards are high. If our program standards are high, then we encourage the very best students to enter into the field—those students know that we are dedicated to the choral art and dedicated to education. It is then our responsibility to teach lifelong learning so that they will make informed decisions throughout their career.

In closing, I believe that our biggest dilemma is perhaps not high standards and increasing graduates, but instead our dilemmas include raising public awareness about investing in education and, specifically, music education, as well as working with public school personnel so that districts hire highly qualified teachers and not just anyone with an emergency credential.

This article originally appeared in the November/ December 1999 issue of the Maryland Music Educator. *Reprinted by permission.*

Fostering a New Generation of Music Educators
Lissa May

Each semester, as I meet with the young music educators in my student teaching seminar who are embarking upon undoubtedly the most critical semester of their entire college education, I am struck by the many emotions they are experiencing. First, they are excited about being done with school and eager to try their wings as teachers At the same time, many are quite apprehensive for a variety of reasons. They often don't feel well prepared, having had seemingly little time to practice and hone conducting skills, piano skills, instrumental techniques, classroom management strategies, etc. Although they have certainly taken plenty of classes, it is difficult to find authentic opportunities for them to practice these skills in the classroom. Additional worries include fitting into a new situation where everyone else knows each other well, establishing a good rapport with students, yet maintaining a professional distance and most important, developing a good working relationship with their cooperating teacher.

Looking at these bright and talented young people, there is clearly unlimited potential, yet they face a critical time in their development, where years of formal study meet the real world. Student teaching will be a time to question beliefs and values about teaching and music, to experiment with instructional strategies and techniques, to come to terms with discipline and classroom management, and, most important, to develop a "teaching personality." They must quickly become immersed in incredibly busy, fast-paced music programs, finding a niche to call their own.

The many music teachers throughout the state who consistently accept the responsibility of mentoring emerging teachers make an invaluable contribution to the music education profession. As predicted teacher shortages become reality, continued efforts must be made to encourage the best and brightest young people into the profession. The need for master music teachers to encourage and nurture young music educators at this most critical point in their education is greater than ever.

The relationship that develops between a student teacher and cooperating teacher plays an important part in the young music educator's attitudes and values about the profession. Although each relationship and each student teaching situation is unique, there are strategies that a mentor teacher can employ to facilitate a successful student teaching experience.

Student teachers often enter their internship highly focused on themselves. "Will I be able to manage the classes? Will the students like me? Is my conducting clear?" and "Did I say the right thing?" are some of the questions that fill their heads. Helping them shift the focus from themselves to the students they are teaching is critical to their development. Encouraging them to ask what their students have learned and what can be done to better facilitate student understanding and performance will help them see that teaching music is not about them, but rather about the students they are teaching.

As young music teachers become more comfortable with classroom management and gain confidence in their ability to utilize their musical skills in a classroom, they are able to concentrate more on what they are hearing musically. I have often been astounded and dismayed when I observe student teachers whom I know to be fine musicians with excellent aural acuity stand in front of ensembles and let a multitude of errors go by. When discussing the rehearsal, I ask why they didn't stop and correct a specific problem and they often admit that they didn't even notice it. I discovered by incorporating an "error detection" unit in my instrumental methods class that it is not a problem for most students in that setting to accurately identify technical and musical errors. Rather, the challenge for them in the classroom is focusing on error detection when they are already struggling to manage the class, remember students' names, adjust to an unfamiliar environment, recall instructional strategies, read the score, conduct effectively, follow a lesson plan, keep track of the time, clearly communicate their expectations, etc. None of this is automatic for a beginning teacher.

As a mentor, it is important to structure student teachers' experiences so that they can build on their successes and gain experience and confidence in the myriad skills and strategies that are needed to teach music effectively. Just as beginning instrumentalists need to have material broken down into manageable pieces, beginning teachers need assistance approaching each of the necessary teacher skills systematically and in controllable segments.

Providing specific feedback is also extremely important. Although there are admittedly many

different ways to reach a goal, young teachers will always benefit from hearing how the experienced teacher might have approached a particular problem. It can be difficult to strike a balance between allowing student teachers the freedom to experiment with their own ideas while at the same time giving them enough guidance to insure their success—and that of your students! I often hear the comment, "I wish that my cooperating teacher would tell me what (s)he is thinking."

One excellent way to begin dialogue about a student teacher's competencies is to videotape a class or rehearsal and ask the student teacher to review it and self-evaluate. That self-evaluation can be used as a starting point to discuss specific strengths and weaknesses that have been observed. A sense of whether the student teacher is aware of problems that might seem obvious to the cooperating teacher can be gained from beginning a conference with a discussion of the student teacher's self-evaluation. Perhaps the student teacher felt the lesson was a success because the classroom was relatively quiet, but had no awareness that the music rehearsed did not improve during the rehearsal, or that many students were confused about a particular concept, or that poor pacing created student lethargy. The hope is that as student teachers continue to grow and gain confidence, self-reflection will become an integral part of their practice.

Communication is vital to a successful student teaching experience. As a mentor, it is critical to talk about what is done in the classroom and why. It is also important to address extramusical issues with student teachers. They will benefit greatly from hearing their mentors' personal histories. Discussions might include questions such as why teach music, what compels one to continue in the profession, or how a career in music education can be balanced with one's personal life. Through the sharing of philosophies of teaching and of music, mentors can help young teachers strengthen their beliefs and values—an important step toward surviving the first few years of teaching.

Data collected from first-year music teachers indicate that many experience feelings of isolation, loneliness, and culture shock. They often feel overworked and overwhelmed by the demands of the job. Many student teachers who do their internships in excellent music programs have no indication of what their first year of teaching may be like. Just as it is important for them to experience success and gain confidence, it's all right if they face some challenges and experience frustration from time to time, especially with a mentor there to help them work through the problems. It is important for them to hear how this excellent program developed. What steps were taken to bring it to the present level of excellence? How long did it take?

Each person must develop his or her unique teaching personality. Undoubtedly, one of the most difficult aspects of mentoring is encouraging that emerging personality in a beginning teacher rather than trying to create a clone of oneself. Truly great teachers and mentors hope to see their protégés think independently, creating and achieving at an even higher level than they did themselves. Open communication that encourages questioning and dialogue and the opportunity for exploration and reflection pro-vides a nurturing atmosphere where young teachers can make connections between theoretical knowledge and practice.

The future of music education is in the hands of the young teachers entering the field. We certainly must do all that we can to encourage the best and brightest to become music teachers, particularly knowing that the current music teacher shortage will likely only get worse. Nurturing those who have chosen to pursue music education as a career and helping them develop fully as teachers may well be one of the most important contributions we can make to the profession.

This article originally appeared in the March 2002 issue of the Indiana Musicator. *Reprinted by permission.*

Tell Them about It
Steve McGrew

If predictions are accurate, we can expect a huge shortfall in the supply of teachers within the next five to ten years. The great majority of career teachers who began their journey in the '60s will be retiring. If you consider class-size reductions and swelling student enrollments, you have what experts are calling a historic turnover in the teaching profession, in which half of the teachers who will be in public school classrooms ten years from now have not yet been hired. Nationwide, about 2.4 million teachers will be needed in the next eleven years (National Center for Education Statistics). Certainly music education will suffer proportionately from this general shortage.

Years ago, I would talk each year with individual students about a possible career in music education. I would explain that they had good skills, practice habits, peer respect, sense of humor, geniality, and an obvious love of music, which made them excellent prospective music teachers. Having said this, I would let it percolate. Many would come back with follow-up questions. Some would take the plunge.

Somehow, in the years to follow, I got away from this formal practice. Those students interested in music careers would come to me and initiate the conversation about their promise as a music teacher. It seems that many students did, in fact, pursue music careers following this practice as well.

Now, however, with what could be a severe teacher shortage looming, it is my opinion that we, as professional music educators, need to be more proactive in our recruiting efforts. We owe it to our profession to encourage the best and brightest of our students to think about music related careers in general, and—most importantly—teaching.

As a catalyst, here is a checklist of possible actions we might take. Each teacher may exercise a little fine tuning and expand upon and tailor it to their own likes.

Identify the students whom you think have the qualities of excellent music educators—common sense, musicality, good work ethic, perseverance, good people skills. Ideally, the identification phase should be during the sophomore year, and certainly no later than the first quarter of the junior year.

Talk honestly with the student(s) individually. Lay it out for them—the stress and rigor of music school; the conflicts in the teaching field, personal and philosophical; the politics in public education; the financial considerations; the balance of personal and professional demands.

Volunteer to speak at Future Teachers Association meetings. Invite members to arrange shadowing projects in elementary, middle school, and high school music classrooms. Be positive and truthful. I have found these students to be very curious and interested.

Initiate cadet teaching at middle school or elementary schools. Prospective music teachers can gain invaluable experience and provide valuable assistance by "minds on" activities (sectionals, student conducting, solo/ensemble tutoring) with elementary or middle school ensembles. Many high schools have programs similar to these under the auspices of their guidance departments.

Of course there is the age-old, time-worn practice of the band room TA. The trick is to select these students judiciously and keep them engaged in all that backstage, unglamorous drudgery that no one sees: library work, inventory, general organizing, news releases, program planning, department-chair details, forms, and more forms. This is a part of reality that the future music teacher needs to experience.

Plan a short unit in music history/appreciation class concerning careers in music. Many of the newer texts already include such topics.

If your school has a career day, lobby to have a session on careers in music. Certainly you will have a room full of "rockers," but plug the session in your regular classes to your own students. Perhaps you will find a few who are curious enough to sign up. That's a start.

Capitalize on community members who earn some or all of their income from music. Invite them in to talk and Q & A with small groups of interested students.

Many schools are extremely deficient in career education. Accrediting associations are placing new emphasis on this goal. Music teachers can and should get in on the bottom floor of this move. There will always be a few students who have the self-confidence and assurance to seek out advice about music careers, but there could be a few more who simply need an encouraging word, and a shot of "You can do this!" If we do not tell them, they may continue to see themselves as always the accompaniment, never the lead.

Where will the next generation of music teachers come from? We can find them. Parents and teachers can encourage them. Guidance counselors can assist them. Our art form is too precious and personal to allow a shortage of fine music teachers to occur. Don't miss the opportunity to "tell them about it."

This article originally appeared in the September 2001 issue of the Indiana Musicator. *Reprinted by permission.*

What Will Keep Our Future Music Educators Persisting Toward a Degree?
Glenn E. Nierman

With a number of districts being concerned about finding qualified music educators to hire and the legislature considering legislation and pay increases for teachers, an article about research in what keeps college students persisting toward completion of a degree qualifying them for certification in music might be particularly timely. It may help you to identify seven to twelve students that you are currently teaching who should be encouraged to pursue a career in music education. What follows is an abstract of a paper delivered at the XXII World Congress of the International Society of Music Education, Amsterdam, Netherlands.

The purpose of this study was to investigate factors which influence the retention of undergraduate music education students and the variability of those factors among different groups of students (e.g., ethnicity, class level, gender) from diverse institutional settings (e.g., land-grant universities, state universities, private universities, state colleges). Students (N = 549) enrolled in four different kinds of higher education institutions served as the subjects for the study. In a series of sixty-six forced choice comparisons, students were asked to select the one factor which most intensified their persistence in music studies for each of the following factors paired in all possible ways: (1) academic or music scholarship, (2) interaction with applied studio teacher, (3) interaction with nonapplied college faculty, (4) grades in academic course work, (5) grades in applied music, (6) love of music, (7) love of teaching, (8) influence of friend/family member, (9) participation in ensembles, (10) impact of field experiences/practicum, (11) academic or music challenges, and (12) membership in professional/social organizations. The one-dimensional scaling solution showed that love of music is the most important factor contributing to degree persistence. Interpretation of two-dimensional multidimensional scaling (MDS) suggested that Music Immersion, Educational Forces, and Social Interaction are perhaps the underlying constructs which determine degree persistence decisions.

Interpretation of two-dimensional multidimensional scaling began by examining the derived stimulus configuration shown in figure 1.

As with factor analysis, the interpretation of MDS plots is a rather subjective process. It involves looking for clusters of factors that are in close proximity on the plot or seem to be in straight lines in any direction. There are a number of factors that seem to cluster together in the

Figure 1. Two-dimensional degree persistence inventory solution.

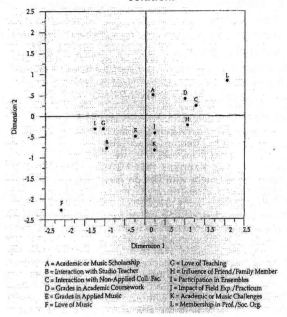

A = Academic or Music Scholarship
B = Interaction with Studio Teacher
C = Interaction with Non-Applied Coll. Fac.
D = Grades in Academic Coursework
E = Grades in Applied Music
F = Love of Music

G = Love of Teaching
H = Influence of Friend/Family Member
I = Participation in Ensembles
J = Impact of Field Exp./Practicum
K = Academic or Music Challenges
L = Membership in Prof./Soc. Org.

lower left quadrant of the figure: Participation in Ensembles, Love of Teaching, Interaction with Studio Teacher, and Grades in Applied Music. This cluster suggests that one of the underlying constructs influencing the retention of music majors might be labeled Music Immersion. All of these factors suggest that involvement with the discipline they want to teach—as individual performers in the studio, as performers in a group, as teachers of music, as listeners—plays a major role in retention. Furthermore, Impact of Practicum, another factor involving interaction with others (one-on-one or in groups) and the making of music, is in close proximity to the lower left quadrant.

Another retention construct for music education students could be defined as Educational Forces. Factors in the upper and lower right quadrants (Academic or Music Scholarship, Grades in Academic Courses, Interaction with Nonapplied Faculty, and Academic or Music Challenges) seem to contain a common theme by virtue of their connection to the formal schooling process. Even Influence of Friend/Family Member is not out of context in this construct. The interaction between students and family member/friend may indeed center around conversation or events involving the educational process such as grades, an upcoming concert, etc.

A relationship among factors may be indicated by the straight line defined by the Membership in Professional/ Social Organizations point and the

Love of Music point. Close to this line lie such factors as Interaction with Nonapplied Faculty, Interaction with Applied Faculty, Grades in Academic Courses, Grades in Applied Music, and Interaction with Studio Teacher. This line seems to define a Social Interaction construct, moving from interaction with groups of students/faculty (upper right quadrant) through one-on-one interactions with the studio teacher to the more personal factor Love of Music.

How does the identification of the Music Immersion, the Educational Forces, and the Social Interaction dimensions aid in the understanding of the issues surrounding retention? First, the Educational Forces and the Social Interaction dimensions are similar to the social and academic dimensions of other models on degree retention (Terenzini & Pascarella, 1980). Thus, music education students seem to be affected by the same retention factors that affect other college students. Unique to the retention model proposed in this study, however, is the Music Immersion dimension. This dimension appears to be the strongest force affecting music education students' decision to persist toward a degree. One wonders if this love-of-subject dimension is unique to music education; or if the study was replicated in another discipline (such as social studies education or visual arts education), would this love-of-subject dimension also appear?

This study was concerned not only with the identification of various factors and dimensions of retention for music education students, but also with influence of selected variables (school type, class level, race/ethnicity, and gender) on these factors and dimensions.

The schools in the sample varied in size from a large land-grant university with over 150 music education majors to several small private universities with fewer than 30 music majors. It would seem that differences in size and type would produce differences in the students' selection of retention factors. Radical differences among the institutional groups were not evident, however. The factors chosen most frequently by all respondents regardless of institution type were those relating to active participation in music. Conversely, those factors selected least often represented nonmusic participation by the respondents. A comparison of the categories revealed that Influence of Friend/Family Member and Interaction with Nonapplied Faculty were among those factors with the greatest variance and among those factors chosen least often.

With respect to differences in retention factors across the variable of class level, there was also some consistency. As shown in figure 2, all class levels selected Love of Music most often as the strongest factor which kept them persisting toward a degree.

Noticeable selection shifts can be found among certain retention factors, however. As students progressed into the upper class standings, Grades in Academic Courses and Grades in Applied Music decreased in importance. This seems consistent with Maslow's theory of movement from "recognition" to "self-actualization." Just as the Impact of Field Experiences increases with class level, so Love of Teaching becomes more of a factor in degree persistence as students achieve higher class levels. This suggests that field experiences are an important factor in the formation of preservice music teachers' attitudes toward teaching, their chosen profession.

Gender and ethnicity/racial groupings have been shown in previous studies to result in differences in emphases on various retention factors. In this study, however, with a similar number of females and males responding to the questionnaire, the percentages of subjects who chose each retention factor six or more times were approximately equal. Thus gender difference did not produce marked shifts in retention selection patterns.

In contrast to the equal number of male and female respondents, the number of white subjects in the study outnumbered nonwhites by a ratio of ten to one. Thus discussion of ethnicity as it relates to degree persistence in music education majors in this study should proceed with caution. non-white subjects seem to perceive that academic and music scholarships contribute more to their degree persistence than white subjects. Compared with all other areas, this factor was unique within the study. When grouped according to ethnicity, nonwhites ranked Academic or Music Scholarships fourth among the twelve factors; for white subjects this factor ranked sixth overall. Interaction with Applied Studio Teacher ranked slightly lower along with Academic or Music Challenges which ranked much lower than scholarships, for nonwhites. Perhaps future research with more equitable representation of all ethnic groups, will reveal other differences regarding retention factors.

Such are the findings of a recent study involving factors which influence undergraduate music education majors to persist toward a degree.

References

Nierman, G. E., Franzblau, R. H., Fredstrom, T., Mallett, C., Sawyer, J., and Young, J. (1996, July). A study of retention factors for undergraduate music education majors using multidimensional scaling. Competitively selected paper presented at the XXII World Congress of the International Society of Music Education, Amsterdam, Netherlands.

Terenzini, P., & Pascarella, E. (1980). Toward the validation of Tinto's model of college student attrition: A review of recent studies. *Research in Higher Education*, 12 (3), 271–282.

This article originally appeared in the April 2000 issue of the Nebraska Music Educator. *Reprinted by permission.*

Figure 2. Percentage of subjects who choose each factor six or more times by class level

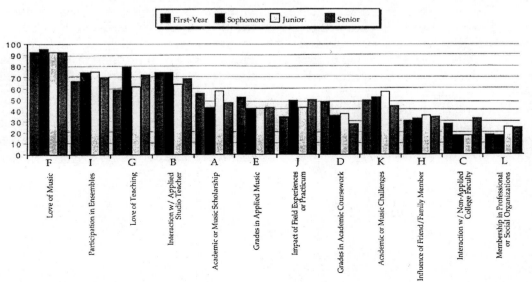

Crisis Management
Dean Peterson

A recent newspaper headline gave me reason for many concerns. The headline stated, "Teacher Shortage Could Become a Crisis in Montana." According to recent studies, rural areas are seeing shortages in music, special education, and foreign languages. When positions are not filled, programs are cut and our musical culture is weakened. Other studies show that the average music educator remains in the profession just three years.

In Montana, low salaries and poor working conditions play a major role for many young teachers leaving the profession, but not the only role. Lack of experience in matters of organizing a choral program, discipline, literature selection, and rehearsal technique can send many young educators out the door. What can you as a choral director do to help stop this alarming trend? Here are some thoughts and ideas that you may wish to consider in order to keep music education from become a thing of the past.

If you have the opportunity to work with young singers either in church, public/private school or in honor choirs, you can help develop future music leaders. Listed below are some ideas that might help inspire our singers to consider music as a career and give them some basic skills to work with even before they have entered college.

1. Make use of student accompanists. Young people with keyboard skills often are the strongest, most musically sound of all our singers. As the skills of an accompanist develop, so can an appreciation for the art of choral conducting.
2. Select and encourage student section leaders. Work with these young people and help them prepare for their sectionals. If they are well prepared, the experience can prove successful and will increase confidence and leadership qualities.
3. Encourage the development of student conductors. Look for students who might have potential to conduct and allow them, under your direction, to conduct the choir from time to time. You may wish to feature a young conductor in concert for one or two pieces.
4. Ask your stronger musicians to help tutor others who might be struggling with music theory or sight singing.
5. Encourage choir members to take on logistical responsibilities for the program. Young people can help with concert-program production, stage setup, recording, uniform care, music filing, and writing news releases to mention a few.
6. Ask your student leaders to create and teach a new warm-up to your choirs from time to time. Some very creative warm-ups can come out of student efforts.
7. Communicate with your singers who show promise. Let them know if you think they might have the right stuff to pursue a career in music education and give them a realistic idea of the skills needed to be a music major.

Beyond encouraging young people to choose this field, you may need to make more conscious efforts in mentoring those new colleagues who are just starting out. Mentoring can be as informal as a simple buddy system where one experienced conductor helps a new conductor with organization information, discipline management, literature selection, and general advice. It may include inviting new teachers into your rehearsal to observe and question. Our Montana CMENC chapter continues to sponsor their own Project Mentor. Consider volunteering to take part in this existing program.

The Iowa Choral Directors Association is implementing a very formal approach this year that includes a specialized training session for designated mentors. The training took place at their summer convention. A good amount of effort and research has gone into their program. To insure that no one is left out of the mentoring, all 1,600 of the state's principals will receive notification of the program and will be asked to encourage young teachers to participate. The ICDA Mentor Program may be something that MCDA may wish to study in order to make a more organized effort to mentor our new colleagues.

This article originally appeared in the January 2000 issue of Montana's Cadenza. *Reprinted by permission.*

Section 3

How can CMENC and Tri-M help?

 Section 3

How can CMENC and Tri-M help?

Tips for a Successful Student MENC Chapter: An Investment in the Future of Music Education
Barbara Brinson

The music education majors who are members of our student MENC chapters across the country are the men and women who will carry the torch well into the next millennium, instilling the joys of music into the lives of children and young people for years to come. Working toward a successful student chapter on a college or university campus, therefore, is an investment in the future of music education. Special programs, activities, and projects undertaken can enhance and enrich our students' music education and their preparation for teaching. This is certainly not a responsibility to be taken lightly!

Lisa Spataro, current president of the Southern Methodist University (SMU) chapter, feels that "the purpose of [student] MENC is to provide music education majors with a sense of what to expect when teaching. MENC should be informative as well as fun in order to draw students in and keep them." Lisa also believes that opportunities for fellowship and fun are important in building an esprit de corps and identity among the members.

Charlotte Mizener, chapter adviser at University of Texas–Pan American, suggests that "the officers cannot build a successful organization alone, nor can the membership be successful without excellent leadership ... the success lies in the ambition and skills of the students." Strong leaders with a vision of clear, achievable goals, and involvement from both officers and members is listed as critical by Shema Armstrong (SMU, and state collegiate president-elect.)

Meetings
First, a meeting time must be established, and this may be the biggest challenge of the year! Music students are notoriously busy and involved in classes, rehearsals, concerts, and practicing (not to mention eating and sleeping!), so finding a time when a majority of students can meet will be difficult. Rotating the meeting times so that everyone in the chapter can attend at least some of the meetings may work for some, while others may prefer a regular meeting time—perhaps once a month. This way, students get into the habit of attending.

Recruitment and Retention
So now you have decided when and where you are going to meet. The next challenge is to attract the students to join MENC and attend the meetings. (Sometimes, not so easy!) Genny Bennetts (Texas Christian University and state collegiate secretary) suggests that "hands-on" activities such as designing resumes or practicing interviewing skills will draw students into the organization because they will see the relevance of the MENC meetings. Scheduling guest speakers seems to be popular at many Texas universities. Professors, state officials, as well as public school teachers from various teaching levels can offer a different perspective and inform college students of the realities of the teaching profession. Current student teachers or a panel of first-year teachers can offer insights into the relevance of what is being taught in college methods classes. These meetings, especially if they are designed as sharing sessions coupled with opportunities for questions, can help to bridge the gap between the college classroom and the "real world." Donny Pinson (TCU, and state collegiate president) says that "this increases interest, and it complements our theme of professional development."

Social opportunities can also attract new members, while at the same time build friendships, nurture and create an identity for the group. James

Ode, chapter adviser at SMU, had several good suggestions. (We all know that food is a definite "draw" among college students.) Ode suggests that providing pizza and soft drinks at the initial meeting will attract a larger number of potential members as well as lend a social atmosphere to at least a portion of the meeting. Going together to a local symphony concert or opera, or a public school production can help build friendships and cohesion among MENC members. And gathering together, perhaps at the adviser's home for a barbeque supper or homemade ice cream, followed by the election of the next year's officers is a good way to end the school year as well as plan for the next one. Printing a monthly newsletter can disseminate important information as well as highlight various members' accomplishments during the year.

Everyone remembers his/her first semester in college—everything and everyone is new and different and things can get a bit confusing. Pairing older MENC members with first-year students to guide them through the maze of new experiences and opportunities can really make a difference. Having a mentor or "big sister/big brother" to count on will make the new students feel important and welcome, and hopefully, will get them involved in MENC right from the beginning. This practice has worked well in the past at TTU.

MENC in the Community
Active involvement was mentioned by several students and advisers as a way to make MENC membership more meaningful. Service projects involving local public schools can be mutually beneficial. Robert Henry (Texas Tech University, TMEA president) suggests offering to usher for band, choir, and orchestra concerts, making posters and bulletin hoards for the music/rehearsal rooms, and generally assisting the public school teachers in a variety of ways. This arrangement can help the teacher as well as educate the college student about the day-to-day needs and routines of a music teacher. Teaching mini-lessons in schools that don't have a regular music teacher can be a real service to school children as well as serve as a laboratory for music education majors to hone emerging teaching skills. And don't forget that sharing our musical talents with shut-ins, neighbors, and nursing homes can lift everyone's spirits! Christmas caroling has been a successful activity of the SMU chapter.

The Convention and Fund-raising
One of the biggest motivators for being an active MENC member, cites Charlotte Mizener, is the annual TMEA Convention in San Antonio. One of the biggest problems is: where do the students find the money to go? Members at UT-Pan American hold fundraisers each fall to provide funds for attending the conference to those who have participated in chapter activities during the year. So what works? Bake sales, book sales, and car washes are tried-and-true standard fare. Designing and selling a music department T-shirt or book bag can make money, build identity, as well as make the MENC group cohesiveness more visible to the music department as well as to the entire school. If enough money is earned over time, a small scholarship may be established for deserving MENC members.

Before the convention, MENC members should meet to plan who will ride and room with whom, and more important, to discuss which sessions they plan to attend. The state officers of the Collegiate Student Section (CSS) have scheduled eight sessions specifically for collegiate this year with timely topics ranging from classroom/rehearsal discipline to the TEKS to writing resumes. In addition to the eight sessions, we have a CSS business meeting at the convention where we have important speakers and elect state officers for the next school. And food is provided!

Attending the convention can be a real turning point for many students as they sense the excitement, see the exhibits, attend interesting sessions, and get a feel for their place in the music teaching profession. Students can talk to students from other colleges/universities about mutual interests, cares and concerns, and a sense of mutual purpose can develop for collegiates on the state level. While in San Antonio, meeting at least once for a meal as a chapter can be a good time for sharing the excitement felt, the ideas learned, the performing groups heard, the All-State rehearsals attended, and the music and materials found.

Coda
Students who participate in collegiate chapters of MENC can gain so much from the experience. Their education is enhanced, they get a bigger picture of the teaching profession and their metamorphosis from student to professional may be facilitated. They are the future music educators, and they are worth our efforts! If you have an active student MENC chapter on your campus, keep up the good work. If you don't, think about starting one, and use some of these tips to help you!

Several student leaders as well as state chapter advisers contributed to the information in this article. Many thanks to Lisa Spataro, Shema Armstrong, and James Ode, SMU; Robert Henry, TTU and TMEA President, Genny Bennetts and Donny Pinson, TCU; and Charlotte Mizener, UT-Pan American.

Fifteen Great Recruiting Ideas

1. Raffle off a free membership to someone who joins your chapter during your recruiting drive.
2. Obtain testimonials of the value of MENC membership from members now teaching and share them with potential members.
3. Invite people who have a conflict with chapter meetings to join as national members so they will still have access to current music education information through *Teaching Music* and *Music Educators Journal*.
4. Host a special "bring a friend" meeting featuring an icebreaker exercise, a brief club orientation, and refreshments. Each member must bring a friend with them to the meeting.
5. Ask your professors to offer extra credit for MENC membership and/or participation.
6. Create a bulletin board display in a prominent place showing pictures from chapter activities, membership information, and a calendar of upcoming events.
7. Display business cards of former chapter members now teaching to demonstrate that chapter members are going on to find jobs in their field.
8. Hand out MENC brochures to students in general music or education classes.
9. Announce upcoming chapter meetings in your music and education classes; invite everyone to attend.
10. Call visitors after they have attended a meeting. Thank them for visiting the chapter and invite them to your next event.
11. Ask members for names of friends and classmates who could benefit from MENC membership. Send these people a personal invitation to attend your next event. Follow up with a phone call.
12. List your upcoming meetings in your college of business newsletter and campus newspaper.
13. Prepare a two-minute talk on the value of doing MENC. Give your presentation to music education classes and then hand out membership applications and information.
14. Set up a table displaying MENC materials at the student activities fair.
15. Provide refreshments at your meetings.

Taken from the MENC list, "50 Great Recruiting Ideas."

This article first appeared in the Winter 1999–2000 issue of Texas's TMEC Connections. Reprinted by permission.

How to Make CMENC Work for You and Your Future
Erin E. Cooper

Now that it is time once again to return to class and to the rigorous schedules we face as music education majors, I want to take this opportunity to remind you about an invaluable tool that is available to you as a future teacher: CMENC. Before you laugh and turn the page to check out the latest Burrage ad, please read on! Both your local and state organizations are places where you can concentrate on musicianship, develop teaching and leadership skills, and make yourself more marketable in the teaching profession.

In a time where teachers are evaluated at every turn, forced to plan lessons with little or no money, and are required to demonstrate that music is an important subject, you should be seeking out as many helpful hints as possible on the path to becoming a successful educator. CMENC is one of those helpful tools.

Through your local chapter, you should have the opportunity to volunteer, attend special lectures, work on projects with your peers, and establish professional contacts that will prove to be valuable to you in the near future. I imagine that many of you are shaking your head at this point and thinking to yourself, "This is not my chapter. My chapter rarely meets, and when they do meet, no one ever attends." Maybe you are thinking, "Everyone attends the meetings, and there are lots of projects to participate in, but they are not the types of events in which I wish to partake."

If you are also thinking right about now that you would like to change the situation, then I have two suggestions for you: go to as many chapter events as possible, and make suggestions to your advisers and executive members about projects you would like to see your chapter work on. I recommend going to as many events as possible for both situations because I know how frustrating it can be to plan an event or meeting and have only five out of forty members attend. This causes a lack of desire to plan more events which causes even less participation. So attend chapter meetings as often as you can. Your executive members will be grateful, and you will be surprised how many people will follow your lead, which will create a rise in meeting attendance.

If, however, you feel that your chapter provides loads of activities, but the events do not seem to be beneficial to you, attend anyway. Decide why the activities do not seem to interest you and then kindly offer your own suggestions for projects, seminars, or meeting ideas. Quite often, the people who plan the activities for the year are hard-pressed for new ideas or are afraid to make changes in what seems to be a popular method for running the chapter, so fresh ideas are graciously accepted. You might also want to consider offering to serve as a committee head, or running for a chapter office. Both running for office and heading a committee are great ways to get involved in your local CMENC chapter and will help to inspire fresh ideas.

I imagine by this point those of you who are advisers and executive members of the CMENC chapters are screaming, "I would love to do more with my group, but I'm strapped for ideas!" I have discovered a few suggestions that I hope will help you out. One is to sponsor a CMENC "membership drive/freshman music major welcoming reception" the first month of the fall semester, which would entice new CMENC members and help incoming freshmen meet their professors and peers. Another suggestion is to sponsor a clinic on budgeting personal finances and planning for the future. The lecture could be sponsored by CMENC, but would be open to all students regardless of major. Your chapter could help run scholarship auditions, organize a group to go caroling at the local hospital before winter break, or hold a "petting zoo" at the local Ronald McDonald House or retirement home where the instruments are the "pets" and the performers are the "ring masters." Your CMENC chapter could even sponsor a fund-raising event to buy instruments for a local elementary school. The key to executing these activities is to invite both members and non-members to participate. This way, you are getting members involved in the community and organization, and you are giving nonmembers a chance to see if CMENC is an organization they would like to join.

This article first appeared in the Fall 1999 issue of the North Carolina Music Educator. *Reprinted by permission.*

Tri-M: Future Hope of Music Education
Cynthia Eady-Paulson

If we strive to cultivate musical sensitivity and perception in our students, we must likewise give adequate recognition for their efforts and achievements. We must inspire them to strive for higher goals. In what better way than by bestowing upon them lifetime membership in a worldwide honorary organization for musical youth?
—Alexander Harley, founder of Tri-M

During the first session at the 2001 Northwest Music Educators convention in Spokane, our national MENC president Mel Clayton asked those who had taught over twenty years to stand. He the requested those who were in their first year of teaching music to do the same. I was immediately struck by the small number of new music educators.

Perhaps it was because of lack of funds that there were not many first-year teachers present, but it is also likely because the teaching profession is not as attractive as at it was when many of us entered it over twenty years ago. The clientele we teach now are definitely different because society has radically changed. The salary for teacher has not kept up with the rising cost of living. Our profession remains one of the few left who receive no financial compensation for completing a required master's degree (costing in the realm of $30,000) so that we can climb the financial ladder and retain our current teaching position. Monetary support for most music programs has been drastically reduced from an amount that was already minimal. The rivalry for prime-time slots in the daily scheduling of classes is highly competitive. Music classes are often considered "just electives" and hardly necessary to the academic, intellectual, social, and creative well-being of students. In our state, only two fine arts (semester) credits are mandated for graduation. Sadly, many of the elementary general music specialists are even viewed as merely planning time for the "real teachers." These factors culminate in discouraging many young musicians from entering the field of teaching.

The career of being a music educator remains exciting, rewarding, and challenging. But at times it is also demanding, exhausting, and frustrating. Still, the quality of music educators has steadily improved. It is apparent, however, that if those of us who are well established do not take the time to encourage exceptional young people to take their talents and turn them toward teaching as a career, music education will become a lost, or at minimum, a diluted art form.

Every person who becomes an educator has accepted a career that will influence hundreds, yes, even thousands of futures. As music educators we are also affecting the aesthetic part of our students' lives. We must all realize the far-reaching overtones of what we give to our pupils.

I made a decision early in my life to become a music teacher. Starting in my own secondary school years, I was honored to have had marvelous and dedicated music teachers such as Jeff Mitchell and Gene "Sarge" Huber. Then, as I entered college as a music major, I studied with Raleigh McVicker, Ralph Mutchler, Dr. Theodore Turner, Floyd Standifer, Dr. Gordon Ohlsson, Paul Christiansen, Weston Noble, Eric Christiansen, Dr. Larry Wyatt, and Robert Priez to name a few. When I became a public school teacher, I was graciously mentored by wonderful musicians such as Leo Dodd, Judi Filibeck, Roy Cummings, Andre Segovia, Jimi Haslip, John Mowad, Garry Walker, Dr. Robert Dietz, Neil Leurance, Randi Peterson-Adolph, Jack Halm, William Livingston, Larry Vandel, Greg Boehme, Dave Cross, Mel Clayton, and many others. The influence of these great teachers went far beyond merely instructing me in the mechanics of music and performance. They each took their vocation seriously and blended their immense talent with a great love for teaching and the art of music. Showing through example what we do is exceedingly important; it is how our influence spreads out into the world. In this manner, they inspired me and many other students to join them in this noble profession and to continue on in the unique calling of being a music educator. Over my career of twenty-plus years, I have aspired to carry on this tradition by transferring the vision of teaching. Gratefully, at least one student each year has chosen to carry on the light of this amazingly wonderful career.

Tri-M: One Way to Influence
Becoming actively involved in starting and pro-

moting a Tri-M Music Honor Society in your school is a vitally important step in this direction. Tri-M is the International Music Honor Society for Secondary School students (middle/junior high and high school) that motivates and recognizes musical achievement and musicianship. Founded in 1952 by Alexander and Frances Harley, Tri-M has helped young people provide years of service through music in thousands of schools throughout the world. Through nearly 3,500 international chartered chapters, thousands of students have received recognition for their efforts and been honored for their musical accomplishments.

There were 2,000 new members just this year, bringing the total to over 17,697 members.

The three M's in Tri-M stand for Modern Music Masters. It is a sanctioned program of MENC. Tri-M offers a complete system of rewards that help motivate effort and recognize excellence in individuals and chapters. With this system, the group builds strong communication and critical thinking skills, and provides for a channel of personal fulfillment. It will strengthen your school's music program by its visibility and prestige, building awareness of the importance of music in your school and community through service, increasing teamwork among instrumental and vocal students, and providing great leadership opportunities for music students. Research is showing that kids who study music are much less likely to get into trouble and are more likely to feel pride in their school and in their other studies. Students who have studied music score higher on the SAT. Belonging to a highly recognized group of respected students also lends itself to building strong, positive self-esteem and healthy work ethics.

Starting a Tri-M Chapter
Beginning a chapter is easy. The student entry fee to join Tri-M is $10.00 for the initial year and $3.00 thereafter. A student must have a cumulative GPA of 2.5 and maintain at least a B average in the performance group he/she belongs to (band, choir, orchestra, ensembles). Students must also have the recommendation of their conductor regarding their integrity, their commitment to individual progress, and their commitment to the well-being of the performance group of which they are a part. With this membership, the students receive a newsletter twice each year, a Tri-M gold pin, and a card and certificate.

Currently, students who are active members of their local Tri-M society have the opportunity to audition for the first ever MENC/Tri-M International Honors Ensembles. They will perform at the fifty-eighth MENC National Biennial Conference in the spring of 2002. MENC and ASCAP have also provided Tri-M participants full membership into JAM (Junior ASCAP Members). Through this they receive benefits which make them eligible for discounts on music merchandise and other products. They can use the JAM Web site (www.ascap.com/jam) which will allow them to access up-to-date music news, interviews, and contests. They can research rock, jazz, and symphonic musical styles, and gain information on developing their songwriting skills and beginning a music career.

Our Chapter

At Lincoln High School in Tacoma, Washington, we have over forty-eight members. The hardest part for my students has been coming up with the initial fee of $10.00. I have to wait until March to send in our membership fees because this is usually when my students are able to pay. Even so, they continue to keep actively working in varied projects in the community. They have been singing and playing at retirement residences and local hospitals, working at the rescue mission during the holidays, planting trees in a reclamation area, painting at the YWCA, performing in many concerts, participating in community parades, and volunteering in numerous city projects.

For a recreational activity, many of the students recently attended the Tacoma Opera Company's production of *Don Giovanni* in English. The opera guild provided us with complimentary tickets. In June we hope to visit the Experience Music Project at the Seattle Center. Our next on-site project goal is to design our own Web page so that we can communicate with other Tri-M chapters across the world.

Our chapter is currently working on attaining

the "Seven Cs for Success" in our groups:

1. Clear conception of what we want
2. Confidence with competence
3. Concentration that is focused
4. Consistency
5. Commitment to good attendance
6. Character to stay ethically on course
7. Capacity to enjoy the process along the way

At the end of the year the Tri-M members will be recognized at our final concert and also at the school-wide awards dessert banquet. Parents are invited to attend, and specific awards are given for attendance, community service, and musicianship. Each student is encouraged to keep a detailed and extensive portfolio beginning in his/her freshman year, covering his/her achievements within Tri-M, other academic studies and service to family, school, community, and state. Scholarships in music are sought out for students to apply for. Audition tapes and videos are prepared. Practice interviews are also available by myself and colleagues. The seniors will be given the representative pink cord and tassel of music to wear for graduation exercises.

Give It a Try

There are over twenty chapters of Tri-M in the state, but only five are currently active. It is a wise choice to become a part of an exciting organization that can increase interest in your music program and assist your students in achieving high levels of creative and academic performance. Please consider starting or reactivating Tri-M for your students. It is the best way to encourage and reward them for their dedicated efforts and also to ensure that there are quality music educators for the future.

This article first appeared in the May 2001 issue of Washington's Voice. *Reprinted by permission.*

Section 4

How do we educate music teachers?

 Section 4

How do we educate music teachers?

'Competence' in Music Education
Charles Chapman

One of the first concepts concerning testing that we learn in music education classes is that of validity. A test which is valid has been proven (or, unfortunately, often "assumed") to test that skill or knowledge which it claims to test. An invalid test is at best worthless—a waste of time for everyone concerned, the test giver, the test taker, and the person who makes decisions based on the resulting score. Invalid tests which determine suitability for academic entry into a discipline can at worst mislead students into unfortunate career choices or prevent a student with excellent potential from realizing it.

Legislative and otherwise state-mandated actions of the last ten or so years have imposed a complex array of so-called "competency" hurdles on all students who would be teachers. The first of these hurdles is a body of academic requirements and/or exam score levels which sift them according to various criteria, most of which are based upon scores rendered by standardized tests in language and mathematics. These tests are generic and assume that all disciplines require teachers who possess the same basic skills. (Mistake number one.) It is no accident that this list of desirable skills conforms to those abilities prized by corporate America or established for more academically self-serving reasons by the science/math establishment.

During their university degree work, students who wish to become music teachers may use only a small number of their music courses (those identified as liberal arts), such as music theory and music history, to establish the necessary minimum grade point average for entry into teacher education. Increasingly restrictive requirements in general education continue to crowd courses in the fine arts to the rear of the academic bus, so that

students who would like to dance, sing, paint, act, or play an instrument as a career must complete essentially the same general education program as that required of budding engineers and chemists.

Those who fall under the minimum grade requirement in these so-called liberal courses usually have the alternative of sitting for a standardized exam, such as the PPST. They must then achieve a minimum score in several areas, again dominated by language and mathematics skills far beyond those necessary for competence in fine arts. Success on these exams always requires good reading and comprehension skills, since they are usually constructed of multiple-choice test items.

The student who clears these hurdles and receives a degree (which carries the implied blessing of the music faculty of the school), must then sit for the state "competency exam." This exam is also mostly multiple-choice format, and therefore language-centered.

The original set of objectives according to which the music exams are supposedly written were crafted over many months by a large committee of music educators. This list then was changed in its format and balance by the testing company and/or the state, after the committee was dissolved. Test items generated from these objectives, (sometimes by employees of the testing company who are neither music educators or professional performance musicians), provide hours of head-shaking discussion in music education circles.

Such questions as, "Where does one place the tubas in a marching band?" or, "Which vowel is best for vocalizing?" (the "correct" answer was EE!!) are not even the worst selections from test items supposed to measure the competency of a new teacher to practice the craft he has learned in school.

It seems obvious that the measure of validity for a competency exam is that persons who achieve a passing score are competent music teachers. (Do I see smiles on the faces of experienced music teachers?) Any exam which renders low scores to students who later become successful teachers is by definition an invalid test. A test which renders passing scores to students who prove incompetent is likewise invalid.

My careful observation of the state's competency exam in music, based not just upon my university's students, but many from other areas of Oklahoma, is that the present exam is most certainly invalid from two perspectives. A large number of students who score well above the minimum on the exam are neither successful nor competent. A few of these find other jobs, others simply drift to an isolated corner of music education where their incompetence and unhappiness are not obvious enough to warrant their dismissal.

On the contrary, a larger number of students who are gifted musicians, who have excellent performance skills, who demonstrate fine interpersonal relationships as group leaders, who are fine conductors with discerning ears, and who have language skills that are easily adequate to the needs of music teaching, must wade through this "competency" exam many times, trying to reason where to put the tubas and why EE is the best vowel for vocalizing.

The content of the present exam seems to have little correspondence to actual music teaching. Students who are good at "book learning," score well, regardless of their musical skills or ability to transmit these skills. The student who possesses a high order of music skills and additionally seems to have a teaching personality, but who is less "left-brained," will consistently have trouble passing the exam.

Such a large percentage of a music teacher's normal day tests skills of conducting, analyzing student performance, motivating (cheerleading), playing keyboards, singing, and generally making music, that any valid competency exam must measure these items, not the person's ability to read a multiple-choice question and successfully to determine the "correct" answer a nonmusician has copied out of context from some methods text: an answer which may not even represent the consensus of successful music teachers.

There is some indication that there are plans afoot to broaden the competency exams in the near future, which of course will mean that a choral director must master the calculus in order to train people to sing. Common sense? Not to me!

As long as those of us who practice the fine arts allow, with very little political action to the contrary, persons unrelated to our endeavor to impose impractical and unrealistic standards upon a profession about which they know little, we will be severely limited in the quality and number of music teachers we can produce.

An article in a recent issue of *The Daily Oklahoman* listed music as one of the fields with a shortage of teachers. As I write this article, I have inquiries from six public school administrators whose classes begin next Monday and who need a band director, a choral director, or a general music teacher.

Summary of This Issue's Editorial:

(1) Competency in music education (Chapman's quick definition) is the ability to develop competent musical performance skills (including the ability to read music notation) among students; to lead students to seek, especially in their adult lives, constant repetition of all the musical behaviors, listening, composing, performing, etc.; and to develop the students' abilities to deal with a broad spectrum of musical styles in the context of all these behaviors. Said simply, a competent music teacher produces good student performers, good music ensembles, and students who listen often, in a somewhat analytic mode, to a wide variety of musical styles—they "like" music.

Dialogue

Question: Can competency in music education be measured by standardized tests?

Answer: Emphatically, NO.

Q: Can competency in music education be measured or perhaps estimated *before* a student actually practices the profession for a period of time?

A: An informed, unbiased panel of professional music teachers who know the student in question (a university faculty) can make educated predictions that will be about 70 percent accurate, provided they look at the students' complete academic records and the quality of leadership and personal relationships exhibited by them. The remaining 30 percent inaccurate predictions constitute a problem. Should we not simply "let nature take its course?" How many ultimately good music teachers would be lost in this excluded 30 percent?

Q: The competency exams lean heavily on language ability and the content of the music exams leans toward music history and theory, because they are more easily tested by the format of the exams. Are the scores rendered under these conditions adequate bases for prediction of competency?

A: My answer would have to be that these scores are relatively useless. They may indicate a form of general intelligence, but are not specific (perhaps even negatively related) to musical intelligence. All teachers should be able to write letters, memos, and instructions with acceptable grammar and syntax. All teachers must be able to accomplish simply arithmetic. Beyond these primitive requirements, the task is mostly right brained. A competent music educator need *not* know algebra and need not perform well on multiple-choice exams.

Q: What, then, is the answer? How is competency predicted?

A: Students who successfully complete an undergraduate degree in music education and who receive the recommendations of the music faculty should be considered provisionally competent until their first several years of experience prove otherwise. A college degree should be the only required mark of competence. Whatever the past problems of elementary education, English education, math education, and the generic "professional education" area, the past record of Oklahoma universities and colleges in music education is very good. Music education is the *most* publicly accountable discipline taught in public education. Incompetence can be hidden only in very small, isolated communities, whose patrons have no reference to other programs or whose musical tastes require only the most superficial entertainment service from the music program. With the present shortage of music teachers, one might suggest than in those schools who have ten coaches and one multidiscipline, multilevel music teacher, even a marginally competent teacher is preferable to none at all.

Statistically it may be that a test of general intelligence will, in a primitive manner, with a *big* + or -, predict teaching success. My problem, especially given the crucial shortage of good teachers, is with the large number of students who are excluded from music education by exams that are not musically valid, and the students who are allowed entry who have insuperable problems of personality or lack of musical skills.

Music education should seriously consider class-action against the companies who design and market the SCAT, ACT, PPST, and the state competency exams. We have an excellent case for these exams being invalid predictors of teaching competency in music.

This article originally appeared in the Fall 1997 issue of Oklahoma Music. *Reprinted by permission.*

Preparing Music Teachers for an Urban Setting
Scott Emmons

When comparing the music teacher training I received twenty years ago to the teacher training given to students today, I find many changes. Most music education curricula now include courses in American popular music, world music, and teaching creativity (improvisation and composition). These experiences did not exist in my training.

Unfortunately, I still see many similarities in curricula that make the knowledge of music teachers entering the profession in urban settings largely irrelevant. Even with the curricular changes of recent years, the majority of music teacher preparation course requirements are designed to teach future music educators a very narrow range of literature from a small cultural perspective. Our beginning teachers are well prepared to provide experiences in choir, band, orchestra, and general music from a western European tradition. This training alone, however, will not be enough for motivating the vast majority of students found in urban schools that do not grow up listening with this cultural perspective. In addition to this problem of preparing teachers to teach a culture with which their students will not identify, preservice teachers tend be taught motivation skills that will only work in ideal settings with ideal students.

Music teacher training programs must identify the needs of students in urban settings and then prepare teachers with strategies to overcome unique problems. Only by doing this will we prepare teachers that are ready to experience the unique rewards that exist in urban music education.

Teacher Training Needs
The most common problem identified by urban school music teachers is that so much instructional time is devoted to classroom management. Urban teachers are frequently frustrated that learning seems secondary. Teacher preparation programs must invest greater time and energy in providing students with management strategies that are successful in urban settings.

Our future teachers need to understand that management problems come from student frustration, boredom, lack of attention, and inability to fit concepts being presented with their own interests. Those involved in teacher preparation programs can identify master teachers in urban areas and determine what works. Music education students interested in succeeding in an urban environment can work closely with these master teachers in fieldwork experiences that are much more extensive than the normal observation and student teaching requirements currently mandated. Guided practice and mentoring are key components in the success of young teachers.

Students being prepared for a music teaching career in an urban setting need much more knowledge and experience with literature that will help them connect with urban students. Preservice training devoted to teaching students how to create and perform in popular music styles has been successful in urban settings in both British and Australian music teacher training programs. They have discovered that success in an urban setting can come from active music making in nontraditional ensembles. These ensembles may include rock, hip-hop, rap, and jazz combos. Like music education majors in the United States, much of the musical experience of these preservice students is in Western styles. To combat this, methods classes focus on preparing teachers to design lessons that will help them connect to urban students. While abandoning our model of performance experience in band, orchestra, and choir is not necessary in an urban setting, much more emphasis needs to be given to linking these styles to the music with which students readily identify. Young music educators need experience in designing active and student focused lessons that will make connections to what urban students know—this means beginning with popular idioms and styles such as rap and hip-hop that will later provide interest in blues, jazz, film music, and yes, classical. It is important for young urban music teachers to know how to design experiences around what motivates students.

Greater use of rote teaching and technology has also proven successful in urban music education. Too many American urban music classes emphasize note reading over active music making. This leads to frustration for both the student and the teacher. Music teacher preparation programs must teach students to make notation a necessity that grows out of active musical experience and interest! One way of providing future educators with strategies for teaching in this manner is by providing them with university experience in ensembles that are traditionally taught by rote, such as world-music drumming ensembles. Music methods teachers can talk about these experiences in class, but there is no substitute for actually making music in this way!

Teacher Commitment

The greatest necessity for any successful music teacher, in an urban or rural setting, is commitment to students and to music. The best way to nurture this commitment is by surrounding young music teachers with others that are successful and positive about teaching music. This requires greater support networks for young teachers from universities, school districts, and community organizations. New teachers in urban settings need constant reminders about their potential value to the students that they teach. They also require reminders that energy and frequent demonstrations of caring will help them gain the respect they need for being successful in an urban teaching environment. Real dialogue with all stakeholders involved (music teachers, parents, administrators, and music supervisors) is necessary for the advancement of the urban students' music education.

This article originally appeared in the January 2003 issue of the Wisconsin School Musician. *Reprinted by permission.*

Music Teacher Preparation for the New Millennium: A Professional Continuum

Don Ester

As we sit at the precipice of a new millennium, teacher preparation in Indiana is facing what promises to be the most dramatic change in decades. With the focus on performance-based assessment resulting from the leadership of the Indiana Professional Standards Board (IPSB), teacher trainees and in-service teachers are going to be required to demonstrate teaching proficiency more than ever before. Initial licensure will no longer result from simply completing a sequence of courses culminating in a degree. Likewise, renewed licensure will no longer result from simply completing six credit hours every five years. Continuous professional growth, as measured by the level at which the educator meets specific teacher performance criteria, must now be clearly demonstrated. How can and should the education profession respond to this new and exciting challenge? As chair of the Ball State committee responsible for developing the institutional assessment system required by the IPSB, I am intimately involved with answering this question. Please allow me to share some information and observations about the new approach to licensure.

The System

Under the new guidelines, teacher preparation programs must assess, evaluate, and document the performance of each teacher-trainee on literally hundreds of specific teacher performances. Undergraduates who meet the minimum required teaching performance criteria will be issued an Initial License to teach music. Teachers with Initial Licenses will enter the profession for a two-year induction period, during which time they will be involved in regular professional development and assessment activities. The induction period will culminate with a portfolio presentation and evaluation. Based on the results of this process, inductees will either be identified as proficient and issued a Practitioner's License, identified as basic and possibly rehired for another year of induction (to reach proficiency), or identified as unsatisfactory and not allowed to continue in the profession.

The Challenge

An effective performance-based approach to teacher preparation requires authentic training and assessment procedures. Apprentice Teachers must have regular opportunities to teach in music classrooms so they can practice and demonstrate the requisite skills. While maximizing realistic teaching experiences has always been a goal of teacher preparation, early and continuous field experience opportunities are now going to be an absolutely essential component of the training process. I believe that this will require an approach to teacher training that has been all too uncommon in the past; an approach similar to teaching hospitals in the medical profession. Music educators of all experience levels, trainees to master teachers, will work side by side in the classroom.

The Continuum of Experience in Action

I am presently involved in a pilot music-teaching field experience project with the music staff at Anderson East Side Middle School: Susan Finger, Bryce Mallernee, Jason Witzigreuter, and Beth Pickard. These Master Teachers, my colleague Dr. Margaret Berg, and I are working with thirteen Apprentice Teachers from Ball State. This team of music educators reflects a wide range of experience levels, from novice freshman to senior student teacher to twenty-year veterans. Each is involved at a level appropriate for his/her experience. This involvement includes observation, administrative tasks, one-on-one tutoring, teaching sectional rehearsals, and working with the entire ensemble for increasing periods of time. Apprentice Teachers observe the Master Teachers and each other. The entire team shares instructional strategies and constructive feedback. The apprentices bring a distinct sense of idealism and energy, along with knowledge of new strategies and technology. The master teachers bring a sense of realism and depth of experience. Each member of the team benefits from the unique knowledge, skills, and perspectives of the others. Early results are very exciting. For example, our initial weekly seminar included an extremely valuable discussion of classroom management strategies. Each of the apprentice teachers shared very specific observations of real-life challenges and solutions. They were then able to go back into the field the next day and apply this information. They are asking very practical questions of the master teachers and me, getting advice, discussing professional issues, and beginning to share ideas of their own. This and other similar projects are "mining the continuum of experience" in a much more profound way than the typical on-campus sequence of courses can.

Conclusion

The music education profession has a tremendous wealth of talent and experience. The performance-based approach to licensure forces us to rethink how we utilize this richness. As one of the "twenty-year veterans," I consider myself lucky to be in the middle of this continuum of experience. It is exciting and energizing to learn from my more experienced colleagues while also sharing my experience with those just entering the profession. I truly believe that the new millennium will see a very positive change in the teacher preparation process, and Indiana is leading the way. I encourage you to seek out your role as we work together to mine the continuum of experience.

This article originally appeared in the March 1999 issue of the Indiana Musicator. *Reprinted by permission.*

Music Teacher Preparation: Fitting the Pieces Together
Elizabeth S. Gould

Late last summer I received a call from a recent music education graduate who had just acquired a position as an elementary music educator, his first teaching position in the public schools. Confronted with the prospect of teaching classroom music at the elementary level, he exclaimed, "What do I do with them!?" His student teaching assignments the previous spring had been exclusively with secondary band programs, but he had very successfully completed my elementary music methods class and taught in the second-grade lab school associated with the class.

Because I had observed him demonstrate a great deal of finesse using several strategies for teaching various music skills and concepts to elementary school students, and knew that he was able to plan and sequence learning transactions, I felt that he would be a very effective teacher at that level. He, however, was not as convinced about his ability to succeed, and relinquished the position shortly after accepting it. I have spent much of the past few weeks thinking about his teacher preparation process, and now believe that perhaps it lacks—or perhaps did not make meaningful to him—one crucial component: understanding the purpose of teaching music in the public schools. He knew what to do as a public school music teacher, but could not discern exactly how to do it, perhaps because he could not articulate a practical rationale for doing it.

Many rationales for teaching music in the public schools have emerged in the last 150 years. As Swanwick has noted, perhaps the most established rationale is based on the notion that as "inheritors of a set of cultural values and [musical] practices,"[1] students learn skills and information necessary to participate in their musical heritage. In U.S. public schools, of course, this is defined in its highest form as Western European art music. The purpose of music education using this rationale, then, is to make students familiar with the musical canon, enabling them to become sensitive to its aesthetic qualities. What is valued here is music as an object that produces aesthetic experiences in students. Child-centered theories of music education using this rationale are to develop students' musical creativity. What is valued here is the process of making music—because it enriches students' lives. Recent cognitive research suggests that not only is music an intelligence or a way of thinking,[2] but that studying music actually alters brain structures and improves other brain processes and academic achievement.[3] What is valued in the former instance is music as cognition. The latter instance reflects the value of music as a means of increasing students' success in school. Other recent theories stress the social relevance of making music in the lives of students, particularly in terms of helping to define their relationships to their communities.[4] What is valued here is making music because it develops students' musicianship so that they may participate in and contribute to the communities in which they live.

Because of its immediacy in terms of behavioral objectives, only the last three rationales can be expressed directly in beginner teachers' classroom practices. Developing students' musicianship literally means making students more musical. When applied comprehensively and coherently, this rationale subsumes all of the others. Teaching to develop musicianship should include study of the musical canon and enjoyment of and participation in its traditions. Further, developing students' musical creativity involves connecting musical study to their everyday lives in ways that are immediately meaningful to them. If the current cognitive research is supported, comprehensive, coherent music education will necessarily result in improved cognitive functions. These things—involvement in musical traditions, becoming creatively expressive, and succeeding academically—are several outcomes of music education. Its purpose, however, is to enable all students to participate in the musical life of their communities; literally, the purpose of music education is to develop students' musicianship.

What exactly constitutes musicianship, of course, probably will never be defined to everyone's satisfaction. When considered thoughtfully, however, musicianship is a reasonably intuitive concept.[5] Musical people are able to sing on pitch. They recognize familiar melodies and are able to reproduce them—particularly with others. Musical people can move their bodies to a beat. They feel discernible beat patterns in music and represent them through movement. When these two skills are sufficiently developed, musical people are able to engage in them expressively.[6] Advanced skills in these two areas, of course, would include solo singing and dancing, respectively. The purpose of music education, then, is to develop these skills and extend them to playing instruments; listening to, notating, and reading music; and evaluating, analyzing, and contextualizing it in terms of its structures and history.

Beginning teachers may approach the classes they are teaching in terms of how those classes will develop their students' musicianship and plan the classes so that this development will occur comprehensively and coherently. Elementary general music teachers carry the broadest responsibility in terms of providing the musical foundation for all music education that will follow. Instrumental music teachers develop specific performance skills, but will enhance these skills if they also continue to develop singing and movement skills. While choral music teachers carry the greatest responsibility for developing singing skills, all music teachers must develop in their students notational and reading skills, as well as evaluation and analysis skills and knowledge about music.

Preparing to become a music teacher is an extremely complex process. Bringing together all of the pieces could be accomplished by focusing teacher preparation programs on enabling teachers to understand the purpose of music education in terms of their public school students—making them more musical—instead of in terms of the music or the things music can do for students, such as involving them in aesthetic experiences or making them smarter. Understanding what makes students more musical provides beginning teachers answers to the pedagogical and musical questions with which they are faced every day. Regardless of the type of music class they teach, they will be able to select repertoire, develop pedagogical techniques, plan and sequence learning transactions, and determine assessment strategies in terms of how all of these may improve their students' musicianship. Teacher preparation courses that reflect this purpose of public school music education enable prospective teachers to develop and use their personal musicianship skills to inform and support their emerging teaching skills.

Endnotes

1. Keith Swanick, *Music, Mind, and Education*, (Routledge: London, 1988), p. 10.

2. See Howard Gardner, *Frames of Mind: The Theory of Multiple Intelligences*, (New York: Basic Books, 1983).

3. See, for example, Frances Rauscher, Gordon L. Shaw, Linda J. Levine, Katherine N. Ky, *Music and Spatial Task Performance: A Causal Relationship*, paper presented at the annual meeting of the American Psychological Association, 12–16 August 1994, ED 390733; and Gottfried Schlaug, Lutz Jancke, J.F. Staiger, and Helmuth Steinmetz, "Increased Corpus Caliosum in Musicians," *Neuropsychologia*, 33 (1995): 1047–1055.

4. See David J. Elliott, *Music Matters: A New Philosophy of Music Education*, (New York: Oxford University Press, 1995); Estelle Jorgensen, "Justifying Music Instruction in American Public Schools: A Historical Perspective," *Bulletin of the Council for Music Education*, 120, (Spring 1994): 17–32; Maxine Greene, *The Dialectic of Freedom* (New York: Teachers College Press, 1988).

5. In developing his tests of music aptitude, expressed as audiation, Gordon measured melodic and rhythmic abilities. See Edwin E. Gordon, *Learning Sequences in Music: Skill, Content, and Patterns—A Music Learning Theory*, (Chicago: GIA Publications, 1993).

6. John Feirerabend, "Kodály Methodology I," class notes, The Hartt School, University of Hartford, West Hartford, CT, July 1996.

This article first appeared in the Fall 1998 issue of Idaho Music Notes. *Reprinted by permission.*

Preparing Elementary General Music Teachers

Kathleen Jacobi-Karna

During the first day of my general music methods class, I always have my students answer the following question: "Today you are the teacher, not a university student. Instead of walking into Hertz Hall 105 for general music methods, where would you be? What level (elementary, middle school, high school)? What area (general music, choir, band, orchestra)?" The vast majority of responses are high school band or high school choir. This does not come as a surprise to me since the high school experience is freshest in their memories and, oftentimes, the choir or band director was very influential in their career choice. My case was no different. I was extremely fortunate to attend a junior high and high school with an exceptional music department. So I, too, entered my general music methods course planning to be a high school choral director. Then everything changed—I discovered the world of elementary general music. Due to this personal experience, I encourage my university students to keep an open mind regarding their age level of choice.

As the quarter progresses we discuss what it takes to be an elementary general music specialist. Here is a brief list from some of our discussions, as well as insights from student teachers in elementary general music.

1. Musicianship—Although I probably won't be getting too in-depth with scale degrees and may never mention a cadential pattern, the ear training I had will be of great benefit, and a musical memory is a must. With an average of four songs per class and potentially six different classes per day, I may have at least twenty-four different songs in my head on a single day.
2. Understanding of child developmental stages— An amazing amount of growth occurs during the elementary school years. I need to be aware of the developmental stages when selecting materials and sequencing the teaching process.
3. Organization— "It's Tuesday—it must be third grade, followed by fifth grade, followed by kindergarten, followed by …" Downtime can be deadly. Not only do I need to have my room ready and materials organized so the students are engaged the moment they walk through the door, but additionally, as my third graders are walking out, the fifth graders are walking into my classroom leaving little time to reorganize.
4. Energy—Many times I will be exhausted at the end of the day. It takes a lot more energy to teach than it does to be a university student. This does not mean I go one hundred miles per hour when I teach. Instead, energy tempered with an appropriate teaching pace is the key.
5. Repetition—Children, especially the young ones, learn from love and repetition. I may be ready to move on to another phase of the lesson, but the students may want to do the song/movement/instrument activity "just one more time."
6. Patience—In many respects this goes hand-in-hand with repetition and developmental stages. I must not become discouraged or impatient when my students don't learn something immediately.
7. Redirecting the discussion—This too requires patience. Young children are so excited to share ideas and experiences with everyone. I need to be prepared to respond to "Yesterday my mom and I … ."
8. Asking the right question—This certainly is a fine art. How I ask a question oftentimes determines the answer. I need to plan my lessons carefully, including the questions I will ask.

There are as many rewards as there are challenges in teaching elementary general music, including watching the "light bulb" turn on when the students understand a new concept, the students' excitement for a particular song or dance/movement activity, and (now I am showing my preference) those angelic voices.

This article first appeared in the March 1999 issue of Washington's Voice. *Reprinted by permission.*

Essential Characteristics of Superior Teachers

S. Gordon Jessop

All students who certify to become music teachers experience similar prescribed course work in their college training. Yet some excel as teachers while others flounder. Why? In my fledgling years of teaching, being naive regarding the incredible complexity of the variables that comprise the instructional process, I hoped to find some simple insight that would instantly deliver me into the realm of teaching excellence. It was not until several years later, when I was involved in an administrative role of screening, interviewing, and recommending applicants for teaching positions, that I began to discern distinctive patterns from which effective teaching could be predicted. Certain commonalities emerged among the diverse configurations of attitudes, skills, and aspirations of those individuals who became the strongest teachers. Now, in the twilight of my career, I have come to believe that there are four preeminent attributes that the most effective teachers possess. These are (1) musicality, (2) the ability to establish caring relationships, (3) carefully thought out instructional priorities, and (4) pedagogical prowess. A brief discussion of each follows with the hope that the ideas presented will be helpful in speeding the achievement of any who are seeking excellence in teaching.

Musicality

The infusion of performance skill with musicality influences virtually all of our musical interactions with students. Possessing solid performance skills provides us with insights for addressing technical problems of producing music.

Possessing a high level of musicality provides us with a vision of the expressive potential of the music being learned. It is imperative that we are knowledgeable, sensitive, and responsive to the expressive potential in the music we teach and help students to progress in their ability to understand and respond to the dynamic tensions and emotional power that is inherent in great music. The level of our performance skill and musicality sets a limit on what our students will be able to achieve under our direction. Individual students may occasionally exceed the level of musicianship of the teacher through private instruction, but the ensemble seldom, if ever, does.

Relationships

The two most important relationships we form as teachers are those with our students and those we foster between students and music. Relationships with administrators, colleagues, and parents are obviously important but less critical to our success. Most relationships can be transacted either horizontally (one human to another) or vertically (superior/subordinate) depending on our preference. The teacher-student relationships that are most conducive to producing effective learning, however, are usually more horizontal than vertical. Reflected in these relationships are respect, trust, warmth, caring, and concern for others. Communication is characterized by more "we," "us," and "let's" phrases, which help students to perceive us as allies working with them on the same side of the musical problem. In such relationships, we feel more inclined to provide opportunities for students to be self-directed and share the responsibility for their learning and for group governance. Nurturing this type of independence is of utmost importance in music education.

In contrast, when we choose to be domineering, self-centered, and authoritarian in our relationships with students, both learning and the relationship are adversely impacted. In this vertical relationship, communication is often laden with phrases such as "I want …," or "Do this for me." Keeping students in a subservient, reliant position may elicit in us feelings of power, control, and importance (even indispensableness) but, in reality, such behavior actually produces weakness in our students and ourselves.

The nature of our interpersonal relationships also influences the type of relationship students have with music. Again, there are two contrasting options: one more dictatorial, and one more directorial. Sometimes we position ourselves between the students and the music so they can only experience the music through us. From this dictatorial position, we make most, if not all, of the musical decisions and require that students be obedient or subservient in carrying out our desires. In such instances it may be wise to ask ourselves this question: When learning and music making is strictly teacher-dependent, are students really being educated? If we choose to position ourselves on the sideline—more like a coach, and let students interact with the music more directly, they have more opportunities to make decisions and be self-determining. Our role as teachers is to intervene when necessary, to direct awareness to important things that are not being perceived, to ask appropriate questions about the music, and to interject insights or suggestions that will increase understanding. Nurturing of this type results in education (informed performance) in contrast to training (performance without understanding).

Instructional Priorities

Our instructional priorities reflect what we perceive to be important for students to learn and, therefore, dictate what the musical curriculum will be. The most effective priorities are based on answers to questions such as: What is the purpose of schools? What is a music education? What constitutes musicianship? What are the most important attitudes, knowledge, and skills that students should develop as a result in being in my classes for three or four years? The convictions that one develops as a result of mining deeply for answers to these questions provide clear long-range goals which, in turn, provide a sense of direction, purpose, and urgency to the instruction. Clear instructional goals and priorities help to focus teacher and student energy and enable the wise expenditure of resources—the most valuable of which is instructional time. Operating from a vantage point of clear vision places us in a proactive rather than reactive position. If we have a clear vision of what should be learned and why, and share that vision with our students, it is much easier for them to "buy into" the goals—which leads to improved cooperation and productivity.

Asahel Woodruff, a well-known educational psychologist in Utah from a former generation, stated that learning is a by-product of goal seeking behavior. That is, we learn what is necessary to help us achieve our goals. This translates into our teaching in different ways. For example, if our goal is simply to perform concerts and get good festival ratings, that goal can be attained without developing in our students substantial musical insights or skills that lead to their musical independence. Is that what a music education should be? Why settle for less when it is possible to have even better performances based on a solid foundation of learning. Whatever our true goals are determines what will be learned. Too often lacking in our instructional efforts are well-defined musical priorities related to both the literature being learned and the development of personal musicianship skills. Teachers and music programs in Utah will thrive when each teacher pays the price to clarify what is important for students to learn and why.

Pedagogical Prowess

The most effective teachers are not only musical, form positive relationships, have clear, well-thought-out instructional priorities, but they also have expertise in essential pedagogical processes. This includes accurately assessing where students are on the developmental continuum, selecting appropriate material to facilitate continuous development, organizing and sequencing experiences for efficient and effective learning, and focusing and unifying students' minds and energy to achieve beneficial learning outcomes. Effective teachers are also adept at implementing learning strategies, monitoring student involvement and contribution, intervening appropriately, and helping students have uplifting and stimulating musical experiences.

This important dimension of effective teaching is too broad to address in detail in the space allotted, but the critical nature of the varied skills that constitute pedagogical prowess should be obvious. These skills comprise the delivery system through which musical dreams are realized. Development of such skills is a long-term project that continues as long as we teach. Things that can facilitate our development include reading professional literature, graduate study, attending in-service workshops and conferences, inviting guest clinicians to work with our ensembles, and thoughtful day-to-day trial-and-error experiences.

As a final thought, the four factors presented above might be used as criteria for informally assessing personal teaching effectiveness. Perceived strength in two of the four areas represents "good teaching"; perceived strength in three of four represents "excellent teaching"; and obvious strength in all four areas represents "superior teaching." Best wishes in your quest for teaching and learning excellence.

This article first appeared in the Winter 2000–2001 issue of Utah's interFACE. *Reprinted by permission.*

Teaching a Skill, Like Cutting Hair
Randy Smith

Last summer, as a member of a university team on teaching and evaluation, I did a lot of reading about "What is good teaching?" and "How do you effectively evaluate teaching?" It wasn't the most exciting way to spend a summer, but I assure you I did have a fabulous two- week vacation in North Carolina where I got a haircut at Floyd's City Barber Shop (Two chairs. No Waiting.) in Mayberry.* Really. No kidding. I've got pictures to prove it!

Reading articles and books about improving teaching reminded me that a teaching certificate is not required to teach at the college/university level. Isn't it a paradox that to teach in a public school you must have a teaching certificate, but to teach in a college/university, where many of us educate future teachers, the minimum qualification is a terminal degree? A college professor is expected to be an expert in a field, but may or may not be an expert teacher. Many new professors have little or no training in the field of teaching. Is it really fair to throw new PhDs into the lion's den (the classroom) without a sword (training)? Which brings me back to my haircut. You can't cut hair, embalm a body, inspect a car, drive an eighteen-wheeler, sell insurance, perform surgery, fill a tooth, or treat an animal without receiving training and obtaining a state certificate. But, you can teach at the college level without any teacher training and without a teaching certificate? What's wrong with this picture?

Teaching is a skill, just like cutting hair. It requires training and practice. Some people have a predisposition for it, but all can benefit from training. Good teachers are grown. They don't just— *poof!*—magically appear. Most universities have a faculty development office that offers workshops and resources on improving teaching. Is teaching a major factor in your annual evaluation? How is teaching evaluated at your institution? Are there workshops and resources available to help you grow as a teacher?

According to Cashin:

> U.S. higher education still pursues the wrong priorities: research and specialization. Graduate programs still socialize their students to aspire to behave like PhDs in some bygone German university, ignoring if not eschewing teaching, especially undergraduate teaching. Specialization has successfully replaced liberal education. (Seldin 1999)

Arrowsmith's (1967) 34-year-old conclusion still seems accurate:

> At present the universities are as ungenial to teaching as the Mohave Desert to a clutch of Druid priests. If you want to restore a Druid priesthood, you cannot do it by offering prizes for Druid-of-the-year. If you want Druids, you must grow trees.

I would like to share with you some quotes and paraphrases from the best source I read last summer: *Changing Practices in Evaluating Teaching— A Practical Guide to Improved Faculty Performance and Promotion/Tenure Decisions* written by Peter Seldin and Associates. Seldin (1999) conducted a study of 740 academic deans at liberal arts colleges and found that 97.5 percent of the 598 who responded listed classroom teaching as a major factor considered in evaluating overall faculty performance in liberal arts colleges (see figure 1). But to evaluate teaching, characteristics of good teaching must first be defined. So, just what is good teaching?

But before you can evaluate something, you must define it so that it can be measured. Seldin (1998) states that although "no single list of teaching qualities has yet been developed to everyone's satisfaction ... more than 15,000 research studies dating from early in the twentieth century to the present [1998] have arrived at reasonably consistent findings about the characteristics of good teaching."

Figure 1. Frequency of use of factors considered in evaluating overall faculty performance in liberal arts colleges, 1998. (Seldin 1999)

FACTORS*	MAJOR FACTOR	NOT A FACTOR
Classroom teaching	97.5%	0.7%
Student advising	64.2%	2.5%
Campus committee work	58.5%	1.7%
Length of service in rank	43.8%	18.9%
Research	40.5%	13.4%
Publication	30.6%	11.4%
Personal attributes	28.4%	26.9%
Public service	23.6%	9.5%
Activity in professional societies	9.9%	5.5%
Supervision of graduate study	3.0%	74.1%
Competing job offers	3.0%	80.1%
Supervision of honors program	3.0%	63.2%
Consultation (govt., business)	2.0%	51.5%

*In descending order by "major factor"

In the first chapter of his book Seldin offers his own list of characteristics of effective teaching and those of three other authors. These characteristics apply to most teaching situations, be it private, classroom, or ensemble rehearsal. Below are what most agree are characteristics essential to effective teaching.

According to Eble (1988):

> Most studies stress knowledge and organization of subject matter, skills in instruction, and personal qualities and attributes useful to working with students.
>
> If personal characteristics are emphasized, good teachers will be ... those who are enthusiastic, energetic, approachable, open, imaginative, and possessed of a sense of humor.
>
> If characteristics of mastering a subject matter and possessing teaching skills are emphasized, good teachers will be those who are masters of a subject, can organize and emphasize, can clarify ideas and point out relationships, can motivate students, can pose and elicit useful questions and examples, and are reasonable, imaginative, and fair in managing the details of learning. Such characteristics as stupidity, arrogance, narrowness, torpor, cynicism, dullness, and insensitivity are commonly associated with bad teaching, as are shortcomings in command of subject matter or in teaching skills.

Beidler (1997), the 1983 U.S. Carnegie Professor of the Year, offers these qualities of a good teacher. He says that good teachers:

1. Really want to be teachers
2. Take risks
3. Have a positive attitude
4. Never have enough time
5. Think of teaching as a form of parenting
6. Try to give students confidence
7. Listen to their students

Peter Seldin (1999) has developed his own list through personal experience and from others. He believes effective teachers:

1. Treat students with respect and caring
2. Provide the relevance of information
3. Use active, hands-on student learning
4. Vary their instructional modes
5. Provide frequent feedback to students on their performance
6. Offer real-world, practical examples
7. Draw inferences from models and use analogies

8. Provide clear expectations for assignments
9. Create a class environment which is comfortable for students
10. Communicate to the level of their students
11. Present themselves in class as "real people"
12. Use feedback from students and others to assess and improve their teaching
13. Reflect on their own classroom performance in order to improve it

Finally, a definition of effective teaching is provided by Miller (1992):

> Effective teachers personify enthusiasm for their students, the area of competence, and life itself. They know their subjects, can explain it clearly, and are willing to do so—in or out of class.
>
> Class periods are interesting and, at times, alive with excitement. They approach their area of competence and their student with integrity that is neither stiff nor pompous, and their attitude and demeanor are more caught than taught.

Back to my haircut. The barber's name at Floyd's is Russell Hiatt, and he's seventy-seven years old. He received his training at the Winston-Salem Barber School in 1946 and has been cutting hair at Floyd's for fifty-five years. He spent almost an hour cutting what little hair I have left. We talked as he snipped. I could feel and see the pride he took in his skill. He was a real person who was full of enthusiasm. When I thought he was done, he got out the hot shaving cream and straight razor and gave me a shave. He then took a warm moist towel and massaged my scalp and neck to remove all the shaving cream. It was the most memorable and best looking haircut I've ever had. But what would you expect? He's a professional. He had training, experience and ... he holds a certificate.

Update

My statement, "... that to teach in a public school you must have a teaching certificate" is untrue. Upon finishing this article I picked up the evening newspaper for a quick read. A St. Louis AP story, "Missouri Schools Attract Badly Needed Teachers—One Way or Another," in the August 30, 2001, issue of the Kirksville Daily Express, page 3, reported that, "In June, the State Board of Education voted unanimously to revamp the alternative certification program. Like others around the country, the program allows mid-career professionals and new college graduates to head up a classroom right away with a temporary teaching certificate."

So now you don't even need a teaching certificate to teach in a public school. Oh, my ... I wonder what kind of a "haircut" those students will receive?

*Mayberry, NC, is the historic downtown area of Mount Airy, NC, the home of Andy Griffith. *The Andy Griffith Show* was filmed in Hollywood, but the folks of Mt. Airy recreated much of the set in their downtown, even including a replica of the squad car. "Well Golleeeeeeee!!" (Gomer Pyle)

Bibliography

Arrowsmith, W. (1967). The future of teaching. In C. B. T. Lee (ed.), *Improving college teaching* (pp. 57–71). Washington DC: American Council on Education.

Beidler, P.G. (1997). What makes a good teacher? In J.K. Roth (Ed.), *Inspiring teaching: Carnegie professors of the year speak*. Boston, MA: Anker.

Eble, K. E. (1988). *The craft of teaching* (2nd ed.). San Francisco, CA: Jossey-Bass.

Hiatt, Russell—professional barber (2001). Personal haircut, July 30, and phone interview, August 30. Floyd's City Barber Shop: Mayberry (Mt. Airy), NC.

Miller, R. I. (1992). In P. Seldin (1998): Personal correspondence.

Seldin, Peter & Associates (1999), *Changing practices in evaluating teaching: a practical guide to improved faculty performance and promotion/tenure decisions*. Boston, MA: Anker.

This article first appeared in the Fall 2001 issue of Missouri School Music. *Reprinted by permission.*

Expertise in Music Teaching
Lelouda Stamou

Music teacher education has always been a central issue in every proposed educational reform. If music education is to change in any way, music educators are the ones that can make these changes happen. Their education and expertise is crucial if music education is to serve the multiple needs of the growing youth in today's complex world.

Music teaching is multidimensional in the sense that it needs to involve both music and teaching expertise in order to be successful. Being a good musician without being a good teacher, or being a good teacher without being a good musician, is a major weakness for a music educator.

David Elliot (1992, 1995) has proposed a model of what expert music teaching involves and requires. Elliot (1992) defines two basic forms of expertise that a music educator should possess: musicianship and educatorship. Both musicianship and educatorship are essentially matters of procedural knowledge, meaning that they involve not only verbal knowledge but also action-based knowledge. Knowing the physical elements involved in riding a bike is totally different from knowing how to ride a bike. Being able to think-in-action and know-in-action is what procedural knowledge is all about.

Musicianship is the "subject matter knowledge" that a professional music educator needs to possess. Musicianship is basically procedural in nature, meaning that one must possess a working understanding of one or more musical practices. One that can verbally explain or identify different bowing techniques does not possess the working understanding of that matter, unless he/she is able to model this knowledge (to know-in-action). As Elliot (1992) says, "the quality and depth of a teacher's musicianship is demonstrated not in what he or she says about music, but in what he or she achieves artistically in her actions of performing, improvising, composing, arranging, or conducting" (p. 9).

Of course, there are other forms of musical knowledge that can contribute to and promote one's musicianship. Formal musical knowledge, consisting of historical and theoretical knowledge on musical practices, musical works, great musicians etc., can shape and refine one's ability to make music, listen to music effectively, and offers him/her additional tools for conveying knowledge. A music teacher that is capable of both modeling musical concepts and verbally explaining them can better serve the needs of the students, some of which can easily grasp principles nonverbally through the teacher's modeling or through listening to music, while others need verbal explanations in order to acquire a thorough understanding of the principles that are being taught.

Informal musical knowledge is also very important for expert musicianship and is basically acquired through one's experiences of making music in several musical settings. It is the ability to respond with music in a productive artistic context, the ability to think in a musical context and about the musical context in which one makes music. In a more advanced level, this kind of knowledge can become what Elliot (1992) calls "the impressionistic musical knowledge," which is often also called "musical intuition" (p. 11). It is the strongly felt sense that one line of action is better than another or not quite right, the ability to spontaneously and intuitively respond in the best possible way while making music, or while reflecting on specific musical situations. Finally, supervisory knowledge is the ability to deal with unpredictable musical situations and handle them successfully.

Teaching expertise is what Elliot calls educatorship, and consists of the same forms of knowledge that musicianship consists of. Teaching expertise is procedural in nature, in the sense that it requires a practical understanding of the teaching-learning situation, and involves the ability to shape the teaching-learning situation or adjust to it. Knowledge of the subject matter is essential for a teacher to be successful, but the ability to interact with students and convey the knowledge in different teaching situations is what educatorship is all about. The expert teacher is not the one that accurately follows a curriculum and tries to deliver it as a product to the learners. It is the one that has the ability to think-in-action, know-in-action, and reflect-in-action in the context of this curriculum and in relation to the fluid and dynamic situation of music teaching and learning. As Elliot says, "teaching expertise is the flexible, situated ability to think-in-action in relation to student needs, subject matter standards, community needs, and the professional standards that apply to each and all of these" (p. 13).

As in the case of musicianship, expertise in teaching also involves and requires formal knowledge of psychology, philosophy of music education, theories of child development, physiology of learning, etc. Such knowledge can aid the educators in refining their teaching depending on the characteristics of the learner and the learning-teaching situation. Informal knowledge, which is the knowledge acquired through experience in teaching, is crucial and should reach the point of impressionistic knowledge; a point at which the educator can sense or feel what is best to do in a teaching situation and act accordingly. Finally, supervisory knowledge is a matter of professional metaknowledge; it is the ability to combine all the above in a teaching situation. Expert educators possess all the aforementioned types of knowledge.

Musicianship, educatorship, and the types of knowledge involved in them cannot be fully acquired in a four- or five-year teacher education program. These are developed through time, continuous education, and experience. However, the foundations for their development should be solidly placed at the college level. If music teacher education programs do not provide future teachers with the formal and the informal knowledge that is essential to help them develop expertise, it will be very difficult for them to find a way to do so on their own. The broader objectives of a music teacher-training program at the college level are to develop music educators that are strong both as teachers and musicians. Such teachers develop quickly through the everyday teaching experience and are the ones who, most often, carry the educational reforms and contribute to the advancement of music education.

References

Elliot, D. J. (1992). Rethinking music teacher education. *Journal of Music Teacher Education*, 1(2), 6–15.

Elliot, D. J. (1995). *Music Matters: A New Philosophy of Music Education.* NY: Oxford University Press.

This article first appeared in the October 2001 issue of New Jersey's Tempo. *Reprinted by permission.*

Can you make it through the college years?

 Section 5

Can you make it through the college years?

Observe! Observe! Observe!
Jon Boysen

If you walked down the halls of your music building and asked people what they did over winter break, I bet you would get a variety of responses. You would find people that worked, people who caught up on their soap operas, people who drove to North Dakota to visit Aunt May. But I'm willing to bet that you wouldn't find too many people who told you that they went and observed over break and saw four general music teachers, two middle school choir directors, a junior high strings teacher, three high school band directors, two high school choir directors, and two high school orchestra directors. Observing usually isn't one of the top priorities when it comes to how we spend our time during our breaks. Usually our breaks are dedicated to making money or getting rest. Although these things are important, they are not as important in the long run as observing can be. Observing is one of the most important activities we can do as we prepare for our professional careers.

By observing, we can accomplish several things. First of all, observing is a great way to figure out what areas you would like to teach in. Through observation, you might discover you really would like to teach middle school choir and that you might not like high school band. Observing gives you a risk-free chance to look at all areas of music education in the real world. It is a good way to reaffirm what areas you want to go into. You might surprise yourself and discover that general music is what you would like. Oftentimes our concept of what it would be like to teach certain areas comes from what we remember from when we were in school and through our classes in college. The real world offers a whole new perspective on things. Observing allows us to gain a teacher's perspective on our past experiences and allows us to look at things in a different light.

Second, observing allows us to view different teaching styles and ways of classroom management. When you do many observations, you get the opportunity to view many different teaching styles. You get the opportunity to see techniques that you might want to try one day. You also may get the opportunity to see teaching techniques that you may never want to try! Observing also will allow you to see several different ways of handling discipline. You can see a variety of situations where teachers have easy-to-handle and hard-to-handle students. You can also see a variety of ways teachers handle the tougher situations. Observing allows you to see many different approaches to teaching the same concepts.

Take advantage of your observation experience. While you are observing, make sure you have a notebook to take notes in. Ask the teachers you are observing if you can see the materials that they use. You might want to write down the author, title, and publisher in case you want to use these materials later in your teaching career. Also ask to see the syllabus and handouts and see if the teachers you are observing will let you keep a copy of their handouts. If you get a chance, sit down with the teachers and talk about some of the things you observed. You might want to talk about the manner in which a teacher handled a situation or explained a concept.

It is also a good idea to talk with the teachers about things that they do that may not have happened on the day you observed. There are a lot of things that teachers do that would be impossible to observe all in one day. You can also talk to the teachers about how they might handle certain situations. An example might be, how do they motivate students during down days, or what they do when the class gets completely out of control? This is also a good time to see how different schools and school districts operate. Ask to see some of the paperwork that teachers have to fill out. Find out what kind of scheduling system the school has. You may also want to find out if the administration is supportive of the music program. Ask your teachers how this affects their program.

Some observing basics. Always call the teachers you would like to observe ahead of time and make sure it is all right for you to come observe them. Ask them what would be the best time and day for you to observe. You will also need to find out what policies different schools have for visitors at their schools. Many schools require that you sign in at the main office and, in some cases, require you to wear a visitor's badge. Last, make sure that you get the most out of your experience!

This article first appeared in the January 1997 issue of Washington's Voice. *Reprinted by permission.*

Classroom Management
Darlene Fett

Education in America is a hot topic of conversation these days. Just turn on the radio or television, or pick up a newspaper and you will probably find something about education being addressed. Our political candidates each have a unique plan for funding and improving the quality of education. Many national and state leaders have been trying to come up with ways to increase teacher salaries and retain quality educators in our school systems. While these issues are extremely important, there is another educational topic that warrants dialogue. This issue is classroom management in today's schools.

Classroom management is a topic that always generates considerable discussion in my music methods classes. How to control twenty-five or thirty eighth-graders in a required general music class or maintain order within an entire ensemble while rehearsing one section is one of the greatest concerns of these future music teachers. Unfortunately, there is no precise "magical" formula that will guarantee perfect student behavior in the classroom. But, there definitely are things that one can to do to prevent potential behavior problems before they occur.

Perhaps one of the key factors to achieving positive behavior in the classroom is organization. Being organized includes such things as having a seating plan for your class or ensemble members, analyzing and studying your musical scores before the ensemble rehearses, writing out lesson plans for ensemble rehearsals as well as your general music classes, and keeping a log for each individual lesson you teach. Now is the time to begin thinking about and planning the kind of classroom environment in which you want to teach. How much whispering and talking can you tolerate?

Does it bother you to see students chewing gum during rehearsals? Will you allow students to come to class late or without their music? How will you handle students who misbehave? Begin now to identify the kind of behavior you will expect from your students. Determine three or four "behavior goals" that can be stated in a positive manner and write them down for future use in your classroom. Some ideas for "behavior goals" might include being considerate, courteous, and respectful in the classroom; being academically responsible; using language that does not offend others; and caring for school property and the property of others (Taken from "4-For-All" Student-Parent Handbook, Southeast Junior High School, Iowa City, Iowa).

In addition to being organized, here are a few more ideas that experienced music teachers have used to help them manage their classrooms and rehearsals effectively:

1. Begin and end the class or rehearsal on time.
2. Keep the students actively engaged in making music. "Less talk—more performance" is generally a good rule to follow.
3. Maintain eye contact with your students as much as possible. Again, a thorough knowledge of the musical score or your lesson plan will enable you to better interact visually with your students. Don't allow yourself to get stuck behind the desk, podium, or piano. Moving around the classroom and among your students really lets you see and hear exactly what they are doing.
4. Realize that your junior high and high school ensembles aren't going to sound like the college groups in which you performed. Also, they probably won't be able to perform the repertoire that you performed in college. While it is good to have high musical performance standards and expectations for your ensembles, choose literature that is realistically appropriate

for the group's ability and that can be performed with success.

5. Be sure your students leave your classroom with a positive feeling about themselves and what they have learned.

6. Finally, be a good role model for your students. Believe it or not, teenagers can tell immediately if an adult is sincere, honest, and genuine in what he or she says or does. Classroom management problems really *can* be minimized when mutual trust and respect exist between students and teacher.

These are just a few ideas that I hope will be beneficial as you begin thinking about how you might achieve a positive learning environment in your future music classrooms and rehearsals.

This article first appeared in the Spring 2000 issue of The South Dakota Musician. *Reprinted by permission.*

Guidelines for Classroom Management and Discipline Plans
Sherman Hong

(This article is addressed specifically to college students and young teachers. However, all of us can learn from it.)

As future teachers, undergraduate music education students take courses that serve as a foundation for teaching success. Courses are designed to give basics upon which to build your applicable teaching materials, methodologies, and procedures. Of necessity, textbooks used in methods classes are written toward ideal teaching environments and students.

To balance the ideal with the "real" teaching world, most schools require a minimum amount of *practica* in classrooms of various school systems before student teaching. If administered properly, such *practica* enable future music teachers to observe real teaching environments and to determine how teachers manage different teaching situations. In many instances, mentor teachers invite and/or allow observing collegiate students opportunities to make class work more meaningful. Use your experiences to engage your teachers and peers in meaningful discussions on some things that might not otherwise be incorporated within the normal curriculum of the college classes.

As a supervisor of music student teachers, I have observed many who are well-prepared. These are ones who are able to apply and/or synthesize information and observations from a variety of classes—music education courses, professional education work, and yes, from the school's core requirements (e.g., psychology). An excellent teacher has the ability to draw on his/her entire education—not just music methods.

In discussions with student teachers (or young teachers), I have found the main topics of concern address two areas: discipline and classroom management. These topics are frequently not discussed in depth in methods classes. Thus, one of my requirements for student teachers is they write such plans. In their first attempts, students frequently combine the two: however, they are then directed to separate them because they should be separate entities.

Each student teacher's plan is different because discipline and management plans are based on each individual school's environment. As future teachers, you must know it is imperative that in both *practica* and student teaching experiences, observations about what does or doesn't work should be made. Balance your perceptions with knowledge about the schools, environments, and students. Remember—what works in one situation might not work in another! Consequently, few rules about management and discipline are carved in stone. What I prefer to do is have guidelines upon which specific plans can be adapted to various teaching environments. The following guidelines have been found to be helpful to both student teachers and young teachers.

Classroom Management
Classroom management refers to all the things a teacher does to organize students, space, time, and materials so student learning takes place. In other words, you have a routine!

1. Characteristics of a well-managed classroom:
   a. Students are actively involved in learning.
   b. Students know what is expected of them.
   c. There is little wasted time, confusion, or disruption
   d. Climate of class is work-oriented and pleasant.
2. Have classroom ready for student learning.
3. Address the floor space—have the room set up for expected work to be accomplished.
   a. Make sure everyone can see you.
   b. Keep high-traffic areas clear.
   c. Know regulations regarding fire and disaster drills.

d. Have necessary materials in easily accessible areas.

e. Test equipment before you plan to use it.

4. Maximize your own work space to allow access to materials you intend to use.

5. Be present in the room or near the door as students arrive; greet them as individuals or small groups.

6. Post the daily assignment; your first priority is to get students to work quickly.

7. Have a set routine for beginning each class. For example, is some or no talking allowed?

8. Take class attendance—seating charts, have assigned student check roll, etc.

9. Keep accurate records.

10. Decide what you want to record in the grade book; attendance, assignment results, test grades, skills mastery, class participation, behavior marks, and cumulative progress.

Discipline Plans

1. Effective teachers have written rules, procedures, routines and follow them faithfully.

2. If there is no school discipline plan, construct yours and get it approved by your administrator. Plans should be in writing and reflect your rules, consequences, and rewards.

3. Have copies available for students, parents, and administrators.

4. Communicate in both verbal and written form to your students what you expect as appropriate behaviors.

5. It is easier to maintain good behavior than to change inappropriate behavior after it has become established. In other words, enforce your rules from the beginning.

6. The best plan is one based on school-wide discipline plans.

7. Limit rules to a number you and your students can remember—no more than 5!

8. Discipline plans should have consequences.

9. Post your consequences!

10. Consequences can be positive (rewards) or negative.
Example: positive—end lesson early and allow them to socialize.
negative—name on board, detention time assessed

11. Do not stop a class to penalize a student—talk to him/her after class.

12. Use set procedures (rehearsal, announcements, etc.) Reinforce them.

13. Use eye contact and names with students; constantly check to see if students are on task by asking appropriate questions. Utilize their perceptions in discussions.

Note that both guidelines are not music specific but are of paramount importance. An excellent teacher has both management and discipline skills before he/she can teach effectively! Before you student teach or become a young professional teacher, learn as much about these two areas as possible!

This article first appeared in the Spring 2001 issue of Mississippi's MMEA Journal. Reprinted by permission.

Relaxation and Coping Techniques for the Music Education Major

Chris Koenig

This article is taken from an interview with Ms. Jane P. Ehrman, MEd, director of the student health center at Baldwin-Wallace College. Ms. Ehrman is a national board certified diplomat as well as a clinical hypnotherapist.

What kind of techniques can you suggest for relaxation that students can do on their own?

I would suggest, first of all, deep breathing. You have to breathe anyway. Most of us don't breathe efficiently; we kind of breathe with "puppy breaths," shallow breathing from the tops of our lungs. But when you breathe deeply you get more oxygen to everything, and everything functions better. You have more energy. You actually get more oxygen to the brain, so you think more clearly. So deep breathing is a good technique. And no one has to know you are doing relaxation exercises. You can do it anywhere—you can do it at a traffic light, you can do it during an exam, you can do it during a performance. When your mind starts to do a tailspin, you can bring it right back with deep breathing.

What else can we use? For example, is visualization important?

Yes. And you can combine the two. Now I wouldn't suggest combining them if you're in traffic, but you can otherwise. Imagine breathing in a peaceful calm and exhaling the tension, the worry, the hesitation, the anger, or the fear. While breathing in imagine what that peaceful calm looks like. It may be like an ocean wave, it may be a light— any color light—or it may be breathing in little stars. Whatever your own imagination comes up with will be the best thing for you. That's a mini kind of visualization you can do along with the breath. When you have more uninterrupted time, you can do even more imagery. We all use our imaginations. Unfortunately, as we move out of childhood and into adulthood our society impresses upon us the idea that we shouldn't fantasize and we don't have imaginations. This is not accurate; everyone uses their imagination. Adults tend to use it in considering "what if?" "What if a catastrophe happens? What if I don't do well at this audition? Or this jury? Or this competition? What if I don't get a good grade? What if I fail out of school? What if I can't get a job? What if I end up on the street without a home?" Before

you know it they're so far down that road they can't even breathe, let alone think about anything positive. That's marvelous imagination. The better the imagination, the worse it gets.

How can students help themselves in coping with general anxieties such as a test, audition, or solo?

They can use a technique called cognitive restructuring or reframing. Replace the negative word with a positive one. If the word jury, competition, audition, etc. is a negative trigger for fear or hesitation, change it. Maybe you can call it a "special program," or an "event," or come up with something yourself. Students need to stray away from those "what ifs" and return to the original reason why they are there. When you do what you love, it's exciting. It feeds your soul. Focus on "I love this, and I am going to treat this as something sacred." Every time a musician picks up his instrument he needs to let go of everything outside of what he is doing and just live in the moment. We need to re-experience the love that we had the first time we did what it is we love. Let go of all outside thoughts and live in that moment. When you do all that, you can perform at your potential. We're not perfect. The only perfect thing about humans is that we are perfectly human. We have inadequacies. No one can ask you to do better than your best.

With the huge workload and lack of rest of music education students, what are some ways to create and maintain energy levels?

Balance. When we are expected to do more than we can handle our bodies are out of balance and the quality of the product goes down. College is a time when you are developing your character. If your life is not balanced you may become a lopsided individual. Then you might never regain balance. In addition to balance, students need to prioritize. Figure out what really is most important. We all have certain needs. We need to nourish our bodies with healthy food. We need adequate rest—six to seven hours—so that both body and mind can replenish themselves. We also need a while every day just to play. Whatever play is—running, riding a bike, playing basketball, painting, sculpting, swimming, socializing, playing cards—we need it every day. Laughter is great for the body. It helps to build up the immune system, and it's an aerobic exercise. It's hard to be uptight after a fit of laughter. When the body is balanced, it functions better all-around.

Here are descriptions of exercises to deal with

stress and anxiety. (Taken from "Relaxation and Coping Techniques," by Jane Ehrman.)

Minis: Breathing Exercises

1. Ten slow, deep breaths, counting back from 10 to 1. Allow yourself to take a normal breath or two between each deep breath.
- Can be done at traffic lights, standing in line, while on the phone on "hold," waiting for class to start, before a competition, before an exam, when angry or upset, before an important meeting, etc.
- Place blue 3/4 inch round color coding labels in areas frequently used to remind yourself to do "minis" (e.g., on your computer monitor, phone, work area, etc.).
2. Stop—Breathe—Reflect—Choose
- When feeling tension build inside, or when having negative thoughts, take a moment to:
- STOP!
- Take a slow, deep breath.
- Reflect on what is happening and the thoughts going through your mind.
- Choose how you will respond in a positive, more effective way.
3. Deep breathe to a 4-count
- As you inhale, count slowly up to four; as you exhale, count slowly back down to one. Thus, as you inhale, you say to yourself, "one, two, three, four," as you exhale, "four, three, two, one." Do this several times.

Progressive Muscle Relaxation
- Begin with the toes, tightening then releasing and softening.
- Move to ankles, lower legs, and up the body, tightening and softening each part, becoming more comfortable.
- If the mind wanders off, gently bring it back to the moment, focusing on the area and softening there.
- Along with softening, incorporate a slow, deep breath.

Mindfulness
- Focus only on one thing, that which you are presently doing (e.g., walking, dancing, cooking, or any other focused activity)! This is an attitude of being aware and remaining present to what is happening without becoming involved with feelings.

Imagery (Visualization)
- This is using imagination at its best; purposeful daydreaming.
- Take a few moments to get very comfortable, letting muscles become soft, like a rag doll.
- With eyes closed or open, imagine being in a special place or performing a specific task or skill well or reliving an experience or activity or reforming an event in a positive way, etc. Let yourself experience the event or activity as you wish with your senses. Experience how it feels, recall and relive an experience when you performed your best and bring that moment to this moment.
- Not everyone is visual or able to "see" with his or her imagination. But you may hear, smell, and feel the experience (kinesthetic) within your body.
- Avoid the idea of perfection, since as human beings, this is unattainable. Imagine peak performance.
- Imagery should be done in a place where you will not be interrupted.
- Imagery should never be done while operating machinery, as you are not able to put your full attention to the task at hand.
- Stay away from pets—they will be drawn to your relaxation and want to sit in your lap or bother you.

Guided Imagery
- This is the same as imagery, except the experience is guided in a one-on-one session with a hypnotherapist or using an audiotape.
- There are many audiotape resources available on the market.

Other Relaxation/Coping Techniques
- Journalizing
- Massage
- Yoga
- Soothing music
- Sensory awareness—sitting in a park and experiencing the surroundings
- Exercise and play
- Talking with a friend

(For more exercises like these that are related to music and performance, try *The Inner Game of Music* by Barry Green with W. Timothy Gallwey, published by Doubleday, 1986.)

This article first appeared in the December/January 1999/2000 issue of Ohio's TRIAD. *Reprinted by permission.*

Don't Knock It 'til You've Tried It
Anna LaBar

If you're like many of my friends, you presently have no interest in teaching music at the elementary level. I've heard these friends say that elementary students don't understand music, they're too much of a discipline problem, or "they just can't do real music." This list could go on—I assume you probably know what I'm talking about. It's a mystery to me where these ideas originate, because these friends who are so sure they don't want to teach elementary music have never had the experience of teaching at the elementary level—or at the high school level, for that matter. From my own limited experience, I would (could) compare not giving teaching music in an elementary school a chance to someone deciding they don't like ice cream before they have taken a single bite.

I spoke with five music specialists in Putnam County (Kristen Duncan, K–4 music specialist at Northeast Elementary; Kevin Fletcher, K–4 music specialist at Sycamore Elementary; Sherry LaBar, sixth-grade music specialist at Prescott Central Middle School; Clarissa Miller, K–6 music specialist at Baxter Elementary School; and Terri Stone, a K–6 music specialist taking a leave of absence from her job in Alaska to study music therapy at TTU) to see how they felt about their students and jobs. Overwhelmingly, the verdict was, "I love my job, and I wouldn't teach high school for the world!" Now, don't get me wrong. I'm not saying that high school positions are not important or that it's wrong to want to teach high school. I'm just saying you should consider first-hand information before you form your opinion. Have you had any experience on which to base your feelings, or have you arbitrarily decided that you are not going to teach elementary school? If the latter is the case, perhaps you should reconsider your position by hearing what these teachers have to say about the children they work with every day or, even better, being present when the teaching is occurring.

All the teachers agreed that the children's age was not a limiting factor. Clarissa Miller feels that her student's ages do not hinder either herself or them, and that it is often more rewarding to work with her youngest students. Kristen Duncan pointed out that it is more difficult to teach kindergartners because they can't read, but she views this as a challenge rather than a problem. Terri Stone, who taught high school before

teaching elementary, commented that the musicality of the students cannot be as advanced because they simply have not had as many experiences. All three teachers commented that we need to keep in mind that if students don't learn basic musical skills in elementary school, they will have to learn them in high school or unfortunately never. If this is the case then you're not going to be able to develop good musicianship in high school.

While discussing the students' capabilities, I was quite impressed. I recently attended one of Sherry LaBar's school programs, and I must admit that I was completely unprepared for what I heard. Her program was written about various composers. Each song performed was filled with interesting and important facts about the most important composers, and all the music was set to one of that particular composer's most familiar works. What was amazing, though, was that the entire program was conducted by select children, the one hundred nonselect classroom children sang in tune without oversinging, they had fun, and they even played some of their own compositions (some of which were quite impressive). Mrs. LaBar commented that she does not feel at all limited and that she feels that anything she is enthusiastic about teaching, the students will be excited about learning.

I also asked about the improvement and musical growth that the teachers had seen in their children since they had begun to teach. Kevin Fletcher, who began his current job three years ago, said that when he came to Sycamore, his fifth- and sixth-grade choir sang familiar Christmas carols in unison. This year his third and fourth grade choir is singing Mozart in parts. By the time Terri Stone's sixth graders leave her, they can sight sing using solfège, read scores that are unmarked, know the basic forms of music, have studied music history, and can read both bass and treble clef. How many of us wish we could say that we could have done all that in sixth grade? How many of us wish we could do all of that now?

Regarding class control, all of the teachers felt that it is much easier to deal with elementary age students. Mrs. LaBar remarked that, while they're much less inhibited about trying new things than high school students, they also don't have nearly as many attitude problems.

My point is that you never really know how wonderful something is or isn't until you've tried it. I once read somewhere that "A student is limited only by what his/her teacher is willing and able to teach." In other words, children are restricted only by their teachers. As Mrs. Duncan so wisely and laughingly told me, "Don't knock it 'til you've tried it!" and that's all I'm asking of you.

This article first appeared in the December 1997 issue of The Tennessee Musician. *Reprinted by permission.*

When the Teacher Is Ready, the Students Will Appear
Tim Lautzenheiser

We continue to explore the various avenues of teacher preparation in hopes of finding the right combination to ensure a healthy learning experience for all students in their lifelong relationship with music. What are the attributes of a successful music educator? Do the students respond to "what" they are taught or "the way" they are taught? While the answer is always "Yes," we sometimes sidestep the contextual aspect of teaching methodology. Let us focus on the teacher as s/he relates to the students and discover, "When the teacher is ready, the students will appear."

1. Teaching Style: Positive or Negative
We would all like our students to evaluate us as positive teachers. It is important not to confuse the word "positive" with "happy." By definition, positive means honest and with forward motion. There are certainly occasions when we are sure things aren't moving in a forward motion and it calls for some serious candor of an uncomfortable nature. Perhaps we can better understand the question by determining if we enjoy the process of teaching music; we must see it as an opportunity to bring our students to a higher level of creative understanding and expose them to a universal language certain to benefit every aspect of their lives. Conversely, a negative style would emphasize reaching the given goal at all costs and justifying it by rationalizing; the extreme justifies the means. This often creates an environment filled with stress, tension, defensive-survival-behavior, and (in most cases) it is counter-productive to what we are trying to achieve.

2. Motivation by Fear and/or Desire
Is it the fear-of-failure or the desire-for-success that motivates us to excellence? Is it the carrot out front or the whip on his back that moves the plow horse forward?

It is clear we all are subject to both avenues of extrinsic behavior modification. Fear is the quickest way to move or motivate a person for-ward. We are creatures of survival and, as pointed out, we will not elevate to a higher level of behavior until we know our survival is ensured; therefore, any kind of threat will stimulate an action in an attempt to preserve our very existence. The ever-popular and always effective, "If you don't do this, I will …" approach to students generates a quick response and, from an outside perspective, appears to be the most efficient way to "lead" the individual or group to the established goal. However, the aftereffects are usually not as desirable as we might hope. If the student chooses to remain in the class/ensemble following a situation where fear of failure is the dominant motivational theme, (many of them simply quit; the "path of least resistance" syndrome), then a behavior habit has been established that will require an even greater fear to achieve the next level of performance. It can be a one-way street to program destruction at the cost of creative artistry.

Alternatively, the desire for success does not guarantee such instant reactions. It requires a much longer and more patient style of mentoring. The sense of high-level accomplishment is often set aside in favor of rest and relaxation. Entropy is not only a law of nature, but also a predictable human pattern. Ultimately, we all want our students to study, practice, perform, etc., because of their innate love of music. This will only happen when the student desires to take on the responsibility with the understanding it has a personal benefit to his or her life.

Master educators use a healthy dose of desire and a judicious amount of fear as they traverse the endless musical journey with their students. Depending on the relationship that has been developed with the members of the class/ensemble, the application of these two extrinsic motivational tools is effectively administered at the appropriate time, resulting in a more productive work ethic demonstrated by the students; herein lies the key to quality music education/performance.

The only true intrinsic motivation is self-motivation; therefore, our emphasis must always be the stimulation of the individual; to inspire the person so s/he will excel without being threatened or bribed.

3. Quieting the Ego

Is our quest for excellence in music a foundation of our teaching mission or is it a payoff to feed our personal/professional growth pattern?

According to Webster, "The egocentric person is limited in outlook or concern to an individual activity or need." Are we capable of rising above our individual needs to pursue a much higher goal? Can we give unconditionally without expecting or demanding anything in return? Can we get beyond our own ego?

These are uncomfortable inquiries and, even as we ask ourselves, our ego will doubt the validity of the question itself. The "I-Me" preoccupation with "self" is seen in every aspect of our society. The constant tug-of-war for ownership has not escaped our world of music. Students are sparring over chair placement, struggling to beat someone else for a seat in the "top group," jockeying for political favor to be the one "selected" as an officer, and on and on. All too often, receiving a first place, or being deemed "the best" becomes more important than making music. Being number one becomes a higher priority than the benefit of playing/singing/creating music; if so, the process alters accordingly to fit the goal. Students may walk off a festival stage thrilled with their performance, then discover they received a second place rating which immediately throws the whole group into an emotional tailspin resulting in tears, accusations, blame, revenge, disappointment, and a host of other negative reactions. If the ensemble felt a sense of positive accomplishment in preparing the music, and the members of the group dedicated their time and energy to achieving a new performance standard, then why would an evaluator's opinion override the joy of the accomplishment? If the described performance scenario is true, the extrinsic award has become more important than the intrinsic reward. In truth, the rating is secondary. This is not to say there is not an educational value in competitive forums, but the evaluation/judgment only has educational worth when used to help in the preparation of the next performance.

Outstanding educators detach themselves from the outcome. The spotlight is always on the growth and development of the students; the pathway of maturity.

4. Agree to Disagree: Harmony Is the Key

Harmony, balance, and blend are common terms we bring to our rehearsal vocabulary. Are they also a part of our teaching pedagogy? Perhaps the solution to quieting the ego (point #3) is developing the ability to "agree to disagree." The results that come from moving forward in harmony are generally far more beneficial than struggling with the handicaps of disagreement. It is certainly important to "stand up for what we believe," but when it is at the expense of the overall welfare of the organization, we have the option to simply agree to disagree. It does not mean giving up our values, our standards, or our ethics; it simply means we support the dignity of the other party or parties and realize the discussion/argument is holding back the progression of the program.

Independently we rely on energy—an individualistic source of natural power. Interdependently we avail ourselves of synergy—a cooperative act such that the total effect is greater than the sum of the independent parts. This extensive boost in potential only shows up when we are in a "cooperative mode." Rather than waiting (and wasting precious time) to find a group of people who are of like minds, we have the wherewithal to access synergy immediately (with any persons) by "agreeing to disagree," thus establishing a sense of cooperation—the key to creative synergy.

5. Our Mind Leads Us in the Direction of Our Most Dominant Thoughts

Thoughts lead to feelings.
Feelings lead to actions.
Actions lead to habits.
Habits establish character.
Character determines destiny.

The equation is an oversimplification of the programming of the mind. We take actions on our feelings; these feelings are a by-product of our thoughts.

We have all been amused by our fellow music educator (?), Professor Harold Hill, center figure of Meredith Willson's popular musical, *The Music Man.* As you remember, Professor Hill was a capricious con artist who convinced the people of River City of the need for a band; this would prevent the innocent children from being lured to the evils of the local pool hall; a sinful establishment of ill morals! In the story line, Harold was finally confronted with his eager young musicians (with instruments in hand) and challenged to "make music" or face the wrath of the skeptical town leaders who were rightfully suspect of the self-proclaimed maestro. He stood in front of the band-to-be with baton in hand and said, "Think!" Although it was a command of desperation, it was that very action that saved his hide, and also it was (and is) a good lesson for all. "Whether we think we can or whether we think we can't, we're always correct."

It seems we often wait to see what the circumstances are, then we adjust our attitude accordingly. However, the sequence is: believe, then be. With each passing hour we are discovering the power of thoughts/beliefs. The ability to manifest our desired conditions is known and practiced by every great teacher. "The mind leads us in the direction of our most dominant thoughts."

What do you believe is possible for your students, your program, your school, your community? Are there real limits or are there only perceived limits? Are we held captive to our self-imposed restrictions? Any successful person will tell you there is more to this than simply "thinking the right thoughts." The next step is to do the work necessary to complete the goal. It is not, by any stretch of the imagination, a quick fix, but it is a necessary beginning to achieve the aspired goal.

6. One Person Makes a Difference

You make a difference. Every person makes a difference. We might want to ask ourselves, "What kind of difference am I making?" We are either part of the problem or part of the solution, but, without question, each of us makes a difference.

We often become frustrated because we feel as though we are alone in our quest. Our daily teaching schedule demands us to be a myriad of personalities ranging from a fund-raiser to a bus driver, and somewhere in the midst of all of it, we teach music. The never-ending list of responsibilities can be overwhelming and as stress and pressure are brought to bear, it is easy to retreat to the rationalization of, "I'm only one person and I can't make a difference." However, embracing such a notion violates the very goal for which we are striving. Successful educators, in any facet of teaching, are the ones who see obstacles as opportunities for growth. They are not enticed by short-cut solutions, but are committed to reaching their goals and willing to invest whatever is necessary to achieve the given end. Styles vary, from those who are patiently methodical, to those who are enthusiastically leading the charge with trumpets blaring. The one commonality is persistence—the ability to go on resolutely regardless of any inconvenience or opposition; to continue in spite of resistance.

As we look through history, it is evident the only thing that has made a difference is one person. Somewhere in our lives one person, probably a music teacher for many of us, was a catalyst in helping us choose our life's calling—music. "Our teacher" was ready when we appeared. Now we have the chance to return the favor; we can have a positive impact on the young people who eagerly step into our classrooms, for we know: when the teacher is ready the students will appear!

We make a living by what we get; we make a life by what we give.
—*Winston Churchill*

This article first appeared in the Spring 1998 issue of Europe's EMEA Journal. Reprinted by permission.

Music Education Majors, Don't Muddle through the Next Millennium! Amazing Music Education Philosophy for the New Millennium Found in the Basement of MENC Headquarters!

David Leithmann

Yes! In an amazing, quasi-mystical event, a folder containing the soon to be announced philosophy for all new music educators was found behind a filing cabinet in the basement of MENC headquarters (see photo) during the annual summer housecleaning. This important document, found by accident, will soon be adopted by MENC as the official educational philosophy. Yes, my music education friends and colleagues, you are hearing it first in *PMEA News*! In a daring and dangerous move, a "mole" at MENC headquarters faxed me the document soon after it was discovered. I have studied it for countless hours (really, about an hour and ten minutes), and believe it or not, I have adopted the new philosophy to my teaching at Elizabethtown College (see photos). You are probably going "bananas" trying to control your excitement wondering what is the essence and beauty of this philosophy. Well, I was speechless when I read the document and discovered the life changing, career enhancing truths found in the educational philosophy of the Great "Yogi." Who and what, you ask, is the great one? Well wonder no longer, he is Yogi Berra, the baseball legend that played for those "amazin" Mets and for the New York Yankees. I was so impressed with the incredible truths found in his philosophy and cutting-edge educational concepts that I spent an exhilarating week at the little known, but highly respected Yogi Institute of

The basement of MENC Headquarters where the incredible "Yogi" file was discovered

Elizabethtown College music students meditating on the teachings of Yogi

Students soaking up the enlightenment offered by Instructor and Yogi-Master Leithmann

Philosophical and Educational Studies (YIPES). I am risking the ridicule of my esteemed colleagues by adopting the radical philosophy to my teaching, but I am willing to risk all! I will not be swayed or stopped. I have begun using the concepts in my teaching at Elizabethtown College (see photo next page) and the results have been spectacular.

Music education students and student teachers, forget all that esoteric and erroneous material that you studied in your methods classes. I'm sorry, students, your music education philosophy is flawed! Something has been left out, but don't worry. I am going to come to your rescue!

All that you really need is the great guru of philosophy, the fount of all wisdom, the mental magician for the new millennium, the one who is rarely mentioned above a whisper … The Great Yogi!

Listen to his words of wisdom and you will find the answers to all of your problems. So, listen up you young, enthusiastic, energetic, and maybe unconfident music educators.

The Great Yogi Said

1. Baseball is 90 percent mental and the other half is physical.
2. You give 100 percent in the first half of the game, and if it isn't enough, in the second half you give the rest.
3. We made too many wrong mistakes.
4. Anyone who can't tell the difference between a ball hitting wood and a ball hitting concrete must be blind.
5. If you ask me anything I don't know, I'm not going to answer.
6. I really didn't say everything I said.
7. How can you say this and that when this and that haven't happened yet?
8. I wish I had an answer to that because I'm getting tired of answering that question.
9. A nickel isn't worth a dime anymore.

And this is how you can apply these awesome and profound truths:

1. Very simply put, be as prepared as you possibly can, and learn to do as much as you can while

you are a student. Example: Penn State grad Gregory Woodbridge was my student teacher, in fact the best I ever had. Why? He was extremely well prepared. He had obviously worked as hard as he could and was mentally and physically ready for the challenge of teaching music.

2. When you start your first teaching position, if you are not willing to work hard and give it everything you have, then don't start! Success does not happen by accident. It is the result of incredible effort.

3. You will make mistakes! We all do, and that is part of the learning process, but, don't make the same mistake twice! That is a "wrong" mistake.

4. Trust your musical intuition and instincts!! You have to size up your students and groups quickly. Trust your ear, not some graded list of solos or orchestrations. Build with success, and to do that you must pick your music carefully.

5. Be honest. If you don't know something, admit it. If you make a mistake, don't try to "bull" or bluff your students. They know!

6. Don't oververbalize—don't talk your students to death. They want to make music. The fastest way to lose your students is by talking too much. Remember, "a picture is worth a thousand words." Demonstrate what you want from your students.

7. Don't worry about what hasn't happened yet. Have faith in yourself and in your students. Be positive! Think positively!

Students dazzling Instructor Liethmann on the "playing field"

8. You have to make the same point over and over, but be creative! Say it in a different way. Be patient and persistent.

9. Budgets are a fact of life. Make the best use with what you have and spend your money wisely.

You "Old" Teachers Can Make a Hit with the Teachings of Yogi!

Are you stressed out? Are you tired of the trials and tribulations of being a teacher? Are you high-strung and worried that those parents, administrators or students are going to string you up? Lighten up! Don't worry! You can gain peace, tranquility and success if you follow the teachings of the great Zen master—Yogi. Yes, the great sage and speaker of wisdom, Yogi Berra. Yogi has uttered some of the greatest truths ever conceived by modem man. Let me try to guide you to peace, tranquility, and success by studying and applying the wisdom of Yogi. Here is what Yogi said:

Dave Leithmann pictured at the prestigious Y.I.P.E.S. summer sessions

1. This feels like déjà vu all over again.
2. You can observe a lot, just by watching.
3. When you come to a fork in the road, take it.
4. It ain't over till it's over.

1. This feels like déjà vu all over again. The problem that you encounter in your rehearsals, lessons, and in dealing with your colleagues will probably happen again. Therefore, remember how you dealt with problems and situations in the past. Learn from it! You will meet these problems again.

2. You can observe a lot, just by watching. Take time to observe what is happening in your rehearsals and lessons. You can improve your productivity and success by carefully observing the response of your students. You don't need someone else to tell you how to improve. Don't get so preoccupied with small details that you lose the big picture.

3. When you come to a fork in the road, take it. What wisdom! Always have a plan A and B, and maybe even C, D, and E! Don't be afraid to change. If something isn't working in a lesson or rehearsal—change. Don't hesitate to make a decision and move on. There is always a road to success. There may be several "forks" in the road before you attain success.

4. It ain't over 'til it's over. No matter how bad things seem and no matter how impossible the situation appears, don't throw in the towel.

Success and satisfaction are waiting for you. What peace! What tranquility! Don't worry, your students will do well. You will find a way to make the concert a success. Have confidence that it will all work out in the end.

I hope that this brief look at the wisdom of Yogi has brought you a deeper sense of peace and tranquility and that in the coming months you will meditate on the truths of Yogi to help you and your students attain the highest level of success. Remember, when you come to the fork in the road, take it!

This article first appeared in the Winter 1999/2000 issue of Pennsylvania's PMEA News. *Reprinted by permission.*

What Will You Do on Your Summer 'Vacation'?
Alicia Mueller

When you return to "school" this fall of 2002, after your summer "vacation," would you be able to describe some experiences that contributed to your aspirations to be a music educator? Summertime can be a good time to regroup and give serious thought to the following areas, each of which can heavily impact decisions to make the field of music education your "profession" and not just your "college major." First of all, are you entering the music education profession because of your personal desires and interests to eventually teach and instill musical knowledge and enjoyment to a younger generation? Second, how much do you really know now, as a student, about the music education program at your college/university? Finally, have you given serious consideration to specific grade levels and teaching areas of music education you would like to teach?

As the summer draws near, you may have plans to attend summer school, or maybe you need to work to build up finances for next year's school tuition and related bills. As either scenario is pursued in preparation for next year, and depending on where you are in your music education program, you may need to make it your business to become better informed of the music education program from which you plan to receive teacher certification. Do not leave this detailed planning to your adviser or applied area teacher. Become knowledgeable in every aspect of your college/university's degree program. Information can be obtained from college/university catalogs, bulletins, and handbooks. Be aware of the challenge of fulfilling the many requirements of music education curriculums, but, if ever given the opportunity to select an elective course, choose a class that correlates with your future music teaching interests and goals. For example, taking a world music course would diversify and enhance your knowledge of multicultural issues and global perspectives. Keep in mind, in addition, that you will need to implement Maryland's Essential Learner Outcomes, as well as possibly MENC's National Standards for Arts Education, in your future curriculum. Familiarizing yourself with these by incorporating them into methods courses and student teacher lesson plans will reinforce your ability to implement them in your future daily teaching. (Your music education professors may already be requiring documentation of the standards in your lesson plans.)

Gaining experience by working with youth in various areas and levels (PreK–12) can have a profound influence on future teaching decisions. Finding ways to work with children, whether as a volunteer or through a summer job, for example, should occur as early as possible during your college years. The following are only a few suggested settings where you could acquire valuable experiences (some even during the school year):

- Preschool, early childhood, or daycare centers
- Public or private school extracurricular programs
- Summer children's arts programs
- Summer music or arts camps (state, regional, national)
- Public library programs
- City parks and recreation programs
- Private music lessons or tutorial sessions

Finding opportunities to gain these kinds of diverse experiences with youth before completing a teacher certification program will contribute and possibly reinforce your decisions regarding grade levels and music teaching areas. A word of advice, though, would be to develop and maintain an open mind throughout this process. There are jobs that require teachers to teach more than one grade level (e.g., elementary and middle school/junior high; elementary and high school) and in more than one teaching area (e.g., general and choral music; general and instrumental music).

The most important part of these vital career preparations and decisions is the question you need to be able to respond to at every step of this

professional path: "Do I want to be a music educator?" In other words, "Do I enjoy music making, and do I want to share this love and knowledge with others?" Be sure that your affirmative answer is the result of a personal rationale—one that encompasses your own thoughts, desires, and strengths. Spend some time this summer "regrouping" and thinking about your future as a music educator as you not only work, but also play! The following are just a few suggestions as you plan your summer leisure activities:
• Listen to new and different styles of music.

• Learn to play a new and different instrument.
• Take a child to a summer concert.
• Attend a summer musical.
• Attend a summer music and arts festival.
• Attend a small-town "folk" festival.
• Enjoy any kind of music for relaxation!

I wish you a summer filled with many learning, as well as enjoyable, music experiences!

This article first appeared in the Summer 2002 issue of the Maryland Music Educator. *Reprinted by permission.*

The LADDER Model for Emerging Music Educators
Vanissa Murphy

When you visualize the structure of a ladder, you see two long poles with parallel rungs across the poles. You can use this ladder to ascend or descend, or, in other words, to go toward someplace or return from someplace. This article will discuss the use of this ladder as a metaphor for best practices and as an acronym, LADDER, to ensure one aspect of best practices. The discussion will be carried forward within the context of the work responsibilities of a collegiate music educator.

Many CMENC members right now may feel as if they are constantly climbing the ladder, trying to go toward that graduation ceremony, and the climb up the ladder is strenuous! There are so many responsibilities as students—preparing for and attending classes, practicing, performing, participating in chapter CMENC events (!), and teaching. Students must also feel as if they are climbing this ladder of music education with a very heavy backpack, full of books and scores and papers and ideas … all weighing them down and keeping them from climbing faster, so that they can graduate sooner, and begin their professional teaching careers. I think we could take a bit of advice from Thoreau★ at this point and try to not be in such "desperate haste" (if I may so paraphrase).

It is probably wise to pause a bit on some of the rungs, maybe even take a step or two back, returning to revisit some of the rungs (places or situations) and secure some time to:

Reflect
Evaluate
Discover
Discuss

Analyze
Listen
(bottom to top, LADDER)

Listening is the first step on this "ladder of best practices" and is perhaps the most important. Because listening skills are essential to student and teacher success (and for the sake of the brevity of this article), all the other rungs will be discussed within the context of listening. Listening is a skill that can be developed to ensure that we get the most from lectures, attending concerts, practicing, conducting, performing, and teaching. Hearing is only one aspect of listening and may be completely inactive. On the other hand, active listening skills involve interpreting what we hear, evaluating its merits, and responding to those merits in finding ways they are of value. For example, as you are listening to a lecture, be actively alert, attend to the main points the teacher is revealing, and continually analyze the content by asking yourself these questions: What is the point the teacher is trying to make? What do I need to remember about this? Analyze the content against your own ideas or the ideas of other teachers and peers and try to discern facts from opinions. Analyzing the lecture content in this way will make it more meaningful and alive. Have an internal conversation and discuss the value of the information then discover how you can use it in your studying, teaching, or performing. Take notes that relate the main points and your personal discoveries about them. If the above ideas regarding listening seem foreign or extreme to you, it may be time to evaluate your listening habits. Active listening is a powerful cognitive tool that is at the core of excellent teaching and learning. Effective listening habits include such components as: (1) finding (or even creating) something in the lecture that sparks your curiosity, (2) being able to evaluate the main ideas rather than how they are presented, and (3) efficient/summative note taking. Ineffective listening habits include: (1) sabotaging your listening by deciding the subject matter is uninteresting or does not apply to you, (2) faking attention, and (3) inefficient note taking (for example, trying to write everything down without discerning the main points and reflecting upon what has been said).

This brings us to the final rung at the top of our best practice ladder—reflection. Reflect upon your analysis, personal discussion, discoveries, and evaluation(s). Taking just a few seconds to look back upon the main points and how you find them of value will help internalize and abstract the information so that you can find useful ways to generalize it across many situations within teaching and learning.

So, we have climbed the ladder, hopefully stepped back a rung or two, and squelched our "desperate haste" so that we might implement those practices that help us to do our best work as emerging music educators. These practices have been discussed as a ladder to ascend and descend, a journey to listen, analyze, discuss, discover, evaluate, and reflect upon before reaching the top. I could further this imagery, revealing that, at the top of the ladder is yet another longer ladder with rungs that have the following words written upon them:

Student-Centered
Experiential
Reflective
Authentic
Holistic
Social
Collaborative
Democratic
Cognitive
Developmental
Constructivist

But that is another ladder and a different approach ... and, I think, a different article!

* "Why should we be in such desperate haste and in such desperate enterprises? If a man does not keep pace with his companions, perhaps it is because he hears a different drummer. Let him step to the music which he hears, however measured or far away."
—From *Walden*, Conclusions XVIII, Henry David Thoreau

This article first appeared in the April 2001 issue of the Wisconsin School Musician. *Reprinted by permission.*

What's so hard about student teaching?

 Section 6

What's so hard about student teaching?

Student teacher's perspective

Student Teaching: The First Mission
Jennifer Brand

Staring for a long while at a blank computer screen, I tried to determine what snippets of "wisdom" I would try to impart in this article from my student teaching experience. After much deliberation I realized that I had better leave the wisdom to the seasoned teachers and focus on "plain ole honesty" instead. Honesty usually makes for a more interesting story than wisdom, anyway.

The night before the first day I began student teaching was the most difficult for me. I experienced many of the same emotions that trouble first graders before their first day of school, multiplied by a million or so. Will people like me? What will the kids be like? Will I do okay? Will I like this school? What am I going to wear? Compound all of these nagging fears with the fact I did not hear about a single positive student teaching experience for at least two weeks before I began. Everyone felt the need to tell me plenty of stories. They were all about student teachers who broke down and cried, changed their major, or had nervous breakdowns. This type of feedback was less than encouraging.

With all of these mixed emotions I timidly approached the school on the first day, only to find that most of my worries had been a waste of time. I am neither experienced nor perfect. I think, however, that I am going to make it. There is really no need to fear the students because they are the same stereotypical band nerds that we were in junior high and high school. The trumpet players still think that the whole point of music is to blast out high notes so as to drown out the rest of the band. Tuba players are jovial and personable,

yet slightly odd in an endearing sort of way. Guard girls think they are part of an elite club, and flute players cannot keep quiet during class. Even the songs "sung" from the back of the bus are the same, and it is still possible to sing the "Song that Never Ends" for thirty minutes or more at a time.

Although some people learned all they need to know at an early age, I am not one of those advanced pupils. In fact, sometimes I can be quite dense. Life has to beat those lessons into me one at a time before I begin to catch on. But for the benefit of those who learn from the experiences of others, I thought I would share a few of the "lessons" that I learned this semester.

Lesson 1. Constructive criticism is just that—criticism for the purpose of building up. Dish it out when necessary, but be even more ready to receive it.

Lesson 2. Kids have much musical knowledge that they are willing to impart to you—such as that there are three Fs on the saxophone: F sharp, F natural, and F regular.

Lesson 3. Be careful what you mention to beginners in an offhand fashion or you may find your entire class singing Christmas carols at the top of their lungs as each section takes turns playing.

Lesson 4. Although it is necessary to take an instrument repair class, do not be fooled into thinking that you will have the time to actually repair instruments. You will only be able to fix small problems. A multitude of problems, however, can be corrected with a screwdriver, a pair of pliers, and duct tape.

Lesson 5. Learn when it is best to shut your mouth. It is better to be a fool than to open your mouth and let everyone know that you are one.

Lesson 6. Get used to hearing your last name.

Students who are bellowing Miss so-and-so across the practice field do not understand that you had no idea that they were referring to you. They think you are ignoring them.

Lesson 7. Transpositions. Transpositions. Transpositions.

Lesson 8. Be familiar with the phrase "Put your hand down." It is a particularly effective statement in the beginner classes.

Lesson 9. Always carry a Band-Aid.

Lesson 10. I must be both grateful and gracious to my cooperating teacher. For him to either correct or overlook my many mistakes requires the patience of Job.

This article first appeared in the Winter 2000–2001 issue of Oklahoma Music. *Reprinted by permission.*

Student Teaching Experiences or Out in the (Almost) Real World
Christine Judith Deschler

Music education programs explore different methods of teaching. Learning how to reach a student, however, comes from hands-on experience. I currently attend The Hartt School with a double major in music education and flute performance. This semester I'm student teaching in both Avon Middle School with Don Fantozzi and East Windsor High School with Richard Shonty. I believe that student teaching is the most important factor in the completion of an education degree. There are a lot of teaching methods available, but when placed in front of a group of students, a teacher has to cater to many different learning styles.

One of my first memories of student teaching was trying to explain syncopation to an eighth-grade trombone class. I had the knowledge, but putting it into simple words or examples was not easy! There were other instances where I couldn't remember a trumpet fingering or when I had to teach my first sixth-grade percussion class. And, of course, fixing a "broken" saxophone that actually turned out to be assembled incorrectly. I realized later that this situation is very common during band rehearsals!

Having a good cooperating teacher is valuable. Not only is it important to be placed with proficient teachers, but you have to get along with them as well! With this in mind, I consider myself lucky. The examples that they set along with the suggestions that they offered have been very helpful—and fun as well.

The best part of teaching (and the most difficult might I add) is conducting. In my situation, I am working with four separate bands—sixth, seventh, eighth, and high school. Each band is different, and being a new face on the podium doesn't make matters any easier. There will always be issues with discipline, and it takes time to find certain strengths and weaknesses of a group of young "musicians," but how does one reach that group of sometimes seventy-five or more students? Being a flutist as well as an educator comes in handy. Modeling is a good "attention grabber," and it lets students hear an example of how certain passages should be played in terms of articulation, dynamics, style, or expression.

Dealing with a large group of students at one time has taught me a lot of important things. Speaking slowly and giving directions more than once is necessary! Good eye contact, clear downbeats (as well as cutoffs), pacing, and not being afraid to try new ideas are all valuable when trying to learn the best rehearsal techniques. The list goes on and on but taking the time to get to know the students makes this experience worth a lot more.

It's quite different being the teacher instead of the student. I can't just roll out of bed and run to my 8:30 class ten minutes late! Everything I do affects the students I work with. And everything they do affects me. I find myself thinking of new things that I can try with my eighth-grade flute class or how I can get my high school band to really nail the Holst Suite in E flat. Being part of a university has its perks as well. I am part of Hartt's Performance 20/20 program which is an honors chamber music group. Getting these musicians to perform for younger students has a long term value that keeps their interest level up.

I have been student teaching for two months now. It has been the best part of my music education training and I'm anxious to discover where I'll end up going from here. I would like to take this opportunity to thank my teachers at Hartt and the teachers/students that I work with at Avon and East Windsor. It has been a wonderful semester so far!

This article first appeared in the Spring 2000 issue of Connecticut's CMEA News. *Reprinted by permission.*

It's Rainin', It's Pourin', the Students Are Snoring: Classroom Management for Student Teachers

Nalora Steele

The first-grade lesson you taught at 8:30 a.m. was a brilliant success! The children walked out happy, your cooperating teacher was all smiles and inside of you, you just knew that you had this thing called classroom management licked. No more problems, smooth sailing until you graduate!

Segue to 1:00 p.m.: first-grade class, same lesson plan. The entire class was overactive. It was impossible to get all the members quiet at the same time so that you could begin your lesson. You struggled to be heard. You tried to be gentle but firm. You swallowed your sudden feelings of inadequacies. Then a student piped up, "Look, it's raining!"

Rain could cause this remarkable difference? Indeed it can. Seasoned teachers are always aware of the effects of nature on the stability of human beings. Though there is little research on the subject of behavioral changes due to phenomena of nature, folklore does refer to such: "Rain, rain, go away, come again another day," or "It's raining, it's pouring, the old man is snoring," or "It's a full moon tonight" to explain unusual occurrences.

The impact of the weather on group behaviors can be too large an issue to be ignored. When air pressure changes occur, sleepiness is often a result. According to Michael Morgan and Joseph Moran, "As the weather causes increasing discomfort, people become ... less able to perform physical and mental tasks."

But that discomfort manifests itself in various ways in the classroom. While high schoolers may tend to be listless, hard to motivate (indeed, may even nod off), younger children tend to become overactive as a response to climate changes. They may talk excessively, move about randomly, become "silly," all in an attempt to stay awake. At all ages, students may tend to complain of being "bored," since this is a convenient catch-all word to describe any feelings that they do not understand themselves.

Often, the student teacher, also not understanding these issues, will continue to plow through the lesson, feeling defeat and discouragement the entire time. No one can change the weather or its impact, but there are several ways of dealing with it and creating a day of positive teaching and learning:

1. If it begins to snow, stop your lesson and "take five" for everyone to go to the window and look at it. (They will soon be ready to go back to other things!) Acknowledgment of environment and feelings is important.
2. Try to spontaneously work the rain, snow, storm, moon into your lesson.
3. Have high school students walk around the room a few minutes and reconvene for the lesson.
4. Be aware of the weather forecasts for each day you teach.
5. Have a solid lesson plan written down so that when disruptions come they can be handled and you can more easily get the class back on track.

So prepare your lesson well, resolve to meet whatever comes your way cheerfully and with good humor, and, of course, check the weather forecast before you leave home—it may have more to do with what happens when you get to school than how you will get there!

This article first appeared in the Winter 2000 issue of the Massachusetts Music News. *Reprinted by permission.*

Potato, Potahto, Tomato, Tomahto, Quarter Note, Crochet?

Cynthia M. Steiner

Student teaching in England has really opened my eyes. I am at Holland Moor Primary School in Skelmersdale, Lancashire. Currently, I am working with a year six class. After coming to terms with the fact that it is what they call here an inner-city school, I soon found out how to make the students interested. They have not been exposed to much classical music. I had them listen to Mussorgsky's *Pictures at an Exhibition* and reflect on what they felt. The children came up with the most amazing poems and drawings. They are now on display in front of the school.

I was very enthusiastic about coming here to enlighten children's lives with music. Well, little did I know that I would be getting just as much enlightenment as they have been receiving. The first day, a little boy came up to me and asked me if I had a rubber! I just looked at him and asked "Why?" He replied, "I have made a mistake and I need to rub it out." Chuckling, I said, " Oh, I don't have one, but you may get one out of the tray." I soon found out that rubbers are erasers! That was the start to a whole new experience.

As I took a look at the curriculum and various lesson plans from the other teachers, I began to brainstorm on what I could begin with. The children are not introduced to any type of notation until they reach secondary school. This puzzled me, and not knowing exactly what they knew, I decided to see what they did know. The first lesson, I just had them singing the entire time. Of course, they were not used to this either. Many of the children were what I call speak-singing. That is, they were not really singing, but they were not really speaking. I knew where to begin from there on the singing aspect. Then there was the task of figuring out where to begin—with notation, terminology, music history, or beginning instruments. I am still trying to decipher some of those issues.

I found it interesting to understand how the students began on instruments. The particular school I am in only has beginning trumpet or cornet players. These are the only instruments available to them. They have a specialist from a music society come in once a week to give lessons. Currently, there are only four students taking lessons. It was at this lesson that I learned another lesson. The teacher kept referring to crochets. I was very puzzled by this. Then I heard him discuss semibreves. After the child had left, I asked what he was talking about. He did not understand what I was questioning. Finally, I pointed to a quarter note on the method book. He said, "That is a crochet." I smiled again, remembering the rubber story and replied to him, "Oh, in America we call them quarter notes." He chuckled but said nothing. I began to talk with him about the beginning trumpet method book. There was no logical explanation for how it was laid out. I soon found out that we agreed to disagree on a few issues. It is definitely not America, that is for sure.

It has been such a challenge, but I really enjoy the children immensely. I am by no means ready to call the whole thing off.

This article first appeared in the December/January 2000 issue of Ohio's TRIAD. *Reprinted by permission.*

Supervisor's perspective

Guiding a Student Teacher: One Way to Give Back to Your Profession

'Yeah, Yeah, Yeah' to 'Holy Smokes!'
Patricia Bourne

I remember my student teaching experience very well. Like many music majors, I was very involved as a performing musician. Student teaching was one of those "college requirements" that seemed more important to my methods teachers than to me. She and I discussed placement, who I might work with best, what was expected from me, and how I would by evaluated. My attitude was borrowed from The Beatles, minus the enthusiasm: "Yeah, yeah, yeah." I was a good musician, I could make sense out of a score, I'd do fine.

Holy smokes! … I soon found out student teaching was not just "another" college requirement; it was the culminating experience to my preservice training. I also discovered that being a good musician was important but was dwarfed by other skills for successful teaching. I admired the way my master teacher encouraged the band members in his charge and how he helped me forecast impending doom and face the consequences of ill-planned lessons.

Years later, I was the master teacher with a few "yeah, yeah, yeah" student teachers in my charge. I began to realize the sacrifices my own master teacher had made for me—letting me take over his groups required tremendous trust and a commitment to helping me become a teacher. (I wasn't quite as unselfish as he, nor was I willing to let someone make mistakes with my young students!)

Along the passage from student to apprentice to master teacher, I took a turn toward higher education and became a placer and supervisor of many student teachers. (I also became the "methods-teacher-who-seemed-to-care-more-about-student-teaching-than-some-of-my- preservice-wards!") It was as a supervisor of student teachers that I learned the most about preparing teachers for the "real world."

I learned that student teachers need three things: (1) a chance to succeed, (2) an opportunity to correct mistakes, and (3) an allowance to be a "student." I also learned that most master teachers needed three things: (1) respect and trust from the university personnel, (2) ownership in their program/curriculum, and (3) open communication with everyone involved in the student teaching process.

The latest chapter of my eighteen-year progression since student teaching finds me back in the public school setting, looking forward to moving into the master teacher role again. I know there will be a few student teachers who will approach my room and my role as an elementary music teacher with a "yeah, yeah, yeah" attitude and will leave thinking "holy smokes!" It is that realization that will move them from student to apprentice to master in their own right.

A Student Teaching in Your High School Music Department: Have You Prepared?
Ric Pilgrim

One of the true joys of teaching is to see students respond with a look of marvel and revelation to the efforts, ideas, and passions presented to them. These cognitive gasps of awareness are the driving force for many a teacher. Each "Aha!" represents a transfer of knowledge and aesthetic passed to another human being and into the future. We look, hope, and pray for these small epiphanies to occur periodically within our students. And when they do, it's goose bump time! Equally satisfying is to experience this same glow of the "teachers' art," which is manifested through the mentoring of a student teacher.

I have been fortunate to have opportunities to work with several student teachers and other long-term preteacher students. In hopes of easing the fears and trepidations a new mentor teacher might have, I will share some general observations and impressions gleaned from these experiences. Invaluable hints from other middle and high school mentor teachers are also included. Hopefully, these will enhance the student teaching experience for all concerned.

The joys of working with a student teacher can be great. This exhilaration doesn't come without diligent preparation and planning, however. If not careful, a high school music teacher could find his or her program held in stasis (or worse) for three months. Preparation is everything! As any gardener knows, proper cultivation ensures bounty come harvest time. So too with mentoring! Time and energy spent in preparation will bear great fruit, and your program will be better for it.

Prepare Yourself

Okay, so you've been asked to mentor an student teacher! A milestone in your career, right? An indication that somebody knows and admires your teaching, right? An opportunity to have an easy semester, right? Hold on! One of the things you need to consider right away is whether you really want a student teacher. Are you prepared to surrender your classes to someone else?

One of the toughest things for a mentor teacher is to let go of his or her classes. You have established bonds with your students. You have shared the agonies and euphorias of countless performances. You have invested a lot of time and energy into making these students an extension of yourself! To cut the apron strings is not the easiest thing to do. You must be willing to step away from countless situations where:

- Students come to you and say "Mr. Student Teacher is doing it completely different than you."
- You see easy solutions to classroom management problems and want to fix them.
- You can't believe the university didn't teach the student teacher this or that!
- You're certain that the spring concert is going to go down in flames (along with your reputation).
- You can't believe those students who had previously been so musically and socially mature have turned into social deviants.
- And on and on.

You must be able to surrender your classes to someone that, in most cases, you have known for a relatively short amount of time. You must put your faith in the fact that your students are basically good kids, and ultimately they are doing the student teacher a favor by testing him or her on so many fronts. And you must bury your ego and not feel a need to respond to every little incident you think might "destroy" your music program. After all, you were an student teacher once, and somebody allowed you your mistakes.

Prepare the Student Teacher

Remember what it was like your first day of student teaching? The human mind has a wonderful way of blocking out unpleasant memories, doesn't it? Well, suffice it to say that you were probably petrified at the prospect of actually telling students only four years your junior what to do! Or, horrors, you might even have to discipline them! What if they call your bluff?

Many student teachers (and veteran teachers, too) suffer from what is known as Impostor's Syndrome. They can't believe anyone actually takes them seriously. After all, they're just beginners, right? Consequently, their professional persona is less than convincing. This is a tough mindset to break. They've been students for seventeen-plus years. Suddenly dispensing, rather than receiving, information is a major paradigm shift. Some grasp the opportunity with open arms; others more reticently. Short of going to the universities and demanding education departments do something about providing more practical, real-life situations (not a bad idea, and something I feel very strongly about—a whole *Voice* issue in itself!), you might need to instill in your student teacher the sense that he or she is in charge. To help dispel self-doubts, I like sharing the maxim "An expert is simply one who has done something longer than someone else." Thus the student teacher is already an expert at many things. Capitalize on these. This mental set opens a panorama of possibilities previously buried in uncertainty and insecurity. With confidence comes the success that leads to further confidence. Success breeds success!

Note on communication: Determine and address how your student teacher responds to criticisms, both negative and positive. Good communication is critical to establishing meaningful professional dialogue. For example, if your student teacher puts up walls and is defensive every time you suggest an improvement, deal with this defensiveness first and resolve it. I have seen entire student teaching experiences wasted because of the tentativeness and inability of mentor and student teacher to effectively and concisely communicate with each other. My advice: Time is short, cut to the quick and be honest. Judge your student teacher's temperament and proceed accordingly. Don't be cruel, just forthright. You will do everyone a favor.

Prepare Your Students

Just as it is difficult to give up the reins of your classroom, it can be equally difficult for students to give up their teacher. Many successful music programs are, for better or worse, an extension of the teacher. Our classes are electives. Students who stay in band or choir through their senior year obviously want to be there. You start messing with the status quo (e.g., the teacher) and students are less likely to find your class enjoyable. Though students don't often express their feelings in this regard, it exists nonetheless. This bond is one of the great pleasures of our occupation. Severing that bond, even temporarily, can throw some students off-kilter. Prepare them by explaining that this is a unique and powerful opportunity for the student teacher and students alike.

Very important: Make sure your students understand there will be only one boss, and that boss is the student teacher when he or she takes over full-time. Students, even good ones, love to play both-ends-against-the-middle games. Don't allow them the opportunity to manipulate you or your student teacher. If you constantly "fix things," you risk blurring just who is in charge. Yes, intervene when necessary, but with discretion.

In Conclusion

Admittedly, this article is woefully incomplete. Whole libraries can be filled with the subtleties of human interaction in teaching. Just remember— the trinity of mentor, student teacher, and music student exists for but one purpose: the art we call music. Mentor with the passion that first brought you into music, and you cannot fail. Philosopher D.T. Suzuki suggested that for full communion with life and its endless pleasures, we must first view daily living with a "beginner's mind." Can one still be a veteran and take a fresh look at teaching every day? Of course, that's why we are in the arts! And that's what you can bring to being a mentor teacher!

Strategies That Work
Jane Peterson

Supervising teachers have a unique experience each time they work with a student teacher because new teachers bring individual strengths, weaknesses, and personalities into the classroom. As the term progresses, supervising becomes fun and exciting when student teachers' techniques improve. However, analyzing problems and finding workable solutions can be challenging and frustrating. Training our future music educators and seeing them prepared, confident, and excited about teaching brings personal reward and growth to any supervising teacher.

Student teachers must demonstrate solid music fundamentals and will need to improve skills in management and planning due to lack of practice in these areas. Since their only training may be meeting requirements for a university course, some of the following strategies may help to improve new teachers' skills to successful levels.

Educate

The supervising teacher should be prepared to spend a tremendous amount of time discussing, explaining, demonstrating, and analyzing with the student teacher. Student teachers need to read policies and procedures in the school handbook, and the supervisor should discuss individual music classroom rules, procedures, goals, and philosophies. This will give them an opportunity to better understand your ideas and to begin formulating their own personal philosophies and goals.

Encourage student teachers to help with lessons as soon as possible so they are in front of the students. This may be done as simply as having them help with partner songs, work with students on Orff instrumental parts, or guide students by singing a round. Also, student teachers need time to observe the supervising teacher and to analyze lessons for objectives, classroom management style, pace, as well as student skill levels, movement, and expectations.

Communicate

Student teachers come with plenty of enthusiasm and desire but not many materials or resources. Be prepared to share the best materials with them for use during their student teaching and after graduation.

Two weeks is sufficient time for helping with classes, looking at materials, and observing the supervisor. In the elementary setting, one or two grade levels can be turned over to the student teacher weekly. Of course this depends upon how comfortable and successful the student teacher feels after the first few weeks of teaching. By gradually adding new grade levels and classes, materials and plans will not become overwhelming. In addition, they can continue to observe the supervising teacher and analyze from a new perspective once they have done some teaching. Four or five weeks teaching the entire music schedule is usually a university requirement.

Practice

Most student teachers have little practice in planning and writing lesson plans. Make time to confer about creating and organizing plans for variety of activities, movements, and materials as well as to gauge materials for appropriate grade levels. Students need guidance in these areas at the beginning, but they acquire these skills quite quickly once they begin working with the students and a variety of materials. Early lesson plans must be detailed enough to indicate process and procedures. The quantity of materials needed for a lesson often worries student teachers. This concern can be eased by developing brief, quality music activities if lessons run short.

A student teacher needs to be familiar with the district's Student Learning Objectives for Music to help in lesson planning and organization as well as understanding the skill level appropriate for students. Often student teachers will put together lessons with fun activities and songs but neglect to coordinate them around specific concepts and objectives. Once they get used to working with objectives, they will understand how this improves valid teaching.

During the first weeks of teaching, offer your expertise in materials and resources so they have quality materials which are effective with students. The student teacher should search for needed materials by the second or third week of full-time teaching. This gives them additional experience while acquiring the skill to find quality material. They will also understand how much time it takes to plan and create effective lessons.

Evaluate

Both the student teacher and supervising teacher need to critique lessons to strengthen areas needing improvement. Comparison of critiques helps to align expectations. Provide encouragement but always be honest. Some student teachers can monitor and adjust lessons effectively while others will need suggestions on how to alter and improve plans.

Classroom management creates the most difficulty for many student teachers. Be prepared to offer a variety of management strategies with which they can experiment and find a style that fits their personality. Many new teachers struggle with consistency in discipline. They need to define how they want their "ideal" classroom to look and sound, as well as musical expectations and discipline. Until they have set limits and standards they may struggle with discipline and expectations. Student teachers often need help to find their "instructor voice" and their "discipline voice."

Giving student teachers a smattering of different methods of teaching such as Orff and Kodály may help them decide if these are areas in which they will pursue additional study. However, encourage them to rely on their personal strengths and to not copy the supervising teacher. Student teaching provides the opportunity to experiment and find the style that works with the student teacher's personality.

Release

Student teachers need time to teach without being observed to experience a genuine idea of first-year teaching. Supervising teachers may find it difficult to leave the room and release control of "your" students, even with competent student teachers, but the experience is necessary.

University personnel provide additional perspective and analysis for the student teacher. Since the supervising teacher deals daily with the student teacher, he or she has an advantage of knowing the total progress. Conference about concerns, because all involved want the best results possible from this experience. If a student teacher lacks the skills needed for success, document and explain any concerns early in the term to both the student teacher and university personnel. Request more observations by university personnel to confirm or alleviate your concerns.

I am amazed at the creativity student teachers bring into the classroom and have always gained new ideas or methods from their teaching. Working with student teachers makes one scrutinize his or her own teaching more closely. Therefore, I have benefited and grown professionally from my experiences in working with student teachers.

Supervising Student Teachers: From the Perspective of a High School Master Teacher
Paul Brueggemeir

Major Responsibilities

As a master teacher, we have three responsibilities:
1. To Our Students: We must remember that we need to give them the best education we can at all times and that includes the times we have a student teacher.
2. To the Student Teacher: He/she needs to have the best experience you and your students can give and you need to do everything you can to make him/her successful.
3. To the Art of Music Education: This means passing on your passion for teaching and your love of music to your student teacher so the specialness of music continues to be presented to generations of students in the future.

Preparation and Timeline

As I meet with a student teacher for the first time, I try to find out where in the field of teaching music they feel the most comfortable. I talk to their college professors to help me assess the student teacher's strengths and weaknesses. I then talk about a timeline for integrating the student teacher into my students' lives. Below is a timeline that would work for well-prepared student teachers.

A week before the student teacher's arrival. I announce to my students that we will be getting a student teacher. I give them a few positive reports I've received about him/her and how he/she will enhance students' learning. I tell the students why it is important for them to have a student teacher. It gives them the chance to be part of the education of a new teacher. It also broadens the experiences I can give them by bringing in someone new.

First day. I introduce the student teacher. I let the student teachers observe with the understanding that even though they are student teachers, they have my complete backing to monitor student management. I tell the students in my class that they now have two teachers to make them the best they can be in their music-making and in their daily demeanor. Once a student teacher walks into my classroom, he/she will be perceived as a staff member.

First week. I videotape students saying their names and give it to the student teacher so he/she can learn their names quickly. I also have the student teacher meet school administration and other support staff (secretaries, book room and business office personnel, custodians, and counselors). I have him/her help with administrative chores so he/she can become familiar with the school layout and inner-staff workings.

In class I have the student teacher begin to work with the students in sectionals or other small groups for which specific lesson plans can be prepared.

Second week. I continue the above and have the student teacher present lessons. As master teachers we need to find the student teacher's strengths and special expertise. As the master teacher I believe it is best to begin the student teacher's experience with students by starting in areas where he/she is the strongest. This is good for the student teacher and it is good for the students. The student teacher can feel confident the first time he/she meets with the students in the role of teacher because he/she is presenting a class or lesson in an area in which he/she feels comfortable. The students in the class benefit from this approach because they see a confident person who is going to help them be the best they can be and

(hopefully) not an unsure stumbling first effort.

For example, Ryan Amend, my current student teacher, has a strong background in jazz and scat singing, specifically. As part of my introducing him to my students, he and I developed a lesson in which he taught an introductory lesson in applied scat singing. The students were wowed by his scatting artistry, and in their eyes he immediately became part of the team that would now be teaching choral music at Ferris High School.

I have the student teacher start taking roll and perhaps sharing warm-ups.

Third week. I continue the above duties and expand them by having the student teacher begin teaching specific songs to a selected class or two. I usually start a student teacher with a younger choir and have him/her introduce a new song to the class and see how the lesson goes.

From there I will continue to expand his/her responsibilities as we together decide when he/she is ready to handle them.

As the weeks go by, I continue to turn over more and more responsibilities to the student teacher.

By the sixth week. I try to turn the complete scope of the choral program over to the student teacher. One exception I make would be times when I am preparing a choir for a special performance such as an ACDA or MENC conference. Even then I will usually give a student teacher the opportunity to work with that choir. Another class I may not turn over would be a specialty class like my Audio Production Lab.

Some Closing Thoughts

I think that the best time for a student teacher is in the fall. He/she can be in on all of the start-of-year preparations, which usually means starting in the summer with choosing music, meeting with student officers, and having summer rehearsals. I work with the student teacher and integrate him/her into the program as I prepare for my fall concert and fall musical. After that concert, I leave all planning for our winter concert up to my student teacher, and I step back and just observe. After having seen all of the preparation I do for the fall concert, all I usually have to do is help my student teacher plan backwards from the date of the concert, and he/she is all set with short and long-range goals to create the next five weeks of lesson plans.

Our most important job as a master teacher is to make the student teacher successful. We need to closely monitor every step and watch him/her interacting with the students. We need to be there at the first hint of a breakdown in management and be ready to work through the problem with the student teacher.

I personally have never had an incompetent musician, but I have had a few very poor teachers. Just letting the student teacher sink or swim is not fair to your students, nor will it be fair for the student teacher. You need to observe your student teacher on a period by period basis at first and then later on during the experience, perhaps choose one or two classes on a daily basis to observe. You need to take time every day to plan and debrief with your student teacher.

I also recommend never having more than one student teacher a year. It is not fair to your students to have student teachers teach them more than once a year.

This article first appeared in the January 1997 issue of Washington's Voice. *Reprinted by permission.*

Schools Paying Student Teachers to Teach: A Discussion of the Pros and Cons
Paul T. Henley

Missouri is facing a teacher shortage. Nationally, such shortages are acute in three areas: foreign language, special education, and music. To combat this shortage, schools are becoming more likely to hire student teachers as paid, contracted professionals. Financially strapped college seniors are only too happy to oblige in this situation.

When a student teaching situation goes sour, much can be lost. This is true regarding the student, but it is also true regarding music teacher educators. Music degrees typically take five years to complete. As college professors, we put our efforts into these students for longer periods of time than most professors do. We also take a strong personal interest in our students' success. To shorten the final and most comprehensive preparation that we offer may prove detrimental to our profession unless it is done carefully and thoughtfully. It is my premise, therefore, that music teacher educators should act proactively to ensure that (a) such situations happen infrequently and (b) students in such positions are protected from potential pitfalls.

This past semester (fall of 2000) was my first semester at Southwest Missouri State University. Because of this, Norma McClellan and I team-taught Supervised Teaching. This gave us a chance to synchronize our efforts while learning each other's management style. We faced a unique situation: all four of our student teachers were acting as paid professionals. The situations varied from a student teacher working two hours per day to cover a maternity leave to student teachers that had a school's entire K–12 music program. Our mission as the public affairs institution of the State of Missouri, committed us to work with these districts to aid their situation. In all cases, ground rules had been set. Two were most meaningful:

1. There was to be a paid substitute teacher in the room at all times during the first six weeks. This substitute was to handle any difficult disciplinary situations and oversee the management aspects of the classroom.
2. Each school was to provide an in-house cooperating teacher from a related department. In some cases, it was another music teacher. In other cases, it was an art teacher or another classroom teacher.

The four student teachers experienced a range of success. This success seemed to be based on two factors: (1) the size of the paid teaching load; and (2) the support given by the school district in question. In two of these cases, the experience was a positive one. Both of these young teachers are finishing their first year ahead of schedule. Since they began the year with these students, there was less transition to make in their careers—and their lives. A third situation, while satisfactorily taught, remains unfinished due to missing paperwork. However, the fourth situation was particularly egregious.

This teacher was placed in a K–12 position in a very small school district that delivered little, if any, support. My colleague had warned me that this particular placement was facing a rough start. With this warning, I drove to this small town in southwest Missouri to observe her. The student teacher (an honor student) was alone in her classroom. She lacked the discipline skill necessary to control a beginning band of eight students. After this, classes changed, and the high school chorus commenced. Here, 20 students worked diligently to destroy any effort on the student teacher's part to foster learning. Worse, the chorus was partially populated with eleven- and twelve-year-old students that were diagnosed as behaviorally disordered children. Since the last period of the day was the planning period for the resource room, these students were placed in the hands of what was essentially a college student for the convenience of the administration.

Regarding the ground rules, the substitute hired by the district had left after two weeks and had not been replaced. The cooperating mentor (mentioned in the ground rules) was the former music teacher, who had retired. Nobody knew how to contact her on the day of my visit.

The visit finished with a discussion between the student teacher, a new principal, and myself. During our after-school conversation, this student teacher was referred to as a first-year teacher no less than five times in one-half hour. Despite my admonishments that this "teacher" was only a college student, the slips continued. Assurances were made by the school district that the original agreement would be met, that a certified substitute teacher would be in place by the next time we visited. Discipline was also addressed by the school, which (among other actions) removed some of the more disruptive students from the music classroom.

Meanwhile, this student teacher exhibited symptoms similar to post-traumatic stress disorder. She was learning to hate teaching, and we feared that we would lose her from our ranks. My colleague and I each gave one subsequent visit before deciding to change her situation and environment. We moved this student teacher to a more traditional setting with a strong role model as a cooperating teacher. She soon became a more confident teacher. She was even confident enough to return to the initial setting (backed by the full faith and credit of the State of Missouri), and she has begun a successful teaching career.

This situation gives credence to both sides of this issue. On one hand, this situation was potentially damaging for a budding teacher. If allowed to continue unabated, this situation would have most likely driven her from education altogether. On the other hand, eight weeks with a strong cooperating teacher was enough to both instill a strong leadership component and rectify any prior damage to the student teacher's confidence. Perhaps sixteen weeks is not necessary for some student teachers. If this is the case, then we should be offering assistance to school districts in need at the earliest possible opportunity.

Some music teacher educators may hold that student teachers should be banned from such situations. This may initially speak to the problems caused by the above situation; however, such a move forces schools to leave music programs in the hands of those with little or (sometimes) no instruction. I am reminded of a colleague in Iowa that refused such a situation for a student teacher. Instead, the student teacher encountered a typical student teaching placement and took the fully paid position in the middle of the year. In the meantime, the school hired a truck driver that "loved music." This one semester significantly damaged the music program that the new teacher assumed. This hurt both the student teacher/teacher and the students of that school district.

Despite such situations, we need to be guarded at a time when change would have us make hasty decisions. Southwest Missouri State University's School of Teacher Education is drafting guidelines regarding this very practice; however, such guidelines may or may not be pertinent to a music setting:

1. Discipline, a key issue at this level of teacher training, is more difficult in groups of eighty than it is in groups of twenty-five.
2. The public performance aspect of our teaching creates an additional pressure not faced by those in nonperforming academic disciplines.
3. Legal aspects facing an uncertified music teacher (trips, after school activities, contests) could be significant.

Statement 8 of the Housewright Declaration suggests that "alternative licensing should be explored in order to expand the number and variety of teachers available to those seeking music instruction." As music teacher educators, we must strive to create our own set of guidelines. This way, the work is already done when guidelines are needed.

If others are currently using guidelines regarding such a situation, perhaps teacher educators could combine efforts to produce a single, coherent body of guidelines used by all teacher education institutions. Any such guidelines would likely have more impact than those of individual institutions. At the very least, shared experiences lead to better understanding among colleagues. If we do not take initial steps in this direction, we leave important decisions to those who may or may not sympathize with our values.

Student teaching situations vary, whether or not teacher shortages are at hand. The music education community would do well to proactively approach this situation to benefit our students, our communities, and our own interests.

This article first appeared in the Summer 2001 issue of Missouri School Music. *Reprinted by permission.*

Learning to Teach: How Can We Help?

Vicki R. Lind

Several years ago, I interviewed student teachers as part of a study on teacher education. I was amazed at the variety of experiences these preservice teachers described. Each student had a unique story to tell. One preservice teacher, Ann, told of a particularly disappointing experience. Her words still ring through my mind each year as I prepare to work with student teachers.

"Student teaching should be ideal, I mean theoretically. You have someone who is experienced there, the cooperating teacher, to help you and guide you along the way. The university supervisor can give you even more feedback. I thought it would be different, I thought there would be conferences and my cooperating teacher would help me ... instead I'm totally on my own ... the university supervisor just judges me, and the cooperating teacher never seems to care" (Ann).

Ann's struggles raise important questions for teacher education. What does a successful student-teaching experience look like? What are the responsibilities of the university supervisor, cooperating teacher, and student teacher? What works and what doesn't work? The purpose of this article is to suggest answers to these questions. The ideas presented have been gleaned from recent research on teacher education, from my own work with music teacher education, and from teachers in the field.

What Does a Successful Student Teaching Experience Look Like?

Successful models of student teaching involve collaboration. The university supervisor, cooperating teacher, and student teacher work best when they work together to define roles, expectations, and responsibilities. Communication is a key element in fostering collaboration. Each member of the student-teaching triad should take responsibility for keeping the lines of communication open. The following ideas are designed to promote communication among the student-teaching triad.

• The university supervisor should arrange for a meeting with the cooperating teacher and student teacher as early as possible. At this first meeting, the three members of the student-teaching triad can work together to set goals, establish expectations, and define responsibilities. In addition, the university supervisor might use this meeting to review the university policies and requirements. Research on teacher education indicates that teachers prefer frequent, short conferences that allow the triad to keep in touch, but that are not too overwhelming or intrusive. Therefore, it is important to keep this first meeting fairly short and focused.

• Communication between the cooperating teacher and the student teacher is crucial. Many successful cooperating teachers meet with the student teacher on a daily basis to discuss accomplishments, frustrations, and goals. When schedules don't allow for daily meetings, it is helpful for the cooperating teacher to find ways to provide some type of feedback. One teacher I worked with provided a written evaluation after each class. These were short notes outlining what went well and making suggestions for improvements. Each week the student teacher and cooperating teacher would meet and review the daily evaluations. This consistent feedback was extremely valuable to the student teacher.

• Communicating expectations in advance is crucial to the success of most student teachers. Student teachers need time to plan, find materials, determine goals, and develop a teaching sequence. Many cooperating teachers work with the student teacher to develop a time line detailing the gradual increase of teaching responsibilities. This time line helps give the student teacher time to prepare.

• Communication with the university supervisor is often the most difficult aspect of collaboration to maintain. The university supervisor should provide contact information to both the student teacher and the cooperating teacher. This information should include an e-mail address, telephone number, schedule, etc. In addition, the university supervisor should contact the student teacher and the cooperating teacher on a regular basis. E-mail has been a valuable tool in communication. My student teachers send weekly updates via e-mail. These updates serve two purposes: the messages keep me informed about how my student teachers are doing, and writing the updates promotes reflective practice. Student teachers often mention that summarizing their week makes them focus on learning to teach and gives them the opportunity to reflect on their experiences.

What Are the Responsibilities of the University Supervisor, Cooperating Teacher, and Student Teacher?

University Supervisor

In the opening quote, Ann expressed her dismay at being "judged" by her university supervisor. She had hoped the college professor would be a mentor for her, and was disappointed when a mentoring relationship did not develop. The literature indicates that successful supervision involves a combination of mentoring and evaluation. The university supervisor serves as the liaison with the public schools, acts as a role model for the student teacher, and is usually responsible for evaluation.

A primary function of the university supervisor is to act as a liaison between the public-school teacher and the student teacher. Establishing and maintaining contact with public-school teachers is an important step in this process. By visiting music classrooms, attending concerts, and supporting school music, university supervisors can develop the necessary connections with music teachers in the area.

The university supervisor also serves as a role model for student teachers. Preservice teachers consciously and unconsciously learn from what they see happening around them. As Costa and Garmston say, "It is from the walk that student teachers learn, far more than from the talk."[1] This learning takes place in the college classroom as well as in the public-school setting. Students learn about the teaching profession by watching their university professors meet their teaching responsibilities. In addition, the university supervisor can serve as a teacher role model during the student-teaching assignment by teaching a class, conducting a rehearsal, or giving a quick teaching demonstration. I often team-teach classes with my student teachers. Not only does this allow the student teacher to observe how I interact with younger students, the experience helps establish my credibility with the cooperating teacher. In fact, one of the major concerns voiced by cooperating teachers is that the university supervisor is out of touch with the real world.[2] By working in the classroom, the university supervisor can stay in touch with the real world and can alleviate some of the cooperating teacher's concerns about "ivory tower" thinking.

The university supervisor is often responsible for evaluating the student teacher and assigning final grades. This has been a source of tension in many situations. When members of the triad do not agree on expectations, it is difficult to agree on evaluations. To avoid this tension, expectations should be clearly defined and evaluation should be completed through a collaborative process.[3] Evaluation should be a consistent, ongoing process.

Cooperating Teacher

Most teacher-education researchers agree that the cooperating teacher is the primary source of support for the student teacher. Again, the preservice teacher learns consciously and unconsciously by observing the master teacher. This learning takes place during faculty meetings, parent conferences, informal meetings with colleagues, and in the classroom. It is particularly helpful if master teachers discuss the decision making that goes on behind the scenes. For example, I often hear that "my cooperating teacher doesn't plan." This is seldom the case. However, teachers often develop their plans away from the school building. Discussing when, where, and why decisions are made helps student teachers understand what they are observing.

Interacting with colleagues is also an important component of teaching that can be modeled for beginning teachers. First-year music teachers seem to be particularly isolated as they begin their careers. These new teachers are rarely part of a larger department and are often left on their own. Novice teachers are more likely to be successful if they make connections with their colleagues. Cooperating teachers serve as role models for this by visiting with the teachers around them, attending and participating in faculty meetings, and working with colleagues. The teachers' lounge, cafeteria, and local cafe are possible locations for collaboration. It is important for cooperating teachers to include student teachers in these settings so that the preservice teacher learns to work with colleagues.

Recent research in education indicates that reflective practice is a valuable component in teaching.[4] Modeling reflective practice helps the student teacher understand the importance of this process. By keeping a journal, writing notes in the lesson plans, or discussing the decisions made, a master teacher can demonstrate the importance of reflective practice. In addition, master teachers can elicit reflection through constant communication with the student teacher. The master teacher can ask questions regarding the planning process, the effectiveness of instruction, student achievement, and classroom management. Throughout these conversations, student teachers are learning to ask questions about their own work.

Student Teacher

While much has been written about the role of the university supervisor and the cooperating teacher, very little is written about the role of the student teacher. Yet, the student teacher is the key person in the student-teaching triad. It is important for the student teacher to communicate with other members of the triad, ask questions, seek help, and clearly explain expectations. In the opening quote, Ann was able to open up to a complete stranger and express her frustrations. Yet, she never let either the university supervisor or the cooperating teacher know how unhappy she was. Ann perceived her role as a subordinate, one with no authority and no say. While the university supervisor and cooperating teacher do assume leadership roles, the student teacher must be an active participant in the triad.

Conclusion

Those of us who choose to work in teacher education have a profound responsibility to develop programs that contribute to the preservice teacher's knowledge and understanding of a complex profession. This responsibility extends to all members of the student-teaching triad. By working collaboratively, we can meet the challenge of providing meaningful and relevant experiences for preservice teachers.

Endnotes

1. Costa, A., & Garmston, R. (1987). Student teaching: Developing images of a profession. *Action in Teacher Education 9*(3), 5–11.
2. Veal, M., & Rikard, L. (1998). Cooperating teachers' perspectives on the student teaching triad. *Journal of Teacher Education 49*(2), 108–119.
3. Slick, S. (1997). Assessing versus assisting: The supervisor's roles in the complex dynamics of the student teaching triad. *Teaching and Teacher Education 13*(7), 713–726.
4. Bolin, F. (1988). Helping student teachers think about teaching. *Journal of Teacher Education 29*(2), 48–54.

This article first appeared in the Spring 2000 issue of the Colorado Music Educator. *Reprinted by permission.*

Helpful Hints in Preparing Your Classroom for a Student Teacher

- Prepare your classroom students for the experience before the student teacher arrives. Let them know a little about the preservice teacher, explain the purpose of student teaching, and communicate your expectations for the students.
- Contact the student teacher before the placement begins as a friendly introduction and welcome. Invite the student teacher for a previsit if possible. Provide materials that will assist in orienting the student teacher to your classroom. This could include the school handbook, class schedule, seating charts, discipline policy, copies of music, curriculum guides, and other resource materials.
- Arrange a place in the classroom for your student teacher to work and to store keys, purse, coat, or other personal items.
- When the student teacher arrives on campus, take the time to introduce the student to the class, other faculty members, and administration. Also, provide the student teacher with a tour of the building and facilities.
- Know your school's policy concerning student teacher responsibilities and share this information with the student teacher. Clearly outline the student teachers responsibilities regarding extra duties, reporting absences, attending faculty meetings, etc.
- Help the student teacher learn about the backgrounds of the students.
- Begin to delegate responsibility and authority to the student teacher within the first two weeks. This will allow both the student teacher and the pupils to become accustomed to the new situation.

You're Student Teaching Where?

Norma McClellan

Student teaching provides young music educators the opportunity to demonstrate the knowledge and skills acquired in their teacher preparation process. While this opportunity is exciting with possibilities, it is also challenging as students begin to bridge the gap between college and their professional careers.

The purpose of student teaching according to *A Guide to Student Teaching* is "to provide a planned, carefully supervised learning activity for the student that will allow demonstration of the qualities of the teacher/practitioner as a reflective decision-maker" (Sharon, 2002, p. 11). Student teaching is not only a time to apply the knowledge acquired to date but to gather new knowledge during the experience.

It is imperative that the student teacher gathers as much information as possible during this time while seeking guidance from both the cooperating teacher and university supervisor. Because of this important working relationship among the student teacher, the cooperating teacher, and the university supervisor, careful thought and planning must occur to ensure the best possible placement of the student. "Placement is the most critical step in ensuring a high-quality student teaching experience" (Fallin and Royse, 2000, p. 20). Consideration must be given to the student's disposition, music skills, and personal goals. When possible, the student should be included in the placement process. This usually works best when the student can suggest several options (school placements) to later be determined by the placement committee. The committee must consider the student's previous clinical field experience, the location and proximity, the quality of the music program, the experience and personality of the cooperating teacher, the potential for a broad range of experiences, and job potential.

Previous clinical experiences. Practicing teachers suggest adequate classroom experience is the greatest deficiency in teacher preparation today. With our K–12 music certification, it is important that students experience a wide variety of settings. These should include

- urban and rural
- band and orchestra
- choral and general music
- high school, middle school, and elementary school
- diverse populations

With one or two semesters dedicated to student teaching and one or two placements in each setting, it is impossible to experience all of the variety needed. Yet, by taking into account previous clinical placements, the hometown of the student, and the student's area of emphasis, variety is possible.

Location and proximity. Commuting is costly in both dollars and time. When possible, placements should involve one hour or less commute for both students and university supervisors. This maximizes a student's preparation and planning time as well as physical rest. In some cases, it may be preferable for the student to move to the location rather than to commute.

Quality of the program. Every effort is made to place students with master teachers in successful programs. Success of a program is not always measured in numbers and contest results. A successful music program may be one in which the parents and community take ownership and pride in the musical endeavors of the schools. It may be one in which the entire school supports the arts and teachers work collaboratively in an arts based curriculum. It may be one in which one teacher teaches all students in all grades providing cohesiveness and continuity to a child's musical development. Determining the success of a program is, at best, a subjective decision made by the placement team.

Experience and personality of the cooperating teacher. Music teachers with at least three years of experience and some graduate work typically exhibit the professionalism and work ethic necessary to serve as a cooperating teacher. It is valuable to consider teaching style when matching students with cooperating teachers. A student who is organized and structured in their life and approach may be frustrated by a teacher who frequently abandons the written lesson plan to take advantage of the "teachable moment," drawing upon personal experience and a more laid-back teaching style. Such personality differences must be considered when matching the students to cooperating teachers.

Potential for a broad range of experiences. Preservice teachers benefit by experiencing the many facets of public school music education. While in a large metropolitan school, they may be a part of the team of music teachers and staff. By contrast, a small rural school provides experiences at every age level in both vocal and instrumental music. Additionally, students should have an opportunity to teach students with special needs as well as diverse populations. Many times, students have not decided which setting is most suited to their tastes. The student teaching experience can help students with that decision. Therefore, it is important to provide abroad range of experiences whenever possible.

Job potential. In today's market, music teachers are a highly sought after commodity. Some school districts anticipate their needs and place a request for student teachers. This allows the district to preview the student prior to hiring them. It also allows the student to scout out the district to determine its desirability. In such situations, it is still vitally important that the student teacher be placed with a master cooperating teacher who will provide quality mentoring and guidance to the student teacher during the student teaching assignment. Job potential must be taken into consideration whenever the student requests specific assignments based upon that possibility.

The student teaching experience is that transition between being a student and being a teacher. When the experience is carefully planned and the match is right, the results are rewarding for all involved: the student, the cooperating teacher, and the university supervisor.

Sources

Fallin, Jana and Royse, David. (2000). Student teaching: The keystone experience. *Music Educators Journal, 87*(3), 19–22.

Terry, Sharon. (2002). *A Guide to Student Teaching.* Springfield, MO: Southwest Missouri State University.

This article first appeared in the Winter 2002 issue of Missouri School Music. *Reprinted by permission.*

Finding the Right Match
Jon S. Remley

As I write this column in the middle of January, I am reminded that this is the time of year when college students begin getting notices from those in charge of teacher education that they need to make final decisions regarding placement for their student teaching experience. Thinking about this brought me to reflect upon my own choice for a student teaching experience and why, although my experience turned out beautifully, I should warn others not to do what I did.

I had never been counseled, nor had I ever sought counsel, on how to choose a school/cooperating teacher for my student teaching experience. I knew that student teaching was coming up the next semester and that I needed to decide where to go. The Hope High School Band was one of the best around our area. I had met and liked Mr. Wells, the director, so I asked him if I could student teach with him. He agreed, I reported my decision to the powers that be, and it was done. Clean, quick, and to the point. Everything worked out. This is not the way to go about it. Student teaching is one of the most important, career-shaping experiences for any music education major. It should be entered into with considerable planning and forethought. Adherence to the following suggestions should provide a successful student teaching experience.

When possible, students should start the process of selecting a student teaching placement in their freshman year. Remember that every potential employer wants to hire someone who is twenty-five years old with twenty-five years experience. From the first semester of their freshman year, students should seek out ways to become involved with a music program in a local school. If payment for services rendered is available, that is a plus, but students should go into a school and ask if they can help without expecting to be compensated financially. The objectives are: (1) to get experience, and (2) to establish a positive relationship with a local teacher. If students are attending college in a city with more than one local school, they should strive to get varied experiences and establish relationships with several local music educators. This can establish a strong base of trust on which to build a potential student-teaching relationship.

During the beginning of their junior year, students should seek counsel from (1) the person charged with supervising student teaching in the students' respective areas of expertise, and (2) the music faculty person who best knows the local school programs and directors. Both students and counselors should consider the following:
- What type and size of program has been the student's experience to date? Consider middle school, high school, and college experience and all facets of each program, from numbers of students to numbers of directors to administrative set-up and experiences offered.
- What type and size of program does the student

want for a student teaching experience? Similar to her previous experience? Contrasting? It is here where the experience and wisdom of the counselors begin to come into play. Counselors must work to match students with schools that will provide the greatest benefit to the development of students' careers.

- What about personalities? Students should communicate with their counselors if they have specific ideas of where to perform their student teaching. Counselors should know the students' and the local directors' personalities well enough to guide the students into a win–win situation between them and their cooperating teachers.
- Is gender an issue? Students should consider whether there might be a benefit gained by student teaching with someone of their own or the opposite gender. Counselors should also consider whether there is a benefit to any particular student of having a mentor of the same or opposite gender.
- Is lifestyle an issue? Students may be uncomfortable with what they consider (real or perceived) to be part of the lifestyle of a particular direc-

tor. If so, they need to communicate this with their counselor. Honesty in all things must be a part of the counseling process if the student is to get the greatest benefit from the experience.

Once the selection has been narrowed to two or three possibilities, the student should visit each school, observe the director(s), meet with them, and report back to the counselor. A mutually agreed upon decision should then be made as to a first and second choice. Those choices should then be submitted to the official in charge of student-teacher placement.

Following these guidelines will take time for both student and counselor, but it is time worth spending in order to make the right match of student teacher and cooperating teacher. Finding the right student-teaching situation for a particular student is at best an inexact art, which is all the more reason to spend the time and effort to make the best match possible.

This article first appeared in the March 2002 issue of Alabama's Ala Breve. *Reprinted by permission.*

 # Need help finding your first job?

 Section 7

Need help finding your first job?

The Search for the Perfect Job, Part I
Diane M. Falk

With the academic year quickly coming to a close, many college seniors are now contemplating the next step in their lives—that into the professional world of a music educator. Having spent four years, or possibly more, preparing for just this occasion, the thought of entering the work force on a full-time basis with a classroom of eager faces before us can be intimidating. But with a review of our course work, our field experiences, and our skills and talents, we know we have been well prepared. Now it is just a matter of finding a teaching position and beginning our chosen career. Just finding a position? The entire prospect of completing job applications, writing resumes, and obtaining references, let alone becoming aware of open positions, can be overwhelming. Rather than awakening in the middle of the night in the weeks following graduation with a panicked voice running through your head, softly screaming "Now what do I do?" the time remaining before graduation is that in which to carefully plan the means to obtain a first job in the public schools.

April is the month in which many nontenured teachers will receive notice from their school districts that they will not be reemployed for the following year. Therefore, announcements and advertisements noting the availability of teaching positions will soon start to become more and more plentiful, a trend which will continue through the first few weeks of September. After this, job openings normally decrease in number until December or January when teachers, retiring or leaving a position for another reason in midyear, will begin to give notice. Therefore, for students graduating college in May, March is the last opportunity to

prepare your materials so as not to miss being considered for many of these early openings.

Writing Your Resume
A resume is a document which gives a potential employer important factual information about your skills, experience, and education. Contrary to popular opinion, a resume does not have to be limited to one page, providing the information contained in the document is relevant to your possible employment.

The contents should be neatly typed and arranged in an organized fashion with adequate white space separating the different sections. A word processing program and computer will allow you to utilize an appropriate font and point size (ten or twelve is best). Try to avoid using too many special effects when typing your resume. Bold print, italics, or underlining are acceptable for headings but do not use special effects such as outlining, shadowing, or bending words. Obviously, your name, address, and phone number(s) at which you can be easily contacted should appear at the very top of the first page. This information can be centered or kept even with the left margin. Following this would appear the main headings of education, work experience, related experience, honors and awards, and references, arranged in a sensible order which will give the reader the most important information first. (See example 1)

Education
For example, a heading titled Education would be followed by a list of the schools and/or special clinics or summer seminars which you attended, in chronological order with the most recent appearing first. Following the name of each of the schools which you attended or from which you

graduated should be the school's location, the degree you earned, your discipline, and the dates you attended. If your GPA is worthy of special attention, list this as well.

Professional Experiences

Following your educational background should be a listing of relevant professional experience related to the teaching of music. Because many seniors have not been employed as educators, this listing should include all field experiences and any other employment or work experience, including such things as summer camps, music stores, teaching private lessons, directing a church youth choir, and so on. Other types of work experience such as working as a cashier or stock person at the local mall can also be included to show that you are an experienced and dedicated worker who understands the implications of employment. Each entry should be followed by a list of your responsibilities and accomplishments.

Note that each of the responsibilities begins with an action verb, all of which are in the same form (a gerund, ending in -ing). An action verb gives the reader a sense that the applicant actually had direct participation in the instruction of students. The list of responsibilities allows the potential employer to more carefully assess your abilities and past experiences to determine your fit to a particular position.

Activities

Other professional activities, if you have several, can then follow under a separate heading. If you have fewer than three, merely incorporate them into the previous section. This portion can also contain other activities which are relevant to your development as a musician/teacher but were not actual employment. You may include such things as volunteer work or community service, performing with community ensembles, serving as an adjudicator or assistant for festivals or auditions, and membership in fraternities, sororities, or professional organizations. The content for this section of the resume will vary considerably depending upon the interests and talents of each person and will be a more complete reflection your personality.

The remaining sections of your resume should contain a list of any honors or awards you received both in and out of school and a list of references. Dean's list, membership in honor societies, special recognitions, awards won by performing ensembles with which you were associated as a performer or director, and any scholarships or

grants received are all areas which could be contained in the resume section normally titled Awards and Recognitions. As with all of the information contained in your resume, be as precise as possible, listing all pertinent information.

References and Letters of Recommendation

The final section of your resume should be a list of the names, addresses, phone numbers, and position titles of your professional and possibly some personal references. These are people who are familiar with your musical and teaching abilities, have had important personal contact with you, and are aware of your qualifications. Before including anyone's name on your reference list, always approach these people individually. Ask their permission, and then advise them that you would like to include their telephone numbers in case a potential employer needs to speak with them directly regarding your candidacy. It is usually best to avoid the statement "references available upon request" at the end of your resume. A school district with a limited time in which to hire a new teacher may bypass your application in favor of those who have provided references or the names of individuals who can be reached immediately by telephone.

Because many school districts prefer written statements of reference, you also should ask your references to provide a written letter for you which could be used for many different job applications or you can provide them with a generic reference form which frequently can be obtained from the Career Placement Office at your college or university. These reference forms are usually of two types: a Confidential Reference for which the student waives the right to see the completed form and a Nonconfidential Reference which the student can read at any time. If you have selected your references carefully and have been candid with each person and they with you, students should not fear using a confidential reference. Depending on your institution, this office also may develop a file for you containing your references, transcripts, and any other information, such as final student teaching evaluations, which might be valuable for a potential employer to peruse. At your request, and usually for a small fee, the Career Placement Office would forward your documents to a prospective employer. If no such service is available at your institution, you can easily develop a file folder containing the same information, make photocopies of each document, and forward the materials to the school district yourself with your resume and cover letter.

When considering the individuals whom you would desire to approach for a letter of recommendation, it is best to choose those most familiar with your abilities who can make relevant comments on your personal, academic, and/or music capabilities. Cooperating teachers from student teaching or other field experiences; your college student teaching supervisor; a college professor; your supervisor in a teaching, educational, or other work setting; a community or religious leader; or any respected member of the community are all excellent choices to serve as a reference. It is best not to enlist the aid of a friend, relative, fellow student, or someone working at the same job as yourself. For example, if you teach the drum line, it is preferable to ask for a reference from the band director rather than the brass instructor who is also a college student.

Finally, request letters of recommendation well in advance of the date needed and at a point when the individual has sufficient time to write a well-thought-out document. If you wait until graduation, the final day of student teaching, or the morning of a job interview, you will be disappointed. Remember that the people from whom you make this request are busy individuals and will need some time to complete your reference. If you wait too late, both parties will be placed in an uncomfortable situation. To expedite the process, be prepared with all of the appropriate materials including reference forms, and, if necessary, stamped, addressed envelopes.

Other Considerations

After completing your resume, carefully review it on several different occasions in case you have forgotten any of your accomplishments or need to update the document. Be fastidious in checking all dates, information, spelling, grammar, and that the exact same format has been used for each entry. Using a computer with a word processing program will greatly ease your burden each time a correction or update needs to be made. Computer programs for both Macintosh and IBM compatible computers also are available for writing resumes. These programs, which

---

Example 1

Education

William Peterson College, Wayne, NJ
B.M. in Classical Performance with teacher certification
Area of applied concentration: piano, voice
1991–1995
GPA: 3.64

Essex County College, Newark, NJ courses taken towards AA degree 1990–1991 GPA: 3.52

Clifford 1 Scott High School, East Orange, NJ college preparatory track 1986–1991

Professional Experience

Student Teacher—Manasquan High School, Manasquan, NJ, Spring 1995. Responsibilities included directing concert and marching bands in rehearsals and performances, teaching small group and private lessons on all band and orchestra instruments, teaching Music Appreciation and Music Theory classes, assisting at four band competitions, and accompanying concert choir rehearsals.

Drum Line Instructor—Jackson Memorial High School, Jackson, NJ, August 1994–present. Responsibilities included teaching all music to percussion section, assisting with designing and teaching drill, serving as a chaperone at summer band camps, assisting director at all football games and competitions.

Activities

American Choral Directors Association (ACDA) Student Chapter—Westminster Choir College, Princeton, NJ, 1993–1996, President (1995–96), Vice President (1994–95). Accomplishments included instituting yearly choral reading sessions, hosting guest speakers at bimonthly meetings, assisting with Junior High Festival Chorus auditions.

Volunteer day care provider—Happy Times Day Care Center, East Windsor, NJ, June–August, 1992. Assisted teachers with children, ages 4–5, in all daily activities, including music, arts and crafts, and playtime.

typically contain several formats and will arrange your material after you have typed it, may be available at your college's academic computing center or the placement office. Resume Expert, published by A Lasting Impression, available for as low as $49.00, comes in several different versions including one with forty different resume templates, one for cover letters, and editions available for careers in education, and arts and leisure, as well as for student employment. These should be used with extreme caution, however, as an administrator reading similar letters from different applicants will quickly become aware that rather than developing a personal resume and cover letter the potential employee utilized a computer generated document.

Although your resume serves to inform a potential employer of your background and abilities, it should not contain items which are personal in nature. Avoid providing information such as "married for thirteen years with five children," "my father is a rabbi," or "my health is very good." These things are unimportant and irrelevant to your application.

Also keep extra copies of your resume readily available for sudden job openings, taking to interviews, and as a handy reference when speaking on the telephone with prospective employers.

Your resume is one of the most important documents you will write during your college experience. It can open the door to employment or close it. It will speak for you as a teacher, musician, and person when you are still merely a name on a long list of job applicants. No matter how many or few your accomplishments, be confident in writing, professional in language, and, most important, present yourself in a manner which will bring honor to yourself and your college.

This article first appeared in the March 1996 issue of New Jersey's Tempo. *Reprinted by permission.*

The Search for the Perfect Job, Part II
Diane M. Falk

The Cover Letter

At a recent induction meeting of Kappa Delta Pi, an education honor society, it was announced that, on average, one job opening for an elementary teacher results in letters from over seven hundred applicants. Fortunately, the number of applicants for music positions is much lower, although no exact figure is readily available. However, this frightening statistic clearly helps us to understand the need to prepare materials which will cause a prospective employer to request an interview and eventually offer employment.

Once your resume is complete and has been refined, a prospective music educator needs to focus attention on the cover letter, which is attached to the resume and serves as your formal introduction to the employer. Most important is the realization that this letter provides the opportunity to sell yourself and is the means by which a potential employer begins to become familiar with you as an individual. In spite of an outstanding resume, a cover letter can and frequently does affect the school administrator's opinion of you and your skills. Your writing style, use of language and spelling, and the actual content of the letter can either serve as a help or a hindrance. Therefore it is important to give careful consideration to this document and to write a letter which provides a reflection of who you are as person, allowing your personality to be evident.

The letter itself should fit on one page and, depending on length, can be either single or double spaced using a typewriter or computer. Easily read type, avoidance of fancy fonts, and use of a good quality printer are imperative to ensure serious consideration being given to your application. If necessary, find a reference book or secretarial guide which will review the rules of writing a business letter and strictly adhere to these. Be exceedingly careful about grammatical errors, spelling or typographical errors, and use of colloquialisms, slang, or casual language. The sentence "I really think kids are super!" may be acceptable in a casual conversation with friends but does not demonstrate to an administrator that you have made the transition from college student to professional. An unfortunate trend in writing business letters has recently appeared in which a prospective employee fills the letter with cliches or writes as if scripting a television commercial containing three or four exclamatory sentences. Sentences such as "If you've been searching for the perfect choral director and haven't been able to find one, then you're search is over!" or "You haven't seen anything 'til you've seen me!" are not appropriate for inclusion in a business letter in which your trying to present yourself as a worthy prospect.

The Content

The cover letter should begin with the opening

paragraph specifying the title of the position which you are seeking. School districts may have several openings in a given subject area, and the person opening your application will, if necessary, be able to then forward your materials to the appropriate individual. This opening paragraph also may include the source from which you learned of the position.

The body of the letter should clearly state the reasons why you are the best candidate for this particular job, without sounding like a braggart, and how your specific skills, talents, and abilities directly relate to those required for the job and can benefit the school, the district, and, most importantly, the students. In other words, the content of the letter needs to clearly specify what you can do for the school district, not what it can do for you. An administrator justly will be flattered while reading; "I always wanted to work in your district due to its outstanding reputation and excellent marching and jazz band programs." But every candidate would want to work in a district with such programs! An administrator needs to know in what ways your potential employment will further improve the present program and how your particular abilities will interface with those of the other music educators in the district. In other words, teacher candidates must be able to clearly articulate the reasons why they are the right person for this particular job. Provide accomplishments, a summary of work experience, and other pertinent information which will allow the administrator to fully evaluate you. While serving on a committee to hire a teacher, I once encountered a letter from a violist who wrote extensively about her skills in coaching chamber music and conducting orchestras. She mentioned her Master's degree in viola performance from a prestigious conservatory, her private studies and performances in Europe and the United States, and the extensive private studio she was developing. Her letter fully demonstrated that she was an outstanding musician. However, she was not interviewed for the position! This was due to the fact that she never mentioned in either her resume or cover letter any experience or accomplishments in the concentration required for the job—music technology! It is vital that the content of your letter addresses the requirements for the position advertised. If the position you desire is that of a high school marching band director, give specific examples of your skills or experience in this area. If it is for an elementary general music specialist, mention your keyboard skills and work with young children. However, when providing examples of your accomplishments, be honest and straightforward without being an egotist.

Finally, the cover letter should close with a brief statement thanking the administrator for consideration of your application and, if desired, your willingness to be available for an interview. Even though you already included you phone number(s) on your resume, you also may wish to provide it at the close of your cover letter as well.

Supporting Documents

In addition to sending a resume and cover letter to a prospective employer, many potential employees provide other supporting documents, which allow their candidacy to more completely evaluated. If you have been faithful in collecting concert programs, newspaper articles, copies of awards, and other documents about your accomplishments during your college career, you may wish to provide photocopies of some of these to your potential employer. Some administrators may wish to see tangible evidence of your accomplishment and therefore you may wish to send copies of programs for concerts in which you conducted or, to a lesser degree, participated. This does not imply that you should send copies of all the programs for the high school and college orchestra concerts in which you played fourth horn, but rather include those which are meaningful and important. Performing with a choral group at Avery Fisher Hall, conducting a portion of the spring concert while student teaching, or your senior recital are examples of activities which may be attractive to an administrator. In addition to programs, you may also wish to forward to the hiring districts other examples of your accomplishments. These can include but are not limited to a video tape of student teaching, the marching band for which you served as percussion instructor or assisted with the drill design, or any other relevant experience related to your career as a music educator. Audiotapes of ensembles which you conducted or accompanied may also be included. If the cost incurred in reproducing video or audio tapes is excessive, it would be acceptable to provide these tapes only if you are invited to an interview.

Other items you could send include:
• relevant newspaper articles about you and your accomplishments,
• sample lesson plans or instructional materials which you developed and utilized during your teaching experiences,

• copies of awards or certificates of commendation
a photocopy of your teacher certification issued
by the state and any certificates earned for
completing course work in specialized areas of
music instruction such as Orff or Kodály.

An applicant also may find it beneficial to include a copy of the undergraduate college transcript with the initial application since many administrators will request a copy prior to interviewing applicants. Students can obtain an unofficial copy of their records, which is not embossed with a raised copy of the college seal or another official marking. This unofficial copy of your transcript, which should only be utilized in emergency situations until an official one can be obtained from the college or university, could be mailed with your resume and cover letter for use on a temporary basis.

Maintaining files of all relevant materials is also extremely important. Job seekers should keep multiple photocopies of all paper work, printed resumes, and other materials in organized packets so that whenever a desirable music position is announced, the applicant has everything ready for mailing and merely has to attach a copy of the cover letter. Because each cover letter needs to be addressed to a specific person and mention the title or description of each individual position, these must be prepared on an individual basis. Many individuals find that the print merge option in computer word processing programs to be particularly helpful so that one document containing the names and addresses of the persons to whom the cover letters were addressed and application materials sent is merged with a second file contains the cover letter. This allows each cover letter

to be individually prepared with just a few touches on the keyboard. A complete record of your applications is maintained simultaneously.

Finally, remember that the first impression a potential employer will receive of you is the manner in which your materials arrive in the mail. While employed in another state, I once opened applications from those applying for a teaching position. One applicant's materials consisted of a hand written letter with approximately forty unorganized, crumpled scraps of paper, all different sizes, containing notes from colleagues, program information, and clippings of newspapers. Trying to read and organize these materials left all involved in the search for a teacher with a negative impression of the candidate. Therefore, prior to mailing your materials, organize them in the neatest way possible. Rather than using a standard legal envelope, which will require folding your materials, use a large manila envelope with a neatly typed address label. A potential employer will greatly appreciate your materials arriving in this manner.

For many college students, the prospect of graduating and entering a new phase of their lives can be overwhelming. For others it is an exciting time of new challenges to be met and conquered. Regardless of how we feel as we begin our search for a job and become professional music educators, being prepared and confident can make all the difference. I hope that each of you finds the job which is perfect for you and has all the success and happiness possible as a music educator.

This article first appeared in the May 1996 issue of New Jersey's Tempo. *Reprinted by permission.*

Checklist for 'Intelligent' Interviews: Guide from A to Z for Successful Marketing of Yourself
Paul K. Fox

Congratulations, you have made it! You have completed your study of music education, are now certified to teach, and are looking for a full-time job. You send out your letters and resumes, and voila—the requests for interviews start rolling in.

Now what? How do you prepare to present all your talents and schooling to a third person, usually someone who knows little about your content area, get a school district's administration to notice your best qualities, and market yourself for a life-long career in a chosen community?

Many say that during the interview, first impressions are critical, "the first ten seconds will create the interviewer's first judgments about you, and then after four minutes, it's all over." The research also suggests that during the interview, the evaluation of your merit is based 7 percent on what you say, 38 percent on your voice or how you say it, and 55 percent on your facial expressions and nonverbal cues.

However, in this highly competitive marketplace, employers are always screening for those high-end achievers: educators who can demonstrate the potential for mastery of their content areas and essential elements of instruction; show their love of children and teaching; understand the goals, philosophy, and needs of public education; and model the skills of professionalism. They are looking for candidates who have the ability to speak in public, organize their time and manage stress, utilize technology in the workplace, display experience in problem solving and teamwork, and habitually self-evaluate and write down their personal goals and views in a concise, orderly, scholarly, and open-minded manner.

Interviews involve the art and science of public relations, market research, and selling oneself. In short, the more prepared you are, the better. The points below will serve as areas you can study, review, and approach using that familiar process of a good musician—practice, practice, practice!

Preinterview
A. Write down a complete self-assessment of education, accomplishments, skills, experiences, strengths, weaknesses, and qualities you do and do not wish to convey to a prospective employer.

B. Research the school, music program, and community:
1. What do you know about this school district?
2. What music courses and extracurricular activities do they offer?
3. What is the organization of the music curriculum and scheduling?
4. How many periods (not counting lunch) are in the school day?
5. What specialties are emphasized—Kodály, Orff, and/or Dalcroze?
6. What is the average makeup of the community (education and socioeconomics)?
7. What educational, cultural, and sport/leisure activities are available in and around the community?
8. What position(s) is (are) open and what duties are required?
9. What avenues for professional development exist?
10. What percentage of students are involved in the music program?
11. What percentage of students own instruments, take lessons, seek outside ensembles, etc.?
12. What indicators of cooperative parental and community support exist (concert attendance, private teachers, booster groups, community arts organizations, etc.)?
13. What resources are budgeted for music students (sheet music, music technology, field trips, piano tuning, instruments and instrumental repair, teacher in-service, festivals, etc.)?
14. How often is the curriculum updated?
15. What is the school district grading scale and music grading policy/practice?

C. Prepare a list of well-researched questions to be asked of the interviewer(s).

D. Find someone who works in the district; ask him/her about the job opening, the school district's mission statement, work climate, and community.

E. Compile/review an extensive list of personal examples for modeling professionalism (these will become interview questions, so have your views/experiences ready):
1. Statement of philosophy and goals
2. Time and stress management
3. Use of technology
4. Oral and written expression
5. Leadership
6. Teamwork
7. Judgment, problem solving, and decision making
8. Planning and organization
9. Innovation and creativity

10. Personal initiative, energy, and enthusiasm
11. Self-insight and professional development
12. Dependability
13. Adaptability
14. Appearance

F. Practice interviewing techniques (roleplaying, mock interviews, audio/videotaping).

G. Be prepared to familiarize yourself with specific elements of the interview site:
   1. Learn the name, title, and level of responsibility of the administrator(s) and/or interviewers.
   2. Know where you are going (make a trial run).
   3. Arrive early (at least fifteen minutes before interview).
   4. Dress to project an image of confidence and success (wear a suit).
   5. Bring additional materials (transcripts, portfolio, updated resume, etc.).

Interview Process

H. Market yourself with a positive first impression:
   1. Promote a positive and cheerful attitude.
   2. Share a warm greeting and firm handshake.
   3. Build rapport and demonstrate an attitude of openness and sensitivity to the interviewer's style.
   4. Show a feeling of mutual responsibility for creating a comfortable atmosphere and establishing common ground.

I. Treat the interview as an exchange of information between two individuals.

J. Be yourself and demonstrate relaxed speech, posture, and body language.

K. Exhibit positive nonverbal cues:
   1. Respond to the interviewer with an occasional affirmative nodding of the head.
   2. Sit erect in chair with hands, feet, and arms unfolded, leaning forward.
   3. Offer good eye contact and smile appropriately.
   4. Maintain a pleasant facial expression.

L. Provide thoughtful, professional, and firm answers to interviewer's questions:
   1. Back up statements with specific examples.
   2. Share the outcome or solution to a specific problem.
   3. Summarize to emphasize your strengths.

M. Avoid verbal clutter—speak in short sentences or bulleted items (not long paragraphs) using active verbs, concrete examples, summaries, and transitions.

N. Remember the three Cs—be calm, concise, and congenial.

O. Be open, thoughtful, and a good listener of the interviewer's points/questions.

P. Don't go overboard and volunteer too much.

Q. Say what you mean—if you get the job you may be "stuck" with your words.

R. Angle your position so as not to sit directly in front of the interviewer—select a chair beside the interviewer's desk, not across the desk (avoid barriers).

S. Use the person's name when talking—it's the best way to get/keep his/her attention.

T. If you do not know the answer to a question, be honest and admit it—inexperience is not a crime!

U. Interview the interviewer—ask questions that reflect the amount of research you have done rather than your lack of knowledge about the employer.

V. Close the interview with a short summary of why you're the best candidate for the job, thank the interviewer, give him/her another firm handshake, and walk confidently from the interview.

Post Interview

W. Debrief yourself—write down everything you handled right and wrong.

X. Note information you need to include in future correspondence/follow-ups.

Y. Write a personalized thank-you letter (set yourself apart from other applicants.)

Z. Follow-up your visit by making phone calls, sending requested materials, etc.

Some Additional Recommendations

Be ready to respond to several of the most popular questions at interviews:

1. Who had the greatest influence on you becoming a teacher and why?
2. What are the most important qualities of an outstanding educator?
3. What is your personal philosophy of student discipline?
4. How would you assess the learning in your classroom/rehearsal?
5. What purpose does music education serve in the public schools?
6. Describe the importance of continuing professional development and how you plan to incorporate it throughout your career?
7. What are your personal goals in the field of music and music education—where do you see yourself in ten years?

Be aware of the occasional use of stress interviews, an uncomfortable style of the interviewer deliberately introducing "stresses" into the conversation, long periods of silence, challenging your opinions, seemingly being unfriendly or disinterested—all designed to see how you'll react under pressure.

Some administrators have a perception that music teachers are "temperamental" or have big egos. How would you respond to a direct question on this subject?

Avoid describing yourself as a specialist. Underscore your enthusiasm for teaching and love of and proficiency in music. De-emphasize preferences or expertise in a particular music subject, grade level, or performance area (choral director, string teacher, etc.). You teach children.

Don't highlight inquiries on salary, benefits, contract length, etc. Ask these specifics later if they are not offered before signing a contract.

Administrators are always looking for staff members to sponsor extracurricular activities. Make sure you express enthusiasm for participating in school events after the final bell rings. State any interest in coaching sports, directing musicals, charting marching band shows, organizing forensics or speech and debate, working on the school yearbook or newspaper, etc.

Bring to the interview a copy of your professional portfolio with the following:
• recent references
• student teaching evaluation sheets
• sample programs of recitals and concerts
• updated copy of resume
• personal philosophy of music education
• sample sets of lesson plans, original compositions, and student assessment vehicles
• copy of transcripts
• certificates/letters of scholarships and other awards

• informal congratulatory notes on student, substitute, or private teaching, as well as recitals, shows, public speaking engagements, and performances
• Videotape examples of teaching and performances and loan a copy to the interviewer:
• demonstrations of elementary, secondary, general music, choral, and instrumental classes
• senior solo recital
• chamber music recitals
• student teaching experiences of your conducting and piano accompanying performances
• summer music camp and/or private teaching coaching experiences
• public speaking at workshops or PCMEA meetings

Acknowledgements

Carnegie-Mellon University pamphlet *Interviews: Stages and Topics Commonly Asked*; Upper St. Clair School District *Professional Applicant Interview Reference Manual* by Jean L. Rogers, director of Human Resources.

Additional Sources: *Sweaty Palms: The Neglected Art of Being Interviewed* by H. Anthony Medley; *More Power to You* by Connie Brown Glaser and Barbara Steinberg Smaller; *You Are the Message: Secrets of the Master Communicators* by Roger Ailes; *Help! My Job Interview is Tomorrow!* by Mary Ellen Templeton; *Knock 'Em Dead: The Ultimate Job Seekers' Handbook* by Martin John Yate.

This article first appeared in the Fall 1999 issue of Pennsylvania's PMEA News. *Reprinted by permission.*

Who Is Asking the Questions?

Gina Speckmann

During my junior and senior years I often thought about the interview process. I wished that I could gain some type of psychic powers giving me an edge over other candidates when talking with possible future administrators. I spent a lot of time looking for resources concerning tips for resumes and interviews. I went to numerous sessions at professional conferences and completed a massive search for information online. As graduation day grew close, I put forth extra effort to find more information, and it wasn't hard to do. There were an infinite number of resources. I tried to use my time wisely and make the best selections. I hoped the hard work would pay off in the end.

Needless to say, I felt that my resume was in tip-top shape, and I was proud to send it out to prospective schools this last spring. I had practiced my answers to what seemed like hundreds of possible questions administrators would ask. I was very critical of every answer. At this point in the game, I was prepared—or at least I thought so!

It turns out that I forgot one important aspect. At first, I forgot to gather information so that I could turn the tables and interview the school. With each interview I completed, the questions I prepared for the administrators improved. Therefore, I knew a little bit more about each school. In the end, I did choose to teach at the last school with whom I interviewed. I made my decision based on the entire music program, school, and community.

Unfortunately, I do not have a magical list of questions you should ask the interview panel. I think that list probably changes for each one of us. However, I urge you to spend a serious amount of time considering your questions before you interview the school. By including this part of the process, administrators will be impressed by the amount of interest you are taking in their school.

Some of us like surprise more than others. After accepting a position in Anytown, USA, you will be greeted with the element of surprise—some good, some bad. Hopefully, you will be able to minimize the unknowns by thoroughly interviewing your school. Look for information on the Internet. Talk with previous/current band directors or other teachers from the district. They can serve as valuable resources before and after you take the job.

In conclusion, prepare for the beginning, middle, and end of the interview process. Organize your resume, reference list, and credential file as soon as possible. Practice speaking your responses to possible questions out loud. Answers to questions sound differently when you are thinking them through to yourself or speaking them. Collect all of the information you can on your "school candidate." The school district will interview you. Be prepared when it is time to turn the tables.

This article first appeared in the October 2001 issue of the Nebraska Music Educator. *Reprinted by permission.*

Section 8

Are there any mentors out there?

 Section 8

Are there any mentors out there?

Unofficial Mentoring
Jeffrey E. Bush

Most of us can remember some of the interesting (!) experiences we had during our first year of teaching. We did not know who to talk to about what, where anything was; how to get supplies, equipment, etc.; and possibly even where the faculty washrooms were (a particularly interesting story from my own past!). Gradually, over the course of a semester or two, most of us found not only the answers to most of these questions but also "unofficial" ways to fulfill our teaching needs. Primarily, we learned by our errors—a particularly slow educational method.

Many of our new colleagues are currently struggling through this same experience. Beginning teachers often don't know what they don't know; they are not aware of many of the practical matters that experienced teachers navigate through daily. They arrive with a wealth of information and enthusiasm but often have little idea of the pragmatic issues associated with the day-to-day teaching experience. As well, many are reluctant to ask questions for fear of looking like they are dumb or unable to figure out what they think must be simple answers.

In response to this problem, many schools and school districts have instituted formal mentorship programs: senior teachers are paired with beginning teachers. While the objective is laudable, the success is often less than successful. Many times, music teachers are paired with nonmusic colleagues because there are seldom other music teachers in the school. While some aspects of school life remain the same for all teachers, we know the music education world is unique. As well, personality and other personal issues are rarely taken into account when pairing mentors with beginning teachers. In some instances, senior teachers may not view their assignments as anything more than additional labor, may resent the experience, and do little more than the minimum work required.

AMEA Mentorship Program
The Arizona Music Educators Association (AMEA) has instituted a mentorship program for interested new teachers. If you care to review the list of teachers who have willingly agreed to act as mentors, you will realize these are some of the finest music teachers in the state. Yet we receive very few requests from new teachers. From interviews and discussions with novices, it is obvious that many of the same conditions mentioned previously apply: they do not know they need help and may not want to admit they need assistance. As well, many have assigned mentors in their schools and believe that this mentorship is probably all they will need.

Undoubtedly the easiest way to assist new teachers is to simply make informal contact with them. If even a quarter of the AMEA members were to call the new music teachers in their districts, novices would have a huge cadre of unofficial mentors. Psychologically, it is much easier for you to call a beginning teacher than for that individual to call you. Just introduce yourself, tell the new teacher where you teach, how long you have been there, and welcome him/her to the school district. If you ask them how they are doing and what is going well for them, you will find many opening up, as they are eager to have a sympathetic, knowledgeable ear. You might ask them if they have any problems or issues that they want to talk to another music teacher about. Also remind them of deadlines or issues that you know are often problematic in your district or problems that you have seen others grapple with. Relating stories of some of your own first-year experiences often helps new teachers realize that their problems are common. At the very least, provide your phone number and/or e-mail address. Feel free to also recommend the AMEA mentorship program to them.

Other Mentoring Strategies

Another strategy is to have senior music teachers individually take turns inviting novice teachers out socially. A rotating schedule can be made so that every week or two the new teacher gets to meet another colleague. This way, teachers new to the district get to meet a number of their colleagues in a social setting without having to try to associate names with a large number of faces at the same time. As well, when a group of music teachers get together—even if it is to welcome new colleagues into the district—discussion often turns to what they're going to play at the next concert, issues of instrumentation, and voice balance, etc.!

There is absolutely nothing wrong with formal mentor programs. Even if they are successful, the added reassurance of a call from a senior colleague in the school district is beneficial. Taking the few minutes to contact a new member of our profession has the potential to provide much needed help and a lasting friendship. It starts with each one of us.

This article first appeared in the Fall 2002 issue of Arizona Music News. *Reprinted by permission.*

Professional Networking: An Invitation Directed to Active and Retired Music Educators
Jane Forvilly

Throughout our careers, we consistently benefit through various means of professional networking—informal communications with others for mutual assistance or support.

This is one of the ways in which we examine our professional routines and production. Networking is one of the reasons we attend professional conferences. There, we not only grow by hearing and seeing performances and being exposed to the insights of visiting "experts." Equally welcome and productive is the opportunity to exchange ideas with our peers.

What about the times, however, when such professional reinforcement would be useful now and not next spring? ... or when you would like knowledgeable listeners to hear and evaluate your groups with the same critical care you give to the groups heard at conference or festival ... or you would like to talk with someone experienced in a different instructional strategy? The OMEA Music Mentor program, matching experienced retirees to specific inquiries from active teachers, is designed to present that opportunity.

To initiate the exchange, an active teacher communicates with the mentor program coordinator and describes the assignment or specific focus of the proposed visit. The coordinator, in turn, contacts a retired educator who is experienced in that field and asks if they would be interested/able to visit that school. If this is agreeable, then the teacher is urged to contact the retiree, more fully describe the goals of the visit, issue the invitation, and work out a schedule. Despite the term "mentor," the interaction between active teacher and mentor is usually only one or two visits. More visits may be arranged if mutually agreeable.

The requesting teacher is asked to be specific about the goal of the visit, but that menu is broad. It might be listening to ensembles as a prefestival experience, helping strengthen the students' skills in specific areas (example: percussion techniques, tenor vocal range), observing classroom management techniques, suggesting materials/strategies for a new teaching assignment, or just observing and giving some feedback. The mentor could provide students the fresh opportunity and challenge of rehearsing with a different conductor. A variety of auxiliary ideas usually come from the visit. Possibilities could be a different physical arrangement for your room, placement of strong voices within your ensembles, suggesting new materials, offering conceptual teaching strategies and motivational schemes, reinforcement of what is already happening, etc.

The program is not intended to be a vehicle for a teacher in difficulty. It is simply an opportunity for professional exchange between two people with different experiences in the same field of endeavor. No compensation is expected for the retired mentor, although sometimes the courtesy of mileage reimbursement and a cup of coffee are offered.

This article is directed to active teachers and retirees to encourage participation by members of both groups.

Active teachers—Consider how a visit by an experienced retired peer might benefit both you and your students, and perhaps be a refreshing change from the usual routine.

Retirees—You have skills and insights gained

through twenty to thirty years experience. Here is an opportunity to share some of your knowledge. (Besides, being back surrounded by the dynamics of a classroom for a short time is fun and energizing.)

You are encouraged to contact the program coordinator and ask to be placed on the list of people willing to be called to act in the role of an OMEA Music Mentor. (Please note: mentors are usually only called once a year—sometimes not even that—and never more than twice a year.)

This article first appeared in the Fall 2000 issue of the Oregon Music Educator. *Reprinted by permission.*

Mentoring: Thoughts from a Second-Year Teacher
Ellen R. Patrick

Although the first year teaching is always a challenge, my year was made much easier due to the fact that my mentor was a music colleague. Seeing her at one of my schools, we were able to spend some time one-on-one together almost every day. Even when our conversations were short (and most were not), it was wonderful to know that she was there for support and encouragement every step of the way. Because she unselfishly gave up some of her precious time during the day, I was able to learn a great deal from my music mentor in areas inside and outside of music.

During a teacher's first year, procedures and paperwork that many times were not covered in any college class may become overwhelming. Before school began, my mentor and I walked through the school together. She showed me the cafeteria, teachers' lounge, teachers' restrooms, mailboxes, offices, and where all the important papers were located. I never would have known where to pick up my paycheck had she not shown me! Introducing me to every staff member and administrator that we passed, my mind swam with new names and smiling faces. Although I knew that I would not remember everything, she made it clear that she would help me whenever needed.

Throughout the year, my mentor made sure that I understood how to find and fill out the many papers that a teacher uses. Class lists, IEPs, detentions, parent-teacher conference forms, midterm reports, building requests, evaluation forms, surveys, grade sheets, and fund-raising sheets are just a few items she helped to explain.

When I began to make up my rules, handbook, and classroom procedures, she was right there when I needed help.

I cannot imagine how many hours she listened to my joys and frustrations that first year. We had numerous conversations over what was happening in my classrooms. She always tried to give suggestions of different ways to handle discipline problems or teach certain concepts. After discussing some of my concerns with discipline, she shared a few different procedures that she used in her own classroom that I was able to adapt and use with my bands. I am still using some of those procedures and have found them to be invaluable. She took a morning to come to the middle school to observe one of my most challenging classes so she could offer some advice. She even came to my high school band one day before contest, working with them during the class and talking with me after class. These two days were in addition to her required observations for the Entry Year Program. Although we often focused on how to improve many things I was doing, she always helped me to notice the positive aspects of my teaching.

Although my music mentor was a wonderful help in showing me the logistical aspects of teaching, I will never forget the times we spent just talking in her office about the day. We went out to eat several times so that we could spend time getting to know each other outside of school. We shared laughter, tears, and so much valuable knowledge during my first year. I could never begin to show her how grateful I really am for all of her support and encouragement last year.

This article originally appeared in the February/March 2001 issue of Ohio's TRIAD. *Reprinted by permission.*

Mentoring in Music Education: How Do We Keep Them from Bowing Out?

Barb Stevanson

In Homer's famous epic, *The Odyssey*, the goddess Athena, disguised as an old man named Mentor, guides Odysseus's son. To be a mentor teacher is to guide, to listen, to share. In your role as a mentor teacher, you and your mentee will develop your own definition of the mentoring process."★

Teachers who are new to the profession are leaving in astounding numbers. Up to 50 percent of them don't make it past their fifth year in education. With the shortage of music teachers becoming a more common problem in hiring, we must, as a profession, find ways to get new teachers beyond that five-year hurdle. A successful mentoring program is essential for retaining these novices and helping them to become effective and competent educators.

In my district, Austin ISD, we have had a new music teacher mentoring and orientation program in place for over fifteen years. I serve as the district music teacher mentor, leading the new teacher orientation and helping to match new music teachers to a music teacher mentor. I also serve as a mentor trainer for Austin ISD, training mentors in all subject areas.

The tactics used in mentoring new music teachers, whether they are new to the profession or just new to your district, are the same in many ways as they are for all other subjects. There are, however, some specific approaches that can be helpful in dealing with the issues of being a music specialist and being the only person in music on a particular campus. Those approaches are included in the "Components of a Successful Mentoring Program" as they apply to music teaching.

Components of a Successful Mentoring Program

1. **Administrative support and commitment.** The district music administrator and/or the school principal must be a part of carrying out a successful mentor program. It is their initial contact with the new teacher that will give the assurance of someone to turn to for help. The support of the administrator will be important to both the novice teacher and to the mentor.

2. **Time.** The district will need to designate days for orientation for new teachers, usually the days just before school begins. Prior to the beginning of the school year, Austin ISD provides a half day of music orientation at a central

location as part of a district-wide orientation event. Another half day is spent in the music room of a master music teacher going over specific materials and topics. The principal will need to set aside a specific time in these opening days in which to meet with new teachers on their own assigned campus. The music administrator and/or principal will also want to allot time for observing the new teacher in order to provide feedback. Observation is, of course, a part of the state teacher evaluation program, but the new teacher will need and want feedback prior to that time. The music administrator can be especially helpful in preparing a new teacher to be observed/evaluated by a nonmusician principal. Probably the most important time to be set aside for the new music teacher is time for visiting and observing other experienced music teachers in the district. Most music teachers are "one-of-a-kind" on their campus and will need a day or more of substitute leave to observe a fellow music teacher who can help with troubleshooting that is subject specific. In my district, the Fine Arts Department pays for one substitute day, and additional days are covered by the campus of the new teacher. It is also a good idea for the novice to observe other classroom teachers on their campus for help with nonmusic issues such as discipline and faculty planning.

3. **Master teacher as mentor.** Each new music teacher must have a fellow music teacher "buddy," usually from a nearby campus or one with a similar student population, as well as a campus mentor, usually from a different subject area—perhaps an experienced art or P. E. teacher whose schedule may be the same or who works with the same grade levels as the new teacher.

4. **Follow-up meetings and support groups.** New music teachers need each other. They need to have a chance to share successes and problems and to know that others may be having similar ups and downs. A one-hour, after-school meeting within the first month of school is important for "checking in" with new teachers. Additional meetings can be held throughout the year based on needs. These meetings can be held for new teachers only or can be a time for new teachers and their assigned mentors to get together. This type of support should go beyond the initial year into the second year and even the third year as needed.

5. **In-service specific to their needs** . Many problems encountered by new teachers are part

of behavior management issues and can be addressed by the district professional development department. In-services that provide assistance in this area are crucial. Secondary issues are, however usually music-specific and must be addressed by the district music administrator since music in-service is not provided on each campus. A minimum of two such in-services are recommended and should be made available to all music teachers, new as well as experienced. Topics can include anything of current interest or need such as Kodály or Orff methods, assessment strategies, incorporating TEKS, supporting TAAS objectives, etc.

Creating a Music Teacher Survival Guide

The needs of a novice music teacher are seldom met with campus in-service or support. To that end, it is helpful to provide them with a guide or handbook. The book can be used as a resource in knowing who to contact for help specific to the field of music and for basic planning and organizational materials that are unavailable in the local campus mentoring program. In Austin ISD, this guide is prepared by experienced music teachers with the help of someone who has recently entered the profession and who has been through the "trials and tribulations" of being a first-year music teacher. The "Music Teacher Survival Guide" should include:

1. Yearlong calendar of district holidays, activities, and in-service offerings.
2. Names and phone numbers and/or e-mail addresses of people who can help them (music administrator, mentor, personnel office, etc.).
3. In-service resources—school district and region service center, etc.

4. Procedures for grading and filling out report cards.
5. District teacher evaluation policy and copies of forms.
6. Lesson plan formats; year plan formats.
7. District, state, and national standards.
8. Seating charts—require them!!
9. Suggestions on how to coordinate with and support fellow art and P. E. teachers on the campus.
10. District policy on religious observances and how it impacts music performances.
11. Lesson plan ideas for the first week of school.
12. Articles on behavior management, including how to write effective rules and enforce them.
13. Overview of teacher's editions of adopted music textbook series.
14. Just to make it fun, you might want to also provide a "mini-survival kit" that could include items such as aspirin, notepads, chocolate hugs and kisses, a list of ways to say "good job," your favorite teacher cartoon, a map of the district or city, red pen for grading, etc.

In closing, I would remind mentors that our primary job is to be a listener. Offer specific suggestions when asked. Never put yourself in the role of an evaluator or you will have lost the trust of the person you are mentoring. And remember, always remember, what it was like to be a first-year teacher. You made it, so can they!

★From the "AISD Mentoring Handbook," Used by Permission of the Austin Independent School District.

This article first appeared in the Spring 2000 issue of Texas's TMEC Connections. *Reprinted by permission.*

Mentoring
Bob Thompson

How many times have we heard it? "It is so important to be a mentor to new teachers." I know that I have heard it repeatedly over the years and thought to myself, "Yeah right, nobody was there to help me and I survived." Well, my attitude has changed.

What is a mentor? Webster defines it as "a wise and trusted teacher, guide, and friend." I agree with that definition but with the additions of a confidant, a shoulder to cry on, and most importantly, someone to look out for you. Weren't we all there once? Show me the music teacher that hasn't cried on their way home from work (Come on, admit it!) during that first tumultuous year, and I will be the first to shake his/her hand. Such simple things as ordering meal tickets for All County, telling your principal that you need an administrator to ride the bus because you have to judge all day, or getting that solo and ensemble list in on time can become earth shattering events. Suddenly, you have messed up the lives of a cook, vice principal, or supervisor, and they don't mind letting you know that in no uncertain terms.

What does it take to mentor a new teacher? This is really what I want people to think about. It takes remembering those feelings of insecurity and doubt and realizing that there are people directly related to you in your field having those feelings on a daily basis. Going through these growing pains may help us to develop in the long run, but are they necessary? I really don't think so. I will be the first to admit that I haven't been there in the past for new teachers in my feeders. I did have a personal experience with helping a new teacher this year, and it has changed my entire outlook.

We all remember the questions we had but were too embarrassed to ask because that would make us look incompetent. Most generally there are simple answers, but not until you have been down that road. Until that time, it is a frightening experience to deal with free or reduced lunch vouchers, All State registration forms, travel permits, and on and on and on. After we have been down that road, it all seems so simple. Of course, you have to let the custodian know what's going on with your fall concert; yes, those bus requests have to be filled out by you even though it is a county event; and no, the principal probably doesn't realize that the football team uses the stage for weight training after school when you planned to have a mass rehearsal with two hundred kids.

So what exactly does being a mentor take? From my experience, it takes a phone call out of the blue to ask "How are things?" or just asking to leave a few minutes early so that you can stop by the middle school and say hey. It is a matter of being, as Webster said, a friend. Someone to look to for simple answers or to lean on and not feel jeopardized when times get rough, someone to say you are doing a good job, or just a shoulder that understands to cry on. Admit it or not, we have all been there and had those moments of fear, insecurity, and error. Why not take some time and make the life of a new teacher a little nicer next year? It may very well keep a well qualified, talented person in our system.

This article first appeared in the Summer 2002 Maryland Music Educator. *Reprinted by permission.*

How can you survive your first years of teaching?

Section 9

How can you survive your first years of teaching?

Ten Principles of Leadership
Paul-Elliot Cobbs

This article is for the first-year ensemble director, as well as for those older directors like me, who treat each September as if it were the start of their teaching career. I would like to share ten principles of leadership and ten principles of musicianship that I've found to be quite important. Of course, you will also need to learn how to interact with your administration, fellow faculty, and parents, but that's a separate discussion.

The first leadership principle is to (1) **establish meaning**. Why should I take this class? What's in it for me. What will I learn? Is it worth my time and money? As teachers, we made the commitment to our art years ago, but don't forget that the student is still "shopping around."

Once in your class, the newness of it all will hold their interest for a while, yet this initial enthusiasm will wane as the work load increases, unless you can create a (2) **shared vision**. Perhaps it's to be the best group in the history of the school, community, or state. Whatever your vision, allow your students to dream with you, and as you begin the process, their dreams will turn into a shared vision.

The difference between dreams and a vision is that vision has a strategy to bring it into reality. (3) **Shared objectives** are the stepping stones to the future that you dream about today. Perhaps your objective this year is to play a particular composition or earn a superior rating at a particular festival. When one knows what one is working toward, there is a certain focus which is maintained. There is also a feeling of accomplishment when the goal is reached.

If you are going to lead them to victory, you must be a good general. You must (4) **demonstrate competence**. "Have the score in your head, not your head in the score." Show mastery of the work you're conducting, and the ensemble will respect you for it. Lead by example.

Leading by example also means (5) **demonstrating congruity**. Make sure your actions are congruent with your words. Your students will watch to see if you practice what you preach. Do you know your music? Do you come on time? Are you rude to people? Do you speak negatively about your peers, administration, etc.? Never forget it's what you do that carries the most weight, not what you say.

Yes, we all have good and bad days. We're only human, but (6) **constancy** plays a big role in the way students connect with you or disconnect from you. If someone does not know whether you will hug him or curse him from one moment to the next, he will most probably stay away, and that sacred bond between student and teacher will never be completely established.

The most fundamental way to connect with your student is to (7) **demonstrate caring,** and have respect for him/her as a person first and a musician second. "People don't care what you know until they know that you care." So often we forget that we are not really conducting music, we are conducting musicians, and through this interaction we are creating, organizing, and providing an interpretation. Sometimes it will go quite well and sometimes it won't, yet never forget that excellence is a process not an event. Always start formulating a rehearsal strategy with these thoughts: How can I help them be more successful? Do they need to work on music fundamentals more? Do they need to work on discipline and focus? Whatever you decide, do it because it is what the student needs, not Schubert. You might be surprised to discover that by placing the student above the music, the musical level will actually increase dramatically.

Once you begin to develop a student centered

ensemble, it will be a little easier to demonstrate the next principle of leadership, (8) **adaptability**. Each September you will start with an ensemble unique to itself. Perhaps last year's group was older, younger, more disciplined, less disciplined, more self-motivated, or less self-motivated. Whatever the differences, the only guarantee is that it won't be quite the same as last year.

Although you will start the year with a plan already in place, always be prepared to adapt the curriculum to the needs of the present students. There may be more of a need to work on rhythm or balance than you anticipated, but you must change to meet the needs of the students in front of you.

Being able to make changes when it's best for the students brings us to the next leadership principal (9) **flexibility**. Flexibility is vital to the success of all programs. Nothing will ever be 100 percent as you envisioned. Yet, rather than see it as a setback, view it as an opportunity to venture in a new direction. If you have ever worked with an inflexible leader, you know how frustrating and stifling the situation can be, especially if you have ideas you'd like to contribute. Good leadership empowers an ensemble. As I wrote in a previous article, the best groups have leadership from within as well as from the podium.

The final leadership principle is my favorite. The greatest joy of teaching for me is "rediscovery." I'm sure I've conducted Beethoven's Fifth Symphony thirty times or more. Yet each time is a new experience because I see it through the eyes of students. (10) **Inspiration** breathes new life into what you do, and as your students inspire you, your joy will inspire them. I've found that this happiness lasts well beyond graduation. I have students who still refer to the inspirational times during the school musical ensembles as the best in their lives. Many of these students are now in their thirties.

I will continue this article next time with a discussion of the ten principles of musicianship. To the first year teacher—remember, excellence is a process not an event, and lifelong growth, not perfection, is the aim. There is nothing more worthwhile or satisfying than spending your life making positive impacts on thousands of youth, one at a time.

This article first appeared in the March 2002 issue of Washington's Voice. *Reprinted by permission.*

Ten Principles of Musical Excellence for Ensembles
Paul-Elliot Cobbs

This article is a continuation of the writings outlining the ten principles of leadership. Both are meant to be read by first-year teachers. Yet, even though I've taught for thirty years, I've approached each September as if it were my initial year of teaching. Perhaps you more experienced educators may find this interesting as well.

Tone quality
The first impression you make, besides how you look and if your ensemble behaves in a disciplined manner as they come onstage, is the overall sound of the group. Is it full, rich, and supported, or is it thin and without substance?

If your sound is not compelling, few people will be engaged enough to truly hear what else your group has to offer.

Rhythmic accuracy
After establishing a full, rich tone, the next task is creating rhythmic accuracy. Unless the ensemble plays with rhythmic accuracy, chords are not clearly defined, melodic development cannot be understood, and articulation cannot be truly addressed. Rhythmic accuracy guides the ear of the listener and provides the clarity needed to understand the musical complexity.

Articulation
Hearing articulations which match and contrast are essential to understanding the musical work. Imagine someone speaking with marbles in her mouth. The ear cannot distinguish exactly what is attempting to be said. Yet, now imagine an excellent Shakespearean actor who articulates precisely. Who is more compelling?

Close attention should be paid to every dot and dash. Once a motive is articulated in a particular manner, it should be kept consistent throughout, unless the composer desires a contrast—in which case that should be made obvious as well.

Balance
So often conductors spend a great deal of time tuning chords—as well they should—yet, unless a chord is first brought into balance, one cannot properly bring it in tune. If the third or fifth is too

prominent, the chord will not "ring." Start by balancing the root and fifth and add the "color tones" sparingly. Of course like cooking, what you do with the thirds, sevenths, ninths, etc. depends on personal taste. But, a balanced chord always starts with the root and fifth relationship.

Note accuracy

Once you have rhythmic accuracy, wrong notes become much more obvious. Although correcting mistakes often is a matter of home practice, there are also misprints in the score and or parts. Note mistakes will most often occur when playing accidentals and key changes. "Forewarned is forearmed."

Insist that every note be correct. Individual testing and sectional work are ideal in this area.

Pitch accuracy

When a group is playing with a full, rich tone, the parts are balanced, and note accuracy is good, then pitch accuracy can be addressed. If the tone is unsupported, the pitch will not be "true." If some are playing C and others C sharp in a C major chord, it will never be brought in tune.

If you have not guessed by now, this is a systematic process. First things first ... tone, rhythm, notes, balance, pitch.

Musical direction

When music proceeds aimlessly, no matter how precise everything else is, there will be little interest for the listener. One should always hear if the phrase is leading toward a point of tension or away from the tension toward repose. If there is no direction, it should be due to the composer's specified intention and not the lack of attention on the part of the conductor.

Style period awareness

There should always be attention paid to the musical style period. Is this a classical work, romantic work, neoclassical and the like? Mozart and Shostakovich were excellent composers, but it would be a mistake to perform both in the same style. Light or heavy, bright or dark, short or sustained are decisions that must be made according to the stylistic demands of the period and specific to each composer.

Ensemble interaction

I'm always surprised to learn that there are musicians playing the exact same melodic or rhythmic figure simultaneously and do not know it. Very often there is little or no awareness or interaction between the various parts.

Also common is the fact that a phrase might be divided between multiple parts, yet there is often little awareness from the musicians that these parts are connected and should therefore be played as such. Once an ensemble member is aware of everyone else's part, he truly learns how his part fits into the whole.

Convincing performance style

If you don't believe in a musical composition, nobody else will. Joy, sorrow, anger, introspection, and the like must be demonstrated in a convincing manner. It is your responsibility to bring the music to life. If an audience needs to guess how they should respond to a work, you have not done an adequate job.

I wish you well with your ensembles. Never forget that excellence is a process, not an event. Growth should not only apply to your groups, but to their conductor as well.

Fortunately, music is a lifelong pursuit. Excellence takes time, patience, and diligence, but never forget that real joy is in the journey. All the best!

This article first appeared in the May 2002 issue of Washington's Voice. *Reprinted by permission.*

Open Letter: To First-Year Teachers
Richard Fiese

The text of this letter is taken from a letter I drafted to one of my former students who is now a first-year teacher. A colleague suggested that I publish it as an open letter to all first-year teachers. I know what this content means to my former student, and I hope that others will find something of value as they read it as we all begin our new semester.

Dear First-Year Teacher:

I feel compelled, though uninvited, to write this letter to you as you begin this, your first year of teaching. As you will no doubt discover, no matter how much you will try to provide your students with the best instruction you can, there is always the nagging feeling that you would like to give your students just one more lesson, one more hour of rehearsal, or that one last bit of knowledge.

Moreover, there is perhaps a universal need among teachers to somehow really determine if all of the experiences, projects, and lectures have remained with you as more than mere canned platitudes. It was with these considerations in mind that I began this letter.

All of your teachers endeavored to provide you with the skills, knowledge, information, and activities to prepare you for your life as a successful music educator. It was with no small degree of pride that we watched your recent graduation, knowing full well your many accomplishments—academic, musical, and personal—that have been the hallmarks of your undergraduate education. I have personally been consistently impressed with your professional acumen, your maturity, your growing self-knowledge, and your inner strength.

I must also confess to a certain degree of envy as you enter the profession. Your career is entirely before you, free from both success and blemish. You will never again be able to enter the classroom for the very first time. It is somewhat analogous to sight reading. You can only sight read a piece of music once, so you had better make certain that you give it a good reading. Your first year will only happen (often thankfully) once, so make the most of it.

Beginning your first year of teaching is arguably the greatest challenge that you have yet pursued. The anticipation, bordering between excitement and fear is both typical and healthy. Teaching is one of the greatest responsibilities that anyone can seek to shoulder, but it is a mantle that you will wear well.

You have demonstrated your readiness to assume the title of music educator during seemingly countless exercises, drills, papers, tests, and yes, the "notebook from hell." The ultimate test is now before you and it is a test that I will neither write nor evaluate. Therefore I hope you will indulge me and permit me the luxury of addressing you one final time as your teacher, before you assume the role of my colleague, so that I may give you one final review session.

Everything that follows you have heard before in various contexts and nothing is original. I have often told you that I have been blessed throughout my career to be surrounded by very bright and talented individuals (teachers, colleagues, and especially students) from whom I "liberally lifted" all of these ideas. Perhaps some of these familiar words may have a different relevance at this point in time. Irrespective, I hope these words will help you during the test that is yet to come.

- Teaching is a way of life, not merely a way to make a living. Remember that in all of interactions with others, regardless of the setting, you should be the model of what a teacher should be, and a teacher should be a model of what a *person* should be. Certain basketball players may have the luxury of not being a role model, but teachers do not.
- Your job is to teach children through music, about music, about themselves, about others, about beauty, about life.
- The most basic learning is discrimination, and the most basic level of discrimination is same or different. Start there and build.
- Confusion often produces the teachable moment. Don't back away from confusion. Grasp the moment and make the most of it.
- Imagine your classroom and the students exactly as you would like them to be. Then identify everything that you must do to make it happen.
- Blessed are they who expect nothing, for they shall not be disappointed. Don't expect students to know how to enter a room, sit properly, breathe correctly, practice, or display any particular behavior or set of behaviors until you have taught them, reinforced the behavior, and reviewed.
- Never get upset when students cannot do something. They are merely identifying what they need to be taught.
- Remember that you begin all over again every day. Telling or showing someone something once is never enough.
- It is more important to be able to say one thing

a thousand different ways than it is to say a thousand different things each day.

- You can never finish teaching or learning about fundamentals. (Could one ever know enough about tone production?)
- Music is as much about being human as any other characteristic, including language. Each of us is "wired" for music, and every person is to some degree musical, therefore, each and every individual merits instruction in music as a way of maximizing our individual human potential.
- There is an essential paradox in teaching: All students are exactly the same in that each one is unique. Treat them accordingly.
- Recognize what is correct, not just what is incorrect. Balance your approvals and disapprovals during instruction.
- Let the students make music right away. Get to the good stuff! Music is its own reward—use it to your advantage.
- Never compromise on quality in performance or materials. In doing so, make certain that you are striving for excellence—not perfection. Your students will be more inclined to attain excellence if that is where you consistently aim.
- Never enter a classroom without developing a clear plan of where you want to go and how to get there. Overplan and have a back up. You must also know when to abandon any given plan; which is before your performance deteriorates or your personal well being is jeopardized.
- Tell students what your objectives are. If you don't, students will inevitably think they are something else (often at cross purposes).
- A short pencil is more valuable than a long memory. Don't try to remember everything. This is important for your students as well.
- You cannot hear everything that you need to hear in a single listening. Record every rehearsal and use the recording to develop your subsequent lesson plan.
- While it will often seem that you must do everything, you cannot do it all at once. Establish a set of priorities and keep track of what you accomplish—not just what you are unable to accomplish.
- Listen to what your students perform and what they do not perform; also listen to what they say and they do not say. It is often what is missing that is the most interesting and most important.
- Remember that no one is capable of talking and listening at the same time. Make certain that you listen to colleagues, parents, administrators,

other teachers, and especially students. I have often told you that I have learned more about teaching and learning from students than any other source—and it is true. The converse is also true, make certain you have your listener's attention before engaging in conversation.

- When you don't know something—ask! Then decide based on the best information available. Remember that virtually every teacher fails in some way; it is how you react to failure that will help determine your ultimate success as a teacher. Successful teachers look everywhere for answers; less successful teachers tend to withdraw in an attempt to avoid having their "failures" discovered. Ignorance can be overcome, but stupidity is forever.
- If you make a mistake, accept responsibility for it; then move on and do not repeat the mistake.
- Seek out and surround yourself with the best colleagues available. Learn from them. You cannot fly with the eagles if you only work with the turkeys.
- Be active in your profession and its organizations. It is part of the professional commitment you have made.
- Your principal may often be the one student who requires the most instruction. Administrators want what is best for all students, but they may not know what you do or what it is important. Teach your principal well.
- Advance communication is always the key to avoiding misunderstandings and possible conflicts. It may be easier to be forgiven than it is to get permission, but that does not mean that it is preferable. Students, parents, administrators, other teachers, other school personnel, etc., all need to be informed. Never assume that someone knows something about the program or the activities of its members.
- Every individual in a school community is both necessary and important to the educational enterprise. Treat each and every one of them with the respect that they are due. You are dependent on each other to make the school work.
- Be an active contributing citizen in your school. Participate in the life of the school in all of its variety.
- Avoid references to *your* program , *your* students, *your* room. Avoid using "I," "my," or "mine" when discussing the program, the students, or perceived needs.
- Some days teaching isn't fun—get over it. Everything in life can at times become a rut.

You are fortunate that you have selected a wonderful rut! Stick to it and good times will reward you in the long run.

- The ultimate metric of the success of a rehearsal is if every student is able to do at least one thing that he or she could not do at the beginning of the lesson. Remember that evaluation is an integral part of teaching, not peripheral.
- A grade in music stands for something; make certain that it is the right thing. If you want to be taken seriously as a teacher, be serious about the judgments of student achievement.
- Being a good teacher is much more than wishes or desires. No teacher ever set out to be an ineffective teacher. Wish in one hand and spit in the other and see which hand gets full first. Actions are always more important than intentions.
- Enjoy what you do. Find the pleasure in your work. Seek out the beauty that is in all things and all people. This will help you to capitalize on your passion for your art and for teaching.

- Take care of yourself. Your mother told you to eat well, drink plenty of fluids, and take time to rest—do it. Remember that you are the only you that these children will ever have; don't deprive them of the best that you can be.

Thank you for permitting me this last pedagogical hurrah as it were. I can think of a thousand things that could be added, but if we, your teachers, have done our job well, even this brief review is unnecessary. Since the ultimate goal of any teacher is the independence of the students in his or her care, it is with great pleasure that I welcome you to the profession as a certified and independent music educator. It is wonderful to know that you are out there doing what I know you do so well.

This article first appeared in the December 1994 issue of the Florida Music Director. *Reprinted by permission.*

The First Year: Practical Advice for Surviving and Thriving in Your First Music Classroom
Sara Francis

I recall sitting in my college classes, preparing for my music teaching career. I found it easy to let my imagination carry me off to what I envisioned as my future classroom. Everything there was happy and wonderful. The children's eyes lit up when I entered the room. Disciplinary problems were limited to the most minor infractions. By the end of the year, my students (who had absorbed completely all of the brilliant musical knowledge that I had dispensed since day one) were ready to sign a major recording contract.

No, I never really believed it would be like that, but I did allow myself to nurture a distorted mental picture of my first real teaching job. I have a feeling that I am not the only music education major to be guilty of such behavior. It is easy to let assumptions, aspirations, and expectations cloud the reality of a situation, to the detriment not only of one's ego, but also of one's effectiveness in the classroom—the first classroom of your very own. From my new perspective as a "veteran" teacher with one year of experience, perhaps I can help you to see through whatever fantasy you may be harboring!

First of all, do not assume that your first teaching job will necessarily be in your specialty area, or

that your student teaching experience will be an accurate indicator of what your own classroom will be like. I fell into both of these traps. Although my principal instruments as an undergraduate were flute and violin, my field placements (both then and later, in graduate school) convinced me that I wanted to teach K–5 general music.

My student teaching experience, with Lydia Wainright at Maxwell Elementary School in Lexington, was wonderful. I was able to use many of my new plans and ideas. The students were receptive and enthusiastic, and the classroom environment was idyllic. I knew that my own classroom would be just like this! But what I failed to consider was that I was in the classroom of an experienced teacher who had spent many years cultivating and shaping her learning climate, and where she was always present to support me. It is hard to fail in that kind of a nurturing setting where many of the "thorns" that you will encounter in your first year of teaching have already been removed.

Because my new husband (who has a good job in Lexington) and I had purchased a home, I limited my job search to Lexington and its surrounding vicinity. As it happened, there were only two full-time positions available in my chosen area, and there were about twenty applicants for each, many of them veteran teachers. Though my interviews went well, I soon learned that I was not the chosen candidate for either job. So when I was offered a middle school orchestra position, I accepted it gratefully. However, in stark contrast to my daydreams of leading my students skipping delightfully down a flower-lined garden path of musical enlightenment, my first few months of teaching were more like a terrifying struggle in the briar patch.

After having gotten so caught up in all of my expectations, my shock and disappointment were so great that I easily could have allowed myself to fail miserably during my first year. My saving grace was all of the sage advice that I had received over the years from my professors and mentors, and the fantastic support and advice got from my principal and fellow teachers. But what I truly wish is that the "me" that I was then could have had the counsel of the "me" that I am now. What practical advice would I have given myself?

Step 1: Prepare for the Transition

When you enter a music classroom as a first-year teacher, it is difficult to appreciate what a significant change you represent in the eyes of your students. While they have most of their teachers for only one semester or one year before moving on to someone new, often they will have had the same music teacher for several years. In some lucky cases, they will have seen that music teacher every school day during that time. In my case, the eighth grade students had been with Marcia Pendley, an experienced orchestra teacher, since the beginning of the sixth grade. For two years, they had seen her for fifty minutes every school day. Furthermore, some of my eighth-grade students had been under her guidance since the fourth grade. Naturally, they had built a relationship with her, and were accustomed to her methods and teaching habits. When they realized that their familiar teacher had been replaced by this very different person, they were apprehensive, and a few were even hostile.

It is easy to forget that, despite assumptions to the contrary, kids are often very resistant to change. I have learned that middle schoolers in particular, since they themselves are undergoing a whirlwind of emotional and physiological change, are very much in need of stability in their environment and relationships. I spent the first month of the school year trying to "break the ice." Many of the seventh and eighth graders were not at all receptive to me, to my ideas, or to my expectations for their behavior. Not only were they resistant to change, they were testing me to see where my limits were. In retrospect, I realize that there are probably some things I could have done to

alleviate some of the unpleasantness of the transition. My advice is the following.

First, try to arrange a meeting or phone conversation with the teacher whom you are replacing. Discuss important logistical issues, such as budget, instrument rental policy and procedure, music library, etc. But as importantly, ask questions that will give you a better picture of your students and the classroom climate that you are inheriting. Ask the teacher about what sort of daily routines they followed, what their specific guidelines for success or expectations (a.k.a. "rules") were for behavior in the classroom, what kind of discipline plan they had, what sort of music they performed, what methods books they used, and so on. What worked? What didn't? Also, try to find out about special events or traditions at your school in which your group will be expected to participate.

The next step is to compare notes from your discussion with your own ideas about how you want to handle things in your classroom. When you do this, you will probably end up with more questions than you started with. How do your plans for managing behavior line up with your predecessor's? How do your long-range goals fit in with what this teacher was able to accomplish with his/her students throughout the course of the year? What kind of routine will you have and how much freedom will you allow in your classroom? Based on what your predecessor has told you, what teaching materials do you have to work with? Will they help you to meet your goals, or will you have to look for other resources? Which of the former teacher's ideas can you incorporate into your own plans?

Finally, how will you help your students adjust to the many things that you will most likely do differently? Explain, discuss, and be consistent, yet flexible. If you explain to your students how your rules, procedures, and goals might differ from their former teacher's while explaining why you will be doing things the way you are, you will likely increase their responsiveness. I can't begin to count how many times I've heard, "But we did it such and such way when Mrs. Pendley was here. Why can't we do it that way now?" I would always have a moment of self-doubt, knowing that she was a great teacher and that I was only a "rookie," but when I was convinced that my method was best for what I was trying to accomplish, I found that it helped to explain—several times if necessary—why we were doing things the "new way." I think it is important to discuss your policies with your students, but don't be afraid to set your own boundaries and routines and stick to them. Eventually, the kids will do what you ask with little questioning. On the other hand, don't be afraid to go ahead and try the "old way" if it is reasonable and will not undermine what you are trying to achieve. The old way could be better! If it is, then departing from your plan for a better one will help to convince your students that you are flexible and that you have their best interests at heart.

Perhaps most critically, be prepared for the transition that will take place in your own life. Even more than when you were a college student, you will have to find a way to balance your professional life with your personal life. Your first year of teaching will require an amazing amount of planning, communicating with parents and other teachers, and reflection on your own teaching and your students' progress. I think that this is an especially difficult balance for a musician to find because what we teach is so tied into our identities. It's hard to find time for yourself and your own music-making, but it's a struggle that is well worth it. The good news is that your students' music-making will become as rewarding to you as your own, if not more so.

Step 2: Build a Support System

I can't imagine going through the first year of teaching alone. You will need to depend on your family, friends, and loved ones to support you, but you also need the help of those who have been through the same rite of passage that you are about to undergo. Find experienced teachers to whom you can relate. Perhaps this will begin with the music teacher that you are replacing. Here in Kentucky, we are fortunate to have the Kentucky Teacher Internship Program (KTIP), through which you will be connected to an experienced teacher to work with you and mentor you as your "resource teacher."

In my case, my resource teacher, Nancy Campbell, was an experienced orchestra teacher who was always willing to give me great advice, feedback, ideas, and additional resources when I needed them. She was the person who helped me to get my foot in the door of the local string teaching community, explained how local festivals and events worked, and introduced me to helpful professional development opportunities. In this way, I was able to expand my support system to include other professionals in my field—people whom I could contact when I needed to talk, when I needed ideas, or when I needed someone to come and work with one of my groups. It is very important to become involved in a community of your peers, both at the local level and

through professional organizations. In general, when people are involved in a mutually supportive group that shares common goals, they are more enthusiastic about their jobs.

You should also take steps to build a relationship with the administrators at your school. Take time to talk with your principal, to tell him/her what goals you have for your students as well as for yourself during your first year. Discuss your struggles and your victories. You will most likely be discussing these issues anyway as part of the KTIP experience, but it is important to be open and honest with your principal about how things are going in your classroom. After all, your principal is there to help you. When I was really struggling with one particular group of students, my principal listened earnestly as I talked with her about my problems and concerns. She dropped in occasionally to see how things were going and would often stop me in the hall to ask how things were going in that class. She even partnered me with someone from our Safe Schools office who came in and gave me some fantastic advice.

Also, remember to take the time to get to know the teachers within your school. As a music teacher, it is easy to let the hustle and bustle of your daily responsibilities keep you isolated in your own little world. However, it is important to talk with your colleagues who teach other classes. After all, they also teach your students, and they will keep you better in touch with what is going on in the school as a whole. There may also be times when you ask them the favor of calling your students out of their classes for rehearsals or events related to your program. It's easier to do this when you have previously established a good working relationship. Most importantly, communicate and collaborate regularly with the other music teachers at your school. In the music department at my school we have a wonderful collaborative relationship. If one of us needs help on the night of a concert, he/she can count on it. If one of us needs feedback, there is always someone willing to listen and talk. When I was struggling and needed practical advice, someone was always there to offer it. The bottom line is, teachers need other teachers. You will learn a great deal from your colleagues, and your job will be a lot less scary if you know you have their support.

Finally, stay in touch with your college professors and other mentors, and with your longtime musician friends from school. These people will also prove invaluable to you as you need advice or simply need to talk. One of my professors and greatest mentors came during the first few weeks of school to observe and give some much needed feedback. Just knowing that he was willing to provide this kind of support made me feel less overwhelmed. Also, a younger friend who was still a college student came one day and led cello sectionals. My kids loved it, it gave me a chance to work more closely with the other sections, and she got some valuable practical experience.

In short, having a support system will provide you with a net to catch you if you fall, and it will build you up, give you better ideas, and help you keep your challenges in perspective. Just remain humble enough to ask for help when you need it. (I think that this is probably a rule that applies whether you are in your first year of teaching or your twentieth.) And be willing to return a favor.

Step 3: Beg, Borrow, Steal

When you take your first teaching job, you are suddenly going to find that you need more ideas and materials than you ever have before. It is one thing to prepare a lesson plan for a class assignment or for student teaching, but facing long-term planning and short-term planning at the same time for multiple classes, all with different needs, is an entirely different situation. In your plans you will, of course, want to incorporate your own original ideas; however, it will often be helpful (and necessary) to look elsewhere for inspiration. Ask fellow teachers in your field to let you borrow books, lesson plans, anything that you can get your hands on. You will get some useful ideas from colleagues. As I mentioned earlier, my KTIP resource teacher always gave me great ideas and introduced me to teaching resources that I otherwise might not have known about. She loaned me music and materials from which my students and I benefited so much that I ended up ordering sets of it for my own classroom. When you have trouble figuring out how to approach certain concepts with your students, when you need a new way to approach warm-ups in class, or when you are just looking for a creative spin on a lesson, look to other teaching models for guidance. It never hurts to recycle a good idea or reuse an effective plan.

There are also other outlets for getting good teaching materials and ideas. Professional interest magazines such as the *Bluegrass Music News, Teaching Music,* and *Music Educators Journal* will often include lesson plans and insight on how to approach certain pedagogical issues. There are many Web sites, such as the MENC Web site (www.menc.org), that have teaching resources (including complete lesson plans with assessment) organized by field ranging from elementary general music to high school band.

Also, be sure to take the time to search thoroughly through all of the materials in your new classroom. Even methods books that appear old and outdated may have some materials in them that you can use or adapt. Using what you already have and what you have borrowed or taken from outside sources, try to give your students exposure to a wide variety of materials. In this way you can avoid monotony and discreetly review concepts that students may consider themselves too advanced or too "cool" to revisit. Just be sure that what you use is sequential, fitting into your long-range plans. Also (if you are teaching instrumental music) choose a comprehensive method book that you can use consistently in your classroom. There may be a standard method that everyone in your school district uses, as is the case for me. If not, you can try several and ask other teachers what they use and why they like it. Whether you are looking for fresh ideas or simply trying to find a standard method book that works for your students, once again, don't be afraid to borrow from any source you can.

Step 4: Devise a Communication Plan

Thus far, most of my advice has involved good communication, whether it be with your predecessor, your colleagues, or your principal. However, it is vitally important to remember the two most important groups with whom you will constantly be engaged in dialogue: your students and their parents.

To make your program strong and credible, you need to get parents involved. Make sure that you have a means of communicating with them as a group, be it through a newsletter that goes home every nine weeks, through regular letters or progress reports that come back signed, or through mass e-mails (have your technology resource person help you with setting up a mail list on your e-mail account). If you are going to be teaching instrumental music, you especially will need a way to let your parents know about concert details, instrument needs, fund-raising, private lesson opportunities, upcoming events, etc.

Also, be prepared to make plenty of individual parent contacts. It is wise to contact parents via phone any time there is a major discipline problem or incident in your classroom, even if it has already been resolved between you and the student (just be sure to make the parent aware of this resolution). Be prepared to talk with parents face to face. Call a parent/teacher/student conference when disciplinary action and phone calls are not having enough impact. Finally, it's easy to forget to contact parents when students are doing a good job, but this can be very effective. Making such a phone call is a great first step to improving a relationship with a student who has had disciplinary problems in your class. At first, most of my phone calls home were related to negative situations, but the positive phone calls had just as much, if not more, impact.

You will also need to ask your students' parents for help from time to time. I asked for help transporting instruments to events, chaperoning, preparing food for our Holiday Tea and Concert, and help with advocacy for our program. You will find that the majority of your parents are very supportive and ready to contribute.

Communicating with students is one of the most fundamental aspects of teaching. Good, clear communication is essential to establishing a productive learning environment, whether it be in the form of teacher-student dialogue, teacher-guided student discussion, or lecture. It is easy to get so absorbed in trying to share all of your musical knowledge with your students that you forget to communicate adequately what your learning expectations or goals are for them; that is to say, you provide insufficient context for them to absorb what they are learning, why they are learning it, and how it fits into the grand scheme of things. At the beginning of your year, clearly state what your learning goals are for the school year and how you aim to achieve them. And, at the beginning of each class, give your students an idea of what you hope to accomplish with them during the class period. As you teach new concepts, communicate how they build onto or fit in with what the students have already learned.

When it comes to explaining goals and expectations, it is even easier, and more detrimental, to get so involved in what you plan to teach that you fail to establish clearly for your students your clear, concise expectations for their behavior while in your classroom. This is a topic so important that it deserves its own heading.

Step 5: Develop and Communicate a Clear Set of Expectations for Behavior

You would think that after realizing that my first job would be nothing like I envisioned, I would have emerged somewhat from the haze of idealistic anticipation of the college classroom. Yet even as I sat in a seminar on dealing with disruptive behavior in the classroom, a comment that several people had made when I told them about my new job kept reverberating in my head: "Well the good thing about teaching orchestra or band is that that's where all of the well-behaved children are."

There may be some truth to this generalization, but I realize now that I was hiding behind it. I know now that I did not have the kind of plan for classroom management in place at the beginning of the school year that I should have, much less effectively communicate my plan to my students. Part of the reason for this was my own myopic view of the way things were "going to be." However, to risk making excuses for myself, I think that I was partially conditioned to focus more on my students' musicianship than on their basic behaviors in the classroom.

I have noticed that those of us preparing to be music teachers often spend less time on issues of classroom management than do our "classroom" teaching counterparts. I have wondered why this is. Not only do we teach many of the same children that they teach, we also give each one of these children an irresistible noisemaker and then ask them to multitask beyond anything they are expected to do in any other class. And we expect our students to demonstrate patience almost beyond their years by asking them to sit quietly while another section of the ensemble is being addressed.

In actuality, I think that the music classroom is in many ways one of the most difficult to manage, and therefore should have an especially well-conceived and effectively communicated plan, or set of expectations, for behavior. After all, if you establish the right learning climate at the beginning, you will be able to spend more time on musical issues in the long run. That certainly seems like common sense, but it is more difficult in practice than in theory. A well-managed classroom and a positive learning climate will require some careful consideration of how you expect your students to behave in a multitude of classroom situations. Then you will need to express these expectations effectively to your students by putting them in the format of some simple rules or guidelines for success and via careful explanation and discussion. And you will then need a clear, well-defined system for dealing with negative behaviors.

In my case, I had some general "expectations for behavior" (rules) posted on the wall in my room and printed in our Orchestra Handbook. I went over them with my students on the first day of class. But this was not enough. I failed to discuss thoroughly my expectations, or what the ramifications would be if they were not met. In fact, I don't think I had really determined exactly what my system would be for modifying inappropriate behaviors. I certainly paid the price. Students acted out to find where the limits were and to see what the consequences would be, and when there was any inconsistency, they called me on it (as they should have).

About halfway through the school year, I adopted a conduct mark system from another teacher that clearly defined when students would receive a conduct mark and what the consequence would be after they had accumulated a certain number of these marks. The number of marks received also directly affected the conduct grade the students would receive in my class. I posted an explanation of the system on the wall in my room and kept a chart of students' names where I could easily keep track of the number of conduct marks each had received. This method seemed to help a lot, since students knew exactly what to expect if they violated some aspect of our classroom management plan and they also knew exactly where they stood at all times in terms of their conduct grades. Also, as the year went on, I took more time to explain precisely what I wanted from them in terms of their behaviors and our daily routine in the classroom. I adopted more and more of a method called CHAMPs.

The acronym CHAMPs stands for Conversation, Help, Activity, Movement, and Participation. CHAMPs is a proactive approach to classroom management in which students are told exactly what is expected of them in a variety of situations. For instance, when and how is conversation appropriate? Is group conversation OK, conversation with a partner, or no conversation at all? Students are clearly told what they do when they need help. Do they stay seated and raise their hand? Do they come forward to ask their teacher? Can they ask a friend? How do students behave during certain types of class activities? Is the activity meant to be completed with other students, or individually? Students are also told what type of movement in the classroom is appropriate. For instance, does the student need permission to get up and sharpen his/her pencil? How and when are students expected to participate? Furthermore, core principles of the CHAMPs method include:
1. Student behavior reflects classroom organization.
2. It is the teacher's responsibility to teach responsible in-class behavior.
3. The teacher should praise positive behavior instead of lingering on negative behavior.
4. Response to negative behavior should be brief, calm, and consistent in manner.

I strongly suggest that you adopt a strategy, such as the CHAMPs method, that will allow you to establish your behavioral expectations clearly and consistently. Be sure to review your policies and procedures with students often, particularly at the beginning of the year. If you do not, they will likely revert to old behaviors (which can be a bad thing) and they will continually test you to find your limits. Don't just explain, rehearse your expectations for behavior and the consequences, so that there can be no room for misunderstanding. When you are developing your syllabus, clearly set out your behavior expectations and your discipline policy and have an area where both parents and students can sign, agreeing that they have read and understood your policies.

By the time my first KTIP committee meeting rolled around, I distinctly remember feeling like I was sinking in terms of managing my classes, while the musicianship aspect of my teaching needed far less polishing. When I confided this to my university contact person, or Teacher Educator, he told me that he heard almost identical accounts from a vast majority of the young music teachers with whom he had worked. Make a preemptive strike and start thinking *now* about how you will manage your classroom and what strategies you will use. If your college or university offers a course in classroom management techniques, take it. In the end, if you establish high expectations for behavior, show your students how to meet them, and continually reinforce positive behaviors, your students will be more likely to meet higher musical expectations.

Step 6: Protect and Defend

About two-thirds of the way through my first year of teaching, I finally felt like I was starting to get the hang of things. My students' playing had improved noticeably, I had made it through two concerts and several other events, and I was more comfortable in my own skin as a motivator, mentor, and disciplinarian. Then, potential disaster struck.

Due to a massive budget shortfall, the school district planned to cut funding to our school music program, cutting nearly half of the band and orchestra teaching positions. Orchestra and band at the elementary level would be totally eliminated, and I would be jobless. I suddenly found myself in a new role: music education advocate. I started informing my students and parents of the situation. Since my job also includes teaching beginning strings in the fourth grade and intermediate strings in the fifth grade, I contacted those parents, first by phone and then by sending home letters including the contact information of school board members. I sent similar letters to the parents of my middle school students. All of my classes wrote portfolio pieces on why they thought an early start in elementary school was important for budding musicians and then, if they chose, mailed them to the superintendent of schools. Other teachers throughout the county took similar action at their own schools and we all met together to discuss other ways to advocate instrumental music in the elementary school. Local business people and community leaders, who had been positively affected by their own experiences in school music programs, stepped forward and spoke out. Money was raised and an ad was placed in the newspaper. Other newspaper columns and editorials appeared. Hundreds of letters, phone calls, and e-mails flooded the offices of school board members. Finally on the night of the school board meeting when the cut would be discussed, the auditorium was packed full of music teachers, parents, and students. Many spoke before the board. In the end, we were fortunate: the program remained completely intact. I wonder now if we would have been so lucky if so many had not stepped forward to defend the importance of music education in our schools or if music teachers had not acted quickly.

When you enter this profession, you must be aware of this sad fact: music programs are among the first to be cut when money is scarce. Though the public is probably now better informed of the benefits and rewards of music education than it has ever been, we still have a long way to go and a lot of convincing to do. Even though you will already be overwhelmed with your own personal concerns during your first year of teaching, you must be prepared to defend your job, your profession, and more importantly, the many children who are positively affected and enriched by what you teach. Get the lines of communication with your parents established, know the current research on the positive learning effects of music education, and talk with your principal, other teachers, neighbors, and friends. Most importantly, do the very best job you can when teaching your students the rewards they reap from learning music will speak for themselves.

Step 7: Relax and Teach
During your first year of teaching, you are likely to learn more in your classes than your students

will. You are going to make mistakes, and there are going to be bad days—some of them very bad days. There are going to be times when you are simply trying to survive until the end of the class period. There's no way around it: teaching is tough. Your kids are not always going to be little angels who play in tune and remember their key signatures. Instead you are going to be faced on a daily basis with real people who have real problems and flaws, and who have many needs—musically, intellectually, emotionally, and spiritually. The great thing about being a music teacher, though, is that what you are teaching them can help them meet many of those needs at once.

When things get tough, try not to be too hard on yourself. You will learn from your mistakes, and your students will give you the benefit of the doubt and a lot of second chances. Deep down, they realize that you are human, too. Though their behaviors will drive you insane at times, you will grow to care deeply for your students, and you will become very proud of what they are able to accomplish. Sharing your love of music with them will bring you great joy. So on your first day of your first year, when your first class enters the room and you're more nervous than you were on the day of your senior recital, just try to remember: relax and teach. Be yourself, do the best you can, and try your hardest to make sure that your students learn all that they can from their time with you. Each day will be a little easier than the one before it. The first-year experience is nothing for which anyone can truly prepare you, and it will probably be nothing like what you have imagined or assumed. You have to experience it yourself and find your own way. Hang in there!

Suggested Reading
Mullins, Shirley. *Teaching Music: The Human Experience.* Dallas, TX: Tarrant Dallas Printing, 1998.

Sprick, Randy, et al. *CHAMPS: A Proactive and Positive Approach to Classroom Management.* Longmont, CO: Sopris West, 1998.

Wong, Harry K. and Rosemary T. *The First Days of School.* Mountain View, CA: Harry K. Wong Publications, 1998.

This article first appeared in the October 2003 issue of Kentucky's Bluegrass Music News. *Reprinted by permission.*

Wondering about ... Discipline
Ted Hadley

Classroom management and building self-discipline in our students is always a top priority in every teacher's classroom. Several years ago a student teacher sent me some questions about my philosophy and methods of discipline. I share them with you with the following caveats: (1) Your style of discipline must be based on your personality, your strengths, and your weaknesses—know thyself!; (2) Some of these ideas might work well in smaller classes, but would have to be ditched or modified in a very large ensemble; (3) I am thinking mostly from a junior high/middle school band director's perspective—things that work at this level might really frustrate your high schoolers; (4) I am still learning, too. A lot of this is, unfortunately, based on my self-discipline. Sigh. If this article inspires a reaction in you, please write and share with us.

1. How big of a problem do you think discipline is?

Without discipline (both teacher-dictated and self-discipline on the part of the student), learning in the classroom is impossible. If two students or even one student is without self- discipline, maximum learning cannot take place in a classroom. The trick is to get the students to want to learn self-discipline and still retain respect for teacher, fellow students, the subject at hand (music, singing, instruments, etc.), and the whole school process. Sometimes we quell the problem children but sow disrespect for ourselves and our subject among the indifferent and better behaved kids.

It needs to be made clear that the teachers' and administration's (check with them) expectation is that school is what students do in place of going to work; just as their parents go to work, students go to school. The main idea of school is work: not fun, talking, tricks, social contacts, etc. Somehow we need to keep the focus on work and, even though we give time for other stuff (think coffee break), the main focus and attitude needs to be work. This can be a revelation to some students, who think school is some glorified social arrangement. Discipline is first and foremost an attitude thing. Often your problem child needs to hear this kind of thing in a one-on-one situation, as a to-the-class lecture can sometimes end up sounding rather pompous and know-it-all, and will frustrate your better students. And you know that often your problem child really does "want" individual attention (telling them like it really is).

Above all, the teacher must respect the students and thoughtfully act so as not to lose their respect. Just this year, I am personally working to remove sarcastic remarks from my arsenal of discipline strategies. It degrades me and makes me less trustworthy in the eyes of all my students: any student I have, good or bad, needs to know that I will not make fun of them or use their innocent question (e.g., "Where are we?") as a springboard for some funny remark at their expense and to their discomfort.

2. What are the main discipline problems you've encountered?

Mostly talking, in some cases bothering neighbors, lack of preparation, and forgetfulness (the "idle hands" syndrome). Sometimes a student will bring a toy or distracting bauble to class (hackeysack, rubber bands, etc.). In the worst cases, the student is angry and defiant, refusing to do anything he/she is told.

3. How do you deal with these problems?

First of all, I must be careful not to let my reaction add to the problem. If I keep a businesslike attitude (and sometimes it's hard because you get caught up in the emotion and excitement of the music, or the frustration of the impending concert deadline, etc.), then any problem encountered can be handled in a serious, businesslike, matter-of-fact way. The idea to inculcate in the kids is that what you expect is the norm and not a rare and elusive occurrence. Keep your ideal classroom in mind always, but don't get too frustrated and especially don't get exasperated (meaning you've given up hope and are acting that way!) when reality doesn't match ideal yet. Remember, as Scarlett finally realized, "Tomorrow is another day." There is always a new beginning available.

And you must pray to God that He will give you the ability not to learn to hate any of your frustrating, exasperating kids, so that you can always deal with them dispassionately, fairly, and with the expectation that even they can change. The reality is that some extreme kids will not change, because there isn't time to deal with them in the precious few minutes you have with your class. In case of the extreme kid, make a diagnosis ASAP and get help, first from parents, then if needed from administration.

It is helpful to check with administration and ask them bluntly what they consider justifiable reasons for sending a child out of class to the office. Sometimes they may answer you specifically! And remember, the administrators have the most truly frustrating job of all of us. Be kind and considerate of them: handle most of the problems yourself. Treat the administrators as a most helpful resource (you really must cultivate a good relationship with your administrator), and sometimes they can give you suggestions out of their experience and knowing the specific kids you're dealing with. What a joy to have a supportive administrator! Balance this with the fact that they are there to help you, not to teach your class for you. Save the big fights to take to them, not the nitpicky day-to-day stuff.

Dealing with parents can be helpful or extremely frustrating, and you need to develop an intuition about what kind of parent you've got on the line (or across the table). When dealing with a parent, focus on the potential of the child and how the parent can help you help the child to focus in class. Educate the parent as a peer who also has the best interest of the child in mind, and not with you being the superior "educated and highly trained professional," condescending to speak to the "mere mortal" parent. Sometimes the parent can share insights if they feel comfortable. Everything in teaching is communication, which in reality is the main challenge of life! Make your kids' parents feel comfortable.

In the band classes I teach, talking is usually dealt with by waiting for silence, as the students understand that their grade will suffer (consequence #1), and the whole class might have to keep their instruments out until the bell rings to make up for lost time (consequence #2). This only works to a certain point. Lately, I've tried to focus on the kids who are paying attention, speaking in a softer voice to them: "All my "A" students, please raise your hand." A few students will raise their hands. Then, "Now all you "B" students, please raise your hands." A few more catch on. Then call out the "C" students. Then in a fairly loud voice, "The rest of you must be "D" students today, 'cause that's all that's left!?" I don't take it to the "F" level any more; who wants kids who think of themselves as losers in the group, anyway?

A variation of this is to stop the rehearsal and ask who wants extra credit, and start to write the initials of the kids who respond, and actually give them extra credit. Then do it sometime when your talkers can get a little extra credit, too. Let the talkers see that you're not out to get them, and that you're willing to give them extra credit, too. Never make the class sense that it is divided into the "good" kids and the "bad" kids; never speak such an idea out loud no matter how much you think it. You define reality in the class each time you speak: Be careful. Speak what you want, not what "is."

For example, say "It's good to see so many people sitting up with good posture; you're really catching on to how to do this! I see elbows, fingers, and thumbs in good position! Now let's see if we can make the sound match what I see. Concentrate." Be relentlessly positive, but not dopey about it. Remember, businesslike. Dignity, always dignity. You are a dignified person, are you not?

For me, the same discipline tactics do not always work; sometimes you have to write down names in a showy manner so kids understand that their actions have led to some serious consequence; the names written down receive a more serious consequence later. Sometimes you write the good kids' initials on the board for later rewards ("The kids whose initials are on the board can put their instruments away a minute early; the rest of you play from J to the end, then we'll dismiss.") Always think creatively, try it, evaluate it, keep it, discard it. But don't get so experimental that the kids get nervous about what you're going to try next! Keep some predictability in the discipline and do go after the leaders of mischief.

I have gotten away from the punitive "stay till after the bell" stuff. It can backfire and make all the kids think you really don't care about them. One of the best things ever said to me was, "Run the rehearsal like you would like to be rehearsed; treat the kids like you would like to be treated." It seems obvious, but it's amazing how I don't look at myself enough as if I were a student. I may even get enough courage to videotape my rehearsal more—that's when you really grow!

Habitual misbehavior means a phone call home; a trip to the office or counselor, etc. Identify the power people in your school: administrator, secretary, janitor, master teacher—the people who will help you and have wisdom that "education" never provides. You need wisdom, not education. And think, really think, about what you're doing: develop your own wisdom. You'll help yourself, and maybe others someday!

4. What is the school policy of discipline and how does your own policy differ?

The school has a policy that is the basis of mine with my own modifications having to do with the nature of band class. The school policy goes on to the more serious offenses, like weapons possession, assaulting another student, profanity, etc. The school policy outlines consequences for misbehavior that parallel mine. It really helps the discipline of a whole school if there is consistency of what constitutes an offense and what the consequence is throughout every classroom, with modifications (such as absolutely no gum chewing in band) depending on the special needs of the class. Faculty meeting time should be devoted to this; you could be the gentle instigator of some school-wide policies/consequences to be visited upon students for certain classes of misbehavior. That's another secret of success at a school: make sure you know your fellow faculty members and get involved with school-wide and district-wide committees.

5. What do you think causes discipline problems (why do kids do it)?

Most talking is caused by the inevitable fact that talking is easier and more fun than work. Teenagers, adults, and children love to talk; we are created as social beings who derive our meaning from life on the basis of our relationships with other humans. So the most natural thing to do is to talk and socialize.

The agenda of the teacher is, however, to help the student learn the music curriculum materials and concepts, lead the student in practice, correct the student and suggest refinements, and teach the amazing musical heritage we have.

It's a good standing rule to announce at the beginning of the year that if anyone comes to school and knows they're going to have a bad day (they're sick, or the dog got run over, or mom's in the hospital, or they just broke up with their boyfriend/girlfriend, etc.), they tell you before class so you don't come down on them for inattention or talking and end up with a discipline explosion on your hands. Most kids really like this concession of humanity and respect, and it seldom gets abused. Some of our kids live in a tough world.

The way you phrase things in class can also cause discipline problems. Careful how you use these words: "never," "always," "but," "except," "however," and "literally." They tend to "turn off" communication by encouraging disbelief or selective listening.

If you use the word "but," "however," or "except" in the middle of the sentence, it tends to negate everything you said before the conjunction. "You did that articulation well, but … the dynamics were missing." What the student hears is that they didn't do it right. Never mind you started with a compliment; you made them focus on the bad part by using the but. It may seem awkward at first, but say "You did that articulation well, and … the dynamics were missing. Let's try again and get both!"

Kids will turn you off after a while or seldom give credence to anything you say if you overuse "never" and "always," as in "You never bring your reeds to class." Or, "You're always late." If you misuse "literally," it's mostly just comical, as in "You literally made me climb the walls with that sound." Well, maybe that's literally true some days

Good luck in that classroom tomorrow. God, bless us please.

This article first appeared in the Fall 2002 issue of Idaho Music Notes. *Reprinted by permission.*

A Letter from a First-Year Teacher
Stuart Ling

A letter from a first-year teacher in 1964, written to Dr. Stuart Ling, music education professor:

Now that I'm two days away from my first paycheck, I'm beginning to feel qualified to make an objective report of my teaching experiences—hoping you will enjoy this for laughs if not for information.

The situation here is very unsettled. There has been no music supervisor for two years because of money problems—so no one seems to know what my job is—I'm sort of making it up as I go along. If you feel it is an honor to be called a "special teacher" let me hastily say that here this means you belong everywhere and nowhere, you do nothing and everything, and your boss is no one and everyone. I was lost when we were told during orientation to go to our "building meetings"—because I have four buildings—so I went to one for fun and learned all about fire drills, pass periods, and report cards. Seriously, this experience is far different than I had expected—and better than I had ever hoped.

My first task was to visit each principal and arrange a schedule of classroom visitations. I am visiting about thirty different classes a week, all from grades three to six. The sixth and fifth graders will be visited twice a week in some cases. I also prepare weekly suggestions for all grades—given to the classroom teachers. I sent a letter to all teachers describing my job (which I made up myself—what my job is!!!) and asking them to help by using my materials and teaching music the rest of the week also. Teachers seem grateful for the suggestions—I'm finding that the real task, since my time is so limited, is to get people to work for me and not to try to do it all myself. This is a delicate technique in personal relationships with other teachers—new timid ones, old set-in-my-ways ones, and many "I-would-but-I'm-no-good-in-music" ones. Most elementary teachers have had a few courses in music, but they have not studied the basic goals for each grade level. I made copies of the goals found in Elliot, *Teaching Music* (remember pointing this out to us in seminar, Dr. Ling?) and teachers were grateful to have an overall picture at last.

So much for teaching the teachers—the real joy is the children. They are so eager to learn. At the end of the day my feet ache and my throat is dry (and there still is a supper to cook), but it is worth anything to see what music does for these kids. Sixth graders are finding out that Beethoven is exciting—they even could find the development section of the fifth symphony, first movement—also they love square dancing—are singing harmony—love the autoharp as well as The Beatles—each class is different—each child has to be brought out in a sensitive process of communication and understanding—some need prodding, some need to be left alone so they don't feel conspicuous and self-conscious—like one boy whose voice has changed—he sings very quietly, but his eyes show his hesitating thrill to be joining in. We talked about voice changes, casually—so that when it happens perhaps it will not be embarrassing. The boys seemed eager to know and to discuss this.

I could go on telling about other levels—the third graders are darling—but I know you get the idea of how thrilling this is. It's tough work—planning is a real creative task, and you must be ready to reverse yourself according to the mood of the classroom—and this takes real stamina! But the enthusiasm of these children is a big reward, and it makes me dig in and try to top myself—you want to give everything you can, so you don't cheat a single person.

Now that I've blabbered so much, I'm trying to decide whether to send this on. I will, sentimental as it is, but all so true.

Good luck for a good music ed. year—will let you know if this initial enthusiasm of mine changes.

—Sharrie

The above letter came in 1964 from one of my students who went on into a very productive career in general music. She later became a principal. I wonder how much the initial experience for a young general music teacher has changed. I know that such programs in many schools have deteriorated, and that the lack of support for such "special" teachers (in too many schools) has driven many teachers out of the field. It certainly would be interesting to get feedback from people who would be willing to look back on their introduction to general music teaching.—Stuart Ling

This article first appeared in the February/March 2001 issue of Ohio's TRIAD. *Reprinted by permission.*

Ready—Set—Go!
William G. Mack

The intent of this article is to address the first-year excitement and confusion that new teachers are likely to experience. Hopefully, these suggestions can be of assistance to you in preparing for your first job.

Let us assume you have signed a contract as a one person band department in a 1A–2A school district. Hopefully the starting date on your contract will be at least thirty days prior to the opening of the school year. Being totally prepared is vital to having a successful first rehearsal experience. The following suggestions will help you get "ready."

1. Decide who your band instrument dealer is going to be. A loyal, dedicated road representative from a full-service music company can be of invaluable service to your program. Select one whom you trust, who will call on you on a regular basis, and who can offer dependable service. It is important that they offer a wide variety of quality, brand-name instruments. Be sure to check their prices and interest rates on rent-to-own contracts. You do have a responsibility to both students and parents to provide the best all-around instrument acquisition and maintenance program possible.

2. Take inventory of all equipment, music, and facilities. Hopefully your predecessor(s) has kept a computerized "running inventory" of all school-owned equipment including instruments, uniforms, music stands, chairs, electronic devices, and band library (music, books, and recordings). You should do an accurate count on everything, and then check it with the existing inventory list. Report any discrepancies or missing items to your administrators. Be sure to note any nonfunctional instruments for repair or replacement. These instruments should be repaired, replaced, or abandoned. Nonfunctional or nonplayable instruments take up valuable storage space and are of no value to anyone. Your road representative can be of assistance here. Be sure to go through proper administrative channels in transacting any business of repair, replacement, or abandonment.

3. Become aware of your budget allotments. This is important information that you must have for fiscal survival. Know the difference between capital outlay and replacement sheet music and free textbook funds. Is there a repair or maintenance budget? Ask about all financial resources—parent groups, fund-raising, etc.

4. Get all performance dates on the school master calendar. Inquire as to the priority system regarding scheduling conflicts with other departments. Most school systems will have a priority system which resolves these problems. If not, try to implement one.

5. Develop an all-inclusive handbook covering your entire band training system. This should include: a philosophical statement, a curricular outline, procedural policies regarding classroom rehearsal deportment, attendance policies, grading system, a performance calendar, wearing of the uniform, lettering system, and discipline procedures. A well planned handbook can be of invaluable assistance in administering a band program. It should also include a detachable student/parent signature page acknowledging their understanding and agreement to function within the above stated policies and schedules. Be sure to get administrative approval for all items contained in the handbook. Their ultimate backing of the band operating policies is of paramount importance.

6. A before-school get-acquainted party for your band students can be a valuable time and program saver. Young people tend to be standoffish when meeting new teachers. Due to the loyalty factor, some will even drop their band enrollment. This is especially true when a successful teacher has left their position. It is important for the new teacher to establish good rapport as soon as possible. Band parents and student peer leaders saying good things about the new band director can be a great influence in retaining band enrollment.

7. Make a complete plan for your band training system. Know where you are going and how you can get there. A well organized, sequential training program from the beginner level through intermediate and advanced levels is paramount to success. Remember that all learning transpires as a result of an applicable concept of fundamentals. Fundamental mastery should be of constant concern throughout the training program. This system will change somewhat as the new band director gains experience and discovers what is more expedient in implementing the system.

8. Get an accurate listing of band students by grade and instrument. Make a large wall chart showing grade level across the top and instrumentation along the left side. List each student by their respective grade level and instrumentation. This will render a valuable overall personnel view of the program, which is an important organizational tool.

9. If your position entails marching band performance, a before school marching

band camp is required. Enlisting the aid of student leaders and band parents is of prime necessity. Until you know what instrumentation you have to work with, any kind of show design planning is futile. It is always a good idea to "play it safe" at first. Well done simplicity is far more effective than "clobbered complexity."

The foregoing suggestions are intended to assist you in preparing for your first or new job.

Being able to "hit the ground running" the first day of school will show your administrators real planning and organizational skills. Here's wishing you the best possible experience in your new positions, and a hopefully long and successful career in this wonderful profession.

This article first appeared in the Fall 2000 issue of Missouri School Music. *Reprinted by permission.*

Achieving Longevity as a Music Director
John Miller

We all know that there is a tremendous drop-out rate among music teachers. We always seem concerned about the drop-out rate of our students, as we well should be, but we seem to look the other way or put our heads in the sand when we talk about our own stamina and longevity as music teachers. Over the years I have witnessed many great teachers leave our profession, some for better pay and prestige, but most because of lack of satisfaction with what or how they were doing. I certainly don't have all the answers, but may I be so bold as to suggest a few items for self-reflection. Hopefully they will be of some help, and at least they may trigger other thoughts that might just help us retain a few more great teachers in this, the best, most rewarding profession in the world—that of teaching young people music.

Examine your true motives for being a music teacher. Think back to your college days or beyond and try to remember what it was that got you excited about being a music teacher. What was it that inspired you to dedicate a significant portion of your life to the study of music and that set you on a course to become a teacher of music? Once you have identified these events, ask yourself, do you still have these feelings, and are you providing these same kinds of experiences to the students you teach? One of the reasons I teach is because my motives are more pure than if I did anything else.

Develop a true joy for the profession. As music teachers, we may not be the highest paid profession, but we definitely can make an impact on many people's lives. We are in a profession that offers us unlimited opportunities to make positive influences on the lives of our students. Take the time to reflect on what it is that we are really doing beyond teaching music. What we do is much more than to teach notes or songs; we are teaching about life and providing valuable information and guidance to help young people develop rich and fulfilling lives of their own.

Set musical goals for you and your program. How long has it been since you actually performed on your instrument? Keeping your skills honed and being involved in a performance ensemble is one of the best things you can do to keep your love of music performance alive, and it also refreshes your perspective on how your students feel in a rehearsal. There is nothing quite like reversing roles to help you relate to the other's perspective, and it will give you better clarity and purpose in your own rehearsals. Where do you want your program to be in a few years? Have you put a carrot out in front of your group to encourage them to grow musically? Some of the greatest musical growth occurs during trips or in preparation for important performance opportunities. Get your groups out into the world and expose them to quality musical experiences.

Delegate, delegate, delegate. The days of the one-man music program are a relic from the past. Some still teach under the pretense that they are the only ones who can truly teach their students and that to bring in outside help is to admit or declare your incompetence as a director. I propose that the more competent and inspiring individuals we can expose our students to, the better. We cannot be all things to all people, and by putting our students into close contact with others who share our love of music, we are doing far more for them than we could accomplish ourselves. Keep the control and leadership of your program, but put away your insecurities and bring in others who are willing to help. This will have a two-fold effect of helping not only your students, but those who you bring in to help teach.

Parents are not people to be scared of. Booster groups sometimes get a bad rap, but who other than parents have more interest in your students' educational welfare? If organized and channeled into helpful roles, parents can be one of your biggest helps in providing longevity for you and your program. Organization is the key, and you must early on establish yourself as the philosophical and educational leader of the program. Parents can relieve you of hundreds of important tasks that are essential to the success of your program, and they can free up your time and energy to do what you were hired to do—teach music.

Avoid crisis management—organize. Most stress in my life occurs when I am poorly prepared or have failed to put in the advanced work or planning necessary to achieve a desired outcome. Time management is essential to a director's well-being and to the success of their program. Simple things like ordering all your busses for the entire year at one time in the summer can go a long way to assure peace and tranquility during the year. Make the time to prepare for the year. Plan your season, month, or day ahead of time to avoid the last-minute scramble to throw something together. There are many management tools out there; learn to use them to help yourself and your program.

Be like a duck. Thoreau said, "Be like a duck … calm and unruffled on the surface, but underneath paddling with great fury." It is important that we learn to stay calm in the sometimes hectic events that are part of our everyday music world. Students, parents, and administrators can try our patience on the best of days. It does no good to blow up or "lose our cool" when things get tough; on the contrary, when we "lose it," we are showing our weakness and lack of maturity and professionalism. Focus on your goals, and always keep in mind that you are the professional in the situation concerning the music program, and that others might just need a little tender care and kind instruction in what your program is all about.

Network with others. You are not in this game alone. Although you are the one ultimately responsible for your program, there are other teachers willing to help you succeed. Take advantage of other music teachers in your area to seek out their advice and to use them as mentors or to just ask for a listening ear. There is nothing quite so therapeutic as to discover that others have faced your challenges and situations and have somehow persevered and succeeded in this game of music making. Conferences and workshops are great opportunities to network, as well as a nice, quiet golf course. Get involved in your state or local music organizations and help to be part of the solution and not part of the problem. Seek out those directors who are willing to lend a helping hand, or at least to offer encouragement and maybe some sage advice. A word of caution: Chose your contacts carefully, because there are those in our ranks that are very negative and can poison very quickly. Just like the faculty room can become a bed of negativism, some directors seem to delight in helping others join their ranks of mediocrity and misery. Choose your mentors wisely.

Strive for excellence, not mediocrity. Expect the best from your students and don't settle for their mediocre behavior or performance. "Treat a man as he is and he will remain so; treat him as he can become and he will rise to the expectation" is a philosophy that is very applicable to the music world. I am always amazed at those directors who every year produce amazing performance groups with seemingly normal students. "Making a silk bag out of a sow's ear" seems to be the norm for some directors. How do they do it? I submit that it is because their expectation levels are very high, and that they don't accept as a performance level what most of us would be content with. Raise your own personal bar and what you expect out of your students, and you might just be surprised with the result.

Get a life. Music teaching can become an all-consuming endeavor if you let it. What we chose to do, let alone what is required, to produce a quality program can completely take over our every waking moment if we are not careful. I have met many directors who dedicate their entire existence to their programs. Unfortunately, they are those who have a flash of glory and then leave our ranks to chase another challenge or that burn out and become masters of mediocrity. What kind of toll does our profession take on our families and personal lives? When asked by a young director about keeping a balance between family and your musical career, I heard Francis McBeth think for a moment and then say, "Marry wisely or not at all." Needless to say, we must have supportive families, and we need to develop outside interests and hobbies to balance out our lives. Putting "first things first" will go a long way to ensure that we still have the energy and spark that will keep us teaching for years to come.

These are just a few ideas that hopefully will inspire someone to stay in the greatest profession, teaching music to young people. The grass always looks greener on the other side of the fence, but maybe with a little fertilizer and tender care we can make or keep our grass as green as ever, and maybe even influence a few kids along the way.

This article first appeared in the Fall 2002 issue of Utah's interFACE. *Reprinted by permission.*

Some Survival Tips for Beginning Teachers

Michael V. Smith

Welcome new teachers! We hope that your first days in the profession have been exciting and everything that you had hoped they would be back when you first dreamed of having your own music classroom. We also know that these beginning days can be a bit overwhelming and filled with experiences that you never dreamed of!

The Illinois Music Educators Association is very interested in offering you support as you begin in your new profession. We would be pleased to assist in helping you make a connection with a master music teacher who might be able to help you face some of those uncertain and nerve-jarring first days in the classroom. Please feel encouraged to contact me at the address below if that would interest you. As well, we would like to offer some assistance right here and right now. Making it to that bright tomorrow means making it through today. IMEA has a small publication entitled "How to Survive as a Beginning Music Teacher."

For now, here is an excerpt from this little booklet. Perhaps some of the thoughts from these fine mentors will be of some help to you in these opening days of this new year.

Tips from a Choral Music Mentor

- Choose a simple but musically fulfilling piece of music such as a unison song or canon to rehearse first. This will allow the choir to get past the note-learning stage and into the music-making stage quickly. When the choir has had some musical success they will be far more likely to stick with you through sight reading exercises and more difficult compositions.
- Try to find concert programs for recent years to get a feeling for the difficulty level of the repertoire your choir should be able to perform. Call neighboring choral music teachers to get their suggestions for pieces that "work" for a choir of the size and level of experience as yours.
- Be prepared to "sell" every piece you rehearse. Just because it is one of your favorites doesn't mean that your students will instantly fall in love with it. You may motivate your students to perform a piece by exploring the meaning of the text, supplying some interesting background information about the composer, or highlighting some particularly wonderful rhythmic, melodic, or harmonic aspects of the piece.

- Set the year's concert calendar as soon as possible, and inform students and parents of concert dates so that they can plan their calendars.
- Decide on concert attire early in the year so students can make arrangements to have the proper clothing. For example, if you require your young men to wear a jacket and tie, some of them will have to find someone to borrow a jacket from because they do not own one themselves.
- Think through the daily routine. How will you seat the choir? Distribute music? Take attendance?
- Think through your response to common student problems such as "I have a cold and can't sing" or "My brother is getting married the same evening as our concert."
- Decide what the consequences of misbehavior in your classroom will be.
- Find out your district's procedures for ordering music and supplies.
- Arrange for the pianos to be tuned in the fall and spring before concerts.
- Get plenty of sleep and drink lots of water. Avoid singing more than necessary throughout the day. These things are critical for maintaining your physical and vocal health—which are both necessary for you to be an effective teacher.

Tips from an Instrumental Music Mentor

Before school starts, make a reconnaissance visit to your classroom. The first rehearsals of your first year will go much more smoothly if you have visited your room weeks before school actually begins and have carefully thought through some of the logistical matters of organization. Taking a few moments to consider some of the rehearsal routines and concerns while the room is empty, quiet, and not filled with eager and energetic students is time well spent! You will want to give some thought to such matters as:

- Where and how will personal instruments be stored and picked up?
- Where and how will school instruments be securely and efficiently stored and picked up (particularly all of the percussion equipment)?
- How will music stands be stored and distributed?
- Where and how will music folders be picked up and stored?
- Where will instrument cases be kept during rehearsal?
- Are there bulletin boards to decorate and use for sharing information and motivating learning?
- Are there instruments to be repaired or cared for? (Stuck valves and broken drum heads are not things you want to discover as you begin

your first rehearsal.)

- How about the equipment in the percussion cabinet (mallets and auxiliary percussion)—is it in good shape?

A Checklist for Young Instrumental Music Educators

Supplies and Equipment

____ Set stands and chairs in place before the students arrive for rehearsal.

____ Pass out music before the rehearsal. Carefully stuff the folders yourself. Pass out a piece only when you have time to complete the task.

____ Assign parts to each percussionist as music is passed out.

____ Sell reeds, valve oil, etc. before and after school rather than at the beginning of each rehearsal.

____ Number the instrument storage compartments, and assign a slot to each student. Insist each student have a name tag on the outside of his or her case.

____ Examine/repair instruments that are not working correctly before and after school rather than in the middle of rehearsal. It must be the students' responsibility to bring the need to your attention. If something happens during rehearsal, they are to "do the best they can to finger along" until the end of the hour.

Rehearsal Objectives

____ Play and study quality music.

____ "Perform what you've studied" rather than "rehearse what you're going to perform."

____ Keep a lesson plan book. Make note of the pieces or section(s) and specific objective(s) on which you plan to identify what was actually accomplished.

____ List the rehearsal order on the board so students may get their music and instruments (percussion) set. Next to the name of each piece, indicate the specific objective(s) and section(s) to be worked.

____ Stay with a piece until everyone can recognize progress towards the goal.

Maximize Student Participation

____ Greet students at the door.

____ Make name tags to hang over the stands. Even if you know the names of your students, these are helpful for a student teacher, substitute, or guest conductor.

____ Give students three minutes "after the bell" to be ready to start the rehearsal.

____ Stop the rehearsal three to five minutes before the end of the period. This "pack up and talking time" should be reduced by the amount of time students waste by talking during the rehearsal.

____ Orchestrate upbeat, high energy rehearsals. Stand up to conduct.

____ Walk up and down the rows so you are within inches of each student every day. A good time to do this is during warm-ups.

____ Move off the podium and toward a particular section with whom you are working. Be cognizant of the time. Keep all students involved as much as possible.

____ When you are on the podium, expect students to give their undivided attention. Wait until everyone is quiet and looking at you before giving directions. Step off the podium between pieces signaling it is OK to talk.

____ Place sections of the band for musical and nonmusical reasons. If trumpet players are having a difficult time staying on task, (temporarily) move them to the front row.

____ Dress for success. A young teacher, in particular, will achieve greater success in the rehearsal if he or she is dressed "a cut above the students."

____ Pass out all concert dates and expectations for participation at the beginning of the year.

____ Think before you speak. The impact or potential impact of your words and actions plays a big part in how others perceive the music programs and the subsequent degree of support they are willing to lend.

____ Share your class handbook, lesson plans, concert calendar, etc. with the principal.

____ Provide students and parents with detailed and informative reports of progress.

____ Involve parents in the music program.

____ Publish a newsletter to be distributed at concerts or mailed home. Participate in PTO meetings and functions before you need their help.

____ Cultivate personal relationships with all members of the school staff

____ Work out a schedule for lessons or extra rehearsals with the input of the staff.

____ Publicly thank the staff and administration for their support of the music program. They would also appreciate a *To a Grand Staff* cake for lunch.

____ Keep a high profile in the school. Take your turn in the rotation to cover duties that help the school run efficiently (e.g., bus duty).

Tips from an Elementary General Music Teacher

- Seating charts and classroom behavior guidelines

which are written down are a must. Without them, your students will develop their own agendas.

- Adopting and adapting building discipline plans and procedures helps to promote consistency and better classroom management results.
- A substitute teacher should be able to read your lesson plans. Making such things as a key to textbook abbreviations, location of file materials, and accurate seating charts available and clear will mean that someone will be able to effectively take your class when necessary.
- Clearly understand your building's duplicating policies and procedures. If someone else is responsible for making copies, he or she should not be asked to duplicate materials which would infringe upon copyright guidelines.

- Clearly understand your district's meeting policies. Such gatherings are generally mandatory and not optional. Be sure that you know when your attendance is expected.
- Clearly understand your district's administrative hierarchy so that you may work within that structure most effectively—for your students' benefit as well as your own.
- Be careful in saying "yes" to too many extracurricular performing requests. Such appearances should always promote instructional or program outcomes and, if not carefully monitored, can easily become a driving force for your curriculum.

This article originally appeared in the Fall 2001 Illinois Music Educator. *Reprinted by permission.*

If I Knew Then What I Know Now
Joyce Spande

A group met together at the Iowa Choral Directors Association convention in July for a "sharing" session. It included elementary music teachers, students about to begin teaching music for the first time this fall, and undergraduate music students. The students who were about to begin their first year of teaching music eagerly asked what advice we would have for first year teachers. I am sure each of you would have some vivid memories and several suggestion to share. Here area few "bits of wisdom" which were brought up in our session (I have taken the liberty to add a few). They can be reminders to all of us as we begin a new year.

If I Knew Then What I Know Now ... Twelve Tips

1. **Prepare.** Be over prepared. Know exactly what you will do (all materials ready), when and why.
2. **Listen.** Listen a lot—to peers and students. Ask a lot of question. Do not assume anything.
3. **Maintain high standards.** Start out with high standards and stick to them.
4. **Earn Respect.** Do not be concerned that students "like me." Do your job and remember that earned respect is what really matters.

5. **Be organized.** Be organized and keep students on task. Students like to be doing and involved—then they take ownership.
6. **Stay positive.** Try not to get too frustrated if the students do not respond or things do not work out exactly the way you had planned. You likely will have a chance to do the same lesson again and can make corrections and changes.
7. **Take care.** Take care of your voice. Speak high, do not talk too much, drink a lot of water, and train the students with "cues." Keep a list of activities for "bad voice" days.
8. **Believe in yourself.** Believe in yourself—do not take things personally. Just do your best.
9. **Be assertive.** Be assertive and stand up for your program.
10. **Be friendly.** Be friendly with everyone, especially the custodian and secretary.
11. **Use body basics.** Student body basics (students face forward, hands on lap or desk, sit tall) can be very helpful in class management, especially with younger students.
12. **Be enthusiastic.** Be enthusiastic, share your passion for music, enjoy the children, and have fun!

This article first appeared in the September 1998 issue of the Iowa Music Educator. *Reprinted by permission*

Human Relation Skills for the First-Year Music Teacher
Robert T. Stroker

The theory of multiple intelligences developed by psychologist Howard Gardner (1985) examines what it means to be intelligent. By suggesting that people possess seven intelligences, he challenges past beliefs that intelligence can only be measured through verbal and logical thinking. Gardner's seven intelligences are: linguistic, logical-mathematical, spatial, musical, bodily-kinesthetic, interpersonal, and intrapersonal. Most of us have a few intelligences that stand out and others that cause considerable difficulty in our life. However, Gardner feels that every person has the capability to develop each of the seven kinds of intelligences (Armstrong, 1993).

To be successful during the first year of teaching, a large variety of professional competencies and personal qualities are required. The need for musical competence is obvious and is usually stressed the most during teacher preparation programs. One area that is often not stressed but is equally important to musical competence is the development of human relations skills or interpersonal skills, one of Gardner's seven intelligences. Gardner describes these skills as having the ability to understand and work with other people and requiring the capacity to perceive and be responsive to the moods, temperaments, intentions, and desires of others. Someone with a high level of interpersonal skills can see the world from another person's viewpoint.

New music teachers will interact not only with students, but also with parents, faculty, administration, the school board, and the school staff. In dealing with these various groups, a music teacher is frequently faced with sensitive issues and problems requiring the utmost skill and ability in human communication. The essence of being a successful teacher is successful communication in its various forms with various groups.

Executives, managers, and administrators spend a great deal of time engaged in interpersonal communication with superiors, subordinates, and people outside the organization. The best administrators or managers are those who possess the skills to mobilize others toward the group's basic goals. What follows is a list of the various groups with whom a new music teacher must associate and suggestions for improving interpersonal relations with them.

Students
How you communicate with students will help determine how much they learn.

- Give positive reinforcement when possible and where praise is due. Any severe criticism should be done in private.
- Strive to do an excellent job of teaching. Even young students are capable of evaluating competence.
- Challenge students with good literature and materials that stretch their abilities.
- Be enthusiastic and positive about music, and students are likely to respond in the same manner.
- Smile and address students by name. Often we underestimate the importance of these simple, personal touches.
- Treat students like human beings, and be firm but fair.
- Be discriminating in the way you dress and in your grooming habits. Look professional and not like one of the students.

Parents
Parents can pressure administrators and school boards either for or against a new teacher. Therefore, it is important to keep parents well-informed.

- Send progress reports and newsletters home to parents. Always start with positive points, saving the areas needing improvement until the end.
- Don't be afraid to call parents on the phone; however, avoid discussing serious problems through this means. Personal conferences are best for more severe situations.
- Let parents do most of the talking during the beginning of personal conferences. Learn from them, then tactfully make your points very clear while getting to the source of the problem. Show a sincere interest in their child and a desire to do what is best for the child. Never be defensive.
- Sell yourself first as a person to the community. By letting people know who you are, you will also sell the subject you teach.
- Parents will feel important if you are a good listener and if you encourage them to talk about themselves.
- Produce a good "product" through your teaching; this will be the best selling point of all.

Faculty
Getting along with your colleagues creates good lines of communication and may avoid any misunderstandings.

- Show a sincere interest in your colleagues' work. As a result, they will be more apt to show an interest in your classroom activities. The opposite approach, trying to interest people in yourself, is usually less successful.

- Only ask to take students out of classes when it is absolutely necessary.
- Take part in social opportunities with colleagues, and attend other music and nonmusic events in your school and district.
- Be considerate, and convey to your colleagues that you are interested in the students' welfare and not in any personal prestige of the music department, particularly the kind of prestige that is gained by exploiting students.
- Display mutual cooperation and understanding. This builds support for all concerned.

Administration

Principals and music supervisors depend on you to communicate with them about both your successes and your problems.

- Keep administrators informed of special honors, awards, and published articles. Don't be afraid to "blow your own horn" regarding your accomplishments and those of your students.
- Be understanding and sympathetic toward the many problems faced by administrators on a daily basis. They, too, have difficulties and occasionally need a pat on the back.
- Get out of the music room and show an interest in other school activities and problems; attend meetings and sign up to be on committees to address problems facing the entire school.
- Be willing to compromise. Outstanding music teachers have mastered the ability to reach out and resolve conflicts. This ability will enhance your standing with administrators.
- Be an efficient and professional business person. Take care of paper work and phone calls immediately—do not get behind. Often, this is the only way an administrator has to evaluate your effectiveness as a teacher.

School Board

Members of a school board respond to teachers who make an effort to communicate their ideas clearly.

- Work diligently at your job, produce results, and a school board will usually show support.
- Submit businesslike budgets with full details. This approach will help convince a school board that money allocated to the music department will be put to efficient and constructive use for the benefit of the students and the music department.

Service Staff

Throughout the school year you will need to rely on the school support staff—secretaries, janitors, and bus drivers.

- Treat the school support staff as equals and with the respect they rightfully deserve. Always request their assistance rather than give orders.
- Give plenty of advance notice for their services. Be sure to show your appreciation for their assistance.

One of the most complex and challenging situations in life is dealing with people. Teachers continually interact with a variety of people—students, parents, faculty colleagues, administrators, school boards, and support staff. Getting off to a good start in your first teaching position requires developing your skills and ability in human relations.

References

Armstrong, T. (1993). *7 Kinds of Smart: Identifying and Developing Your Many Intelligences*. New York, NY: Penguin Books.

Gardner, Howard (1985). *Frames of Mind*. New York, NY: Basic Books, Inc.

This article first appeared in the Fall 1995 issue of Texas's TMEC Connections. *Reprinted by permission.*

Surviving As a New Music Educator

The pressures on the beginning music educator can be overwhelming. A real sense of isolation, lack of curricular guidance, and a demanding teaching schedule are often reported as reasons for young music educators to leave the profession within the first few years. As veteran teachers, there is much we can do to help these new educators to survive and succeed—mentoring programs, both formal and informal, have been shown to have a profoundly positive effect on the beginning teacher's experience and effectiveness.

Our focus article in this issue concerns the experiences of a first year music educator coupled with the role of mentoring from both peer and administrative perspectives.

Surviving, Thriving … and Going Back for Another Journey!
Jason Kriner

I ran into a longtime friend, a veteran art teacher in another part of the state, who asked me an intriguing question. The question was "Are you going back?" I tried to think of something witty to say, but instead I simply affirmed her interest by answering, "I'm going back." The conversation could have sounded much like that of one who had just returned from a journey through a foreign land. Instead, the friend was inquiring about my first year as a teacher, a journey in itself.

Entering as a beginning educator in September, the comfortable niches of college that supported you for four or five years (or more) are now gone. With virtually no independent experience, you are expected to be an energetic, vibrant, idealistic, aggressive, proactive teacher; with students, peers, administration, and parents watching your every move and expecting spectacular things from you. Indeed, it is a journey … perhaps through a jungle. As I reflect on my first year as a music educator, I can see that certain actions and attitudes contributed to what I feel was a successful beginning. Whether you are a collegiate member, just graduated, or in the midst of your first year of your teaching journey, I hope that some of these thoughts will be helpful for you.

Be prepared. There are so many facets to being prepared, and it starts in college. I absolutely loved my years in college and did not realize that my experiences there, both in and out of the classroom, would be so influential. It's hard to see the big picture when you are trudging through semester after semester of an undergraduate degree, but everything does pay off.

Overplan. During the first few months of the school year it will be important that you are prepared; in fact, I overplanned, ending up with enough material for two lessons at a time. I planned whole units at a time and if something went wrong during one lesson, I always had several more activities that I could use to teach the same concept. I never once found myself in front of a class with nothing to teach. It is a great idea to have some "sponges" in your bag of tricks. Sponges are musically worthwhile, educational "games" that can be played in thirty seconds or stretched to four minutes in order to make the most of time that could potentially be wasted. You should develop these sponges for whatever fits your goals and objectives for your students.

Get involved. Often the music teacher does not relate to anyone else in the building. We have a unique talent and art form. In addition, we have a job assignment that no one else is able to complete. I am not suggesting that you to get wrapped up in teachers' lounge gossip or the social cliques of the school, rather, I encourage you to get involved in the life of your school, your school system, and your state association—VMEA. Don't become a complacent music teacher who is only being a teacher of music. Don't be a music teacher who is unaware, uninformed, and uninterested in the events taking place in the rest of the school. After all, as educators, we are responsible to teach the whole child. As musicians, we are responsible for developing their growth in the art. By becoming proactively involved, you will find that you will have parents, other teachers, and administrators on your side. It will keep you busy, but it will pay off in the end. And that brings me to my next tip.

Find resources. The best thing that you can have going for you is to find great resources. You not only need to find great teaching materials and ideas, but your "people resources" are imperative. I was fortunate enough to have an amazing student teaching experience. Even after a year of teaching, I have almost daily contact with my cooperating teacher. She has become a sounding board for my frustrations, questions, ideas, and stories.

Find music teachers from other schools that you can call on when you need help or just need someone to listen to your woes. Your music supervisor can also be a great resource to answer questions and offer suggestions. The bottom line is, as first-year teachers we are usually working with teachers and staff that have been in the field much longer than we have. Do not be ashamed to seek out resources. It does not make you less of a professional to ask for help from those around you. It will make you a better teacher.

Encourage classroom teachers to give you pacing charts and teaching timelines. Become familiar with the general education SOLs and be willing to integrate them into your curriculum. However, while you are integrating the general education subjects into your music lesson plans, be sure not to sacrifice the integrity of teaching music as a subject. Integrating core subjects while keeping the authenticity of music education will earn you respect with your coworkers.

Indulge yourself. Up to this point, I have recommended you be prepared, involved, informed, and proactive. In one word, busy. But along with all of those things, you must take time for yourself. Teaching is a stressful job and in order to maintain your own sanity, you have to find something that is going to offer you moments of liberation. Find a new hobby, invest in your health, rekindle an interest. I found that when I started teaching, I really missed performing, so I joined a local choral society and rekindled my love for singing in a great choir. I started exercising, not only for my health's sake but also as a release after a long day of stress. If it's not working out in the gym, find any other activity that will allow some type of physical exertion. It truly does relieve the stress in your tired muscles and your exhausted brain.

It is not my intent to say that I'm an expert teacher or that I had the best possible first year. There were trials and tribulations, but I managed to work my way through each of them. Along with those trials, however, came many moments of intrinsic rewards that are a part of the teaching career. Above and beyond the small trials of every day, you will also find the small events that cause you to reflect on your own teaching and the effect you have on your students. In one year I have had so many of those rewarding moments that I cannot begin to share them all. I can only imagine how many of those rewarding moments I will have packed into my memory after thirty years. It's the rewards that make the trials seem smaller. As I write this article in late July, I'm full of new ideas and energy to begin the second leg of my journey. I have learned from my first year and will do some things the same way and will change some things. I look forward to many more years of growth.

Create Your Legacy ... Mentor
Cheryl Toth

As music educators, we face an increasing number of obstacles that draw on our professionalism outside as well as inside the classroom. Gone are the days where all we have to focus on is our immediate school program. With standards-based testing and the No Child Left Behind initiative, it must be our goal to encourage and support qualified music educators entering our schools. One third of beginning teachers quit within their first three years on the job. We would not stand for that kind of dropout rate among students; we can no longer afford it in our teaching ranks (Stansbury and Zimmerman, 2002, p. 10).

Many of those who are entering the field of education initially rely on past experiences as a point of reference. After sitting in a classroom for sixteen-plus years as students, we assume we know the good teaching from the bad. We have preconceived notions regarding what techniques and styles foster the learning process. Student teaching provides a controlled glimpse into the world of teaching in a safe and monitored environment. As experienced teachers, we acknowledge that the realities of teaching are like driving a car; steering is a totally different experience from riding in the backseat (Kane, 1991). New teachers, as well as veteran teachers, enter a new school struggling to adapt and find their comfort zone in both the classroom and within the total school community.

For music educators, this challenge is enhanced by the fact that most of us are a team of one. Unlike the regular classroom teacher, we do not have the benefits of having a grade level team to support us. It is for these reasons that mentoring programs are critical to the success and retention of first-year music educators. Matching each mentee with an experienced mentor provides immediate and appropriate support. This support allows the mentee access to a repertoire of strategies and tools that promote success in the classroom. Equally important is that a mentor be able to model and communicate a genuine love for children (Portner, 1998).

The Role of the Mentor
On reflection, we have all had someone who inspired us, kept us going while showing us the ropes. Successful mentors in music education should be veteran teachers who have been there. It is their wealth of experience that allows them to show their mentee how to:
• Discover their strengths—a mentor looks for the strengths in their mentee. When new teachers feel good about themselves, they are more likely to look at challenges as an opportunity to grow.
• Demonstrate their professionalism—a new

teacher is seeking answers, alliances and is attempting to establish relationships among faculty and administrators. Model and encourage positive communication with others, while gently steering new teachers away from the pitfalls of gossip and blame.

- Make good decisions—encourage risk taking and decision making. Guidance and honest feedback including setting realistic goals and timelines will provide the framework for mentees to develop necessary strategies to succeed on their own.
- Sustain their positive thinking—success feels good and does not command as much energy or wear on our conscience as when we fail. New teachers often internalize and personalize failure. As veteran teachers, we experience failure in the course of our teaching careers and we learn that we can turn the failure into a positive experience
- Listen—a good mentor listens before they speak. Be a friend. Show compassion. We all need opportunities to think out loud. By demonstrating good listening skills, mentees can often clear out the confusion in their own thoughts and begin to find the answers on their own.
- Tap into resources—if you do not know the answer, find the person or resource that does. Encourage new teachers to use the resources in their base school. Special education specialists can provide valuable information regarding special needs students as well as strategies for classroom success. This encourages relationship building that is essential for any music teacher to be effective and successful.
- Observe—mentors observe, not evaluate. Through observation, the mentor can assist the mentee in developing the planning and lesson process that will be evaluated by the administration. The stress of outside observation can be uncomfortable for many new teachers. Providing both parties the opportunity to observe each other helps to reduce those anxieties while building trust and maintaining open, honest communication.

Making the Match

The matching of mentor with mentee is critical. The relationship between the two teachers determines the success of the mentoring process. Relationships must be open and honest. Both parties must be willing to listen, share, and respect each other as educators. Often this professional relationship develops into a deep bond that con-

tinues beyond the mentor/mentee stage.

The relationship between mentor and mentee is one of growth and opportunity. As a result, the role of the mentor changes from providing resources and teaching tips to someone who, through question and dialogue, changes, improves and strengthens teaching effectiveness. I experienced tremendous growth as an educator working with new teachers. For example, five years ago a second music teacher was hired at my school and I was assigned to be his mentor. Every day he came to work with energy and excitement, and we shared a morning cup of coffee as we went over the day's plans. One morning he arrived excited yet apprehensive. As we discussed the plans for the day, he invited me to look over a new lesson he had created for a jazz unit. The lesson was incredible: well planned, engaging, and would really be exciting for the students to experience. And I learned that one could teach an old dog new tricks. I have used that lesson with my upper elementary students and, with permission, have shared it with many of my veteran colleagues.

Most mentoring programs have specific guidelines and requirements in regards to the amount of time that must be spent in planning and observation. One example is the Great Beginnings Mentor Program in Fairfax County Public Schools (FCPS, 2002). This program is designed to provide and maintain support through mentorship to beginning and new teachers during their first year teaching in the county. Music lead mentors coordinate the school-site program. They are responsible for recruiting and assigning mentors to beginning and new teachers. Music lead mentors monitor the mentor program at the schools site to assure that new teachers receive the support they need (FCPS, 2002). Mentors of beginning teachers must spend a minimum of twenty to thirty minutes a day with their mentee. They are required to complete a one-credit Mentoring Novice Teachers course taught by administrators, complete all formal paperwork, observe lessons, and offer feedback. Each mentor of beginning teachers receives a stipend and State of Virginia recertification points (FCPS, 2002). Requirements for mentoring experienced teachers new to the county include spending a minimum of one hour per week with the mentee. Continuing support is given as needed throughout the school year.

Investing in the Future

Successful mentor programs improve teacher retention by enhancing teacher satisfaction. In addition, these programs serve as a drawing card in the competitive market for hiring teachers (Stansbury and Zimmerman, 2002). Encourage and support the new and veteran teachers entering your schools by becoming a mentor. It is your expertise as an experienced music teacher, your ability to connect with children, and your professional musicianship that will inspire, support, and make the difference in the future of music education. Create your legacy … mentor.

References

Fairfax County Public Schools, (2002). Mentor responsibilities and suggestions for helping new teachers 2002–2003. *Great Beginning Teacher Induction Program.*

Office of Staff Development and Training, Instructional Services, FCPS. Ganser, T. (2002). Sharing a cup of coffee is only a beginning. *Journal of Staff Development.* 23(4), 28–30.

Kane, P. (1991). *The First Year of Teaching.* Walker and Company: New York.

Portner, H. (1998). *Mentoring New Teachers.* Corwin Press: CA.

Stansbury, K. & Zimmerman, J. (2002). Smart induction programs become lifelines for the beginning teacher. *Journal of Staff Development.* 23(4). 10–17.

Surviving the First Year: The Administrator's Perspective
Beth Hazelette

Surviving the first year of teaching can be a major challenge. Although student teaching offers a taste of what is to come, entering your classroom for the first time is a totally different situation. Faced with curriculum guides, lesson plans, grading, school policies, and fund-raising, most new teachers barely know where to begin. How can a first-year teacher deal with such tremendous challenges? More importantly, what role does the music education administrator play in a successful first year of teaching? It all boils down to one word: support; this is the key to a successful start for a first year music educator. Being well prepared by the university is essential; however, the most well prepared teacher may find significant struggles without a strong support network.

Most school systems have division-wide mentor programs focused on in-school support, and many have also developed content specific support systems. In divisions not providing content specific support systems, it is critical for the music educa-tion administrator to initiate such a program. Without such support, school divisions are likely to lose teachers with tremendous underdeveloped potential. Formulation of a support system for first year teachers should include three strands: (1) a teacher-mentor system focused on content; (2) administrative support for in-depth content specific instructional issues; (3) a comprehensive New Teacher Orientation program.

New Teacher-Mentor Programs

Many school divisions have mentor programs focused on in-building peer mentoring. Peer mentors can share suggestions as to school policies, record keeping, managing nonteaching tasks, and some elements of classroom management. This type of mentor program is extremely important as often procedures vary drastically from school to school. Just as critical is the content specific mentor, in this case music education. Music mentors can offer a wide variety of support including program planning, lesson organization, and guidance as to appropriate literature that is "tried and true" for a successful first year. Support for curriculum implementation as well as the all important district festival preparation can be provided. The music mentor can become a lifeline for the first year music educator. Music mentors may also be critical in the area of evaluation. As an administrator, I am often asked to assist with new teacher evaluations. It is important for new teachers to have a confidant in a supporting role who is not involved in the evaluation process. It is dangerous for music administrators to attempt to serve as mentor and evaluator.

Administrative Support

As an administrator, it is my job to make certain that the lesson plan format, music education curriculum, and specific instructional strategies are clear and well defined for new teachers. I must also keep abreast of instructional programs being adopted so that I can correlate and assist teachers in formulating their lessons based on the goals of the individual schools. Providing exemplary videotaped lessons, concerts, general music programs, and superior festival performances can serve as a model for new teachers. Another critical need of new teachers is interaction with the music education staff as a whole. Monthly staff meetings can provide these invaluable opportunities. After the agenda is covered, which includes current instructional topics and practices, time should be provided for sharing ideas, materials, and small group conversation.

New Teacher Orientation Programs

Starting the first-year teacher off with a comprehensive New Teacher Orientation Program (NTO) is vital. This provides an opportunity to meet with new teachers and review curriculum, lesson plans, the annual events calendar, instrument rental and repair policies, and introduce the music mentors. This one-on-one time gives new teachers the opportunity to ask questions and talk honestly about their concerns. Included as part of the NTO session, distribution of an extensive packet of informational materials or a New Teacher Handbook will afford the new teacher the opportunity to review the complete information many times during the first month of school as they may be on overload at the conclusion of the NTO sessions.

Conclusion

Getting off to a good start is critical for the first year music educator and having a support system is key. Developing a three-strand support system, which includes a music mentor system, administrative support for instruction, and a comprehensive New Teacher Orientation Program can serve as the foundation for a successful first year teaching experience. Surviving the first year teaching music is quite a challenge; however, having a strong support system can provide the foundation to meet those challenges head on.

This article first appeared in the Winter 2003 issue of Virginia's VMEA Notes. *Reprinted by permission.*

Have you reached burnout yet?

 Section 10

Have you reached burnout yet?

Keeping that Enthusiasm Candle Burning Brightly
Jane Forvilly

OMEA officers were told during a visit to MENC headquarters this past summer that, "Forty-five percent of music teachers leave the profession within the first five years." Other research puts that drop-out rate as high as 80 percent after the first seven years (that may include some who will eventually return). That rather alarming diminution of our ranks prompted OMEA President-Elect Jim Howell to suggest a review of factors that (1) may cause our enthusiasm to flicker and prompt individuals to leave careers or that (2) might help keep the light of our enthusiasm burning bright and steady.

Targeted for this request: Graham Pinard, whose sixth year as band and choir teacher is "his best yet," and me—retired after thirty-two years, teaching mostly high school band and choir but also including adventures at middle school and elementary levels. This review is an attempt to organize thoughts on lessons learned in our own experience, integrate some material written on the subject (there's a lot), and share ideas generated from informal interviews with other music education retirees. None of this information exposed new revelations, but there was significant consistency in the information gleaned. It would seem useful, perhaps even healthy, for teachers periodically to consider their own activities and attitudes in relationship to the balance between constructive and destructive stresses and fulfillment in this career.

My candle burns at both ends;
It will not last the night;
But, ah, my foes, and, oh, my friends—

It gives a lovely light.
—Edna St. Vincent Millay

The Motif, Stress—Putting It in Perspective
Stress is a dynamic and useful aspect of our lives. In proportion, it motivates us to get to a task, to be attentive, and to strive for improvement. (Without it, some of us may never have worked through Arban's or Klose—trumpet and clarinet students, respectively.) In excess, it leads to discouragement and the abandonment of original goals, even after years of preparation and anticipation. That extreme degree of discouragement seems to be greatest in the caring professions: nursing, childcare, police, and education (within education, music has the greatest dropout rate). It is a problem for those who care the most and often may include those who are doing a good, perhaps exemplary, job.

Contributing Factors and Symptoms
The following, listed with minimal augmentation, are present in most recitations of factors that became discouragingly negative. Beyond the first three, they are not listed in any order of dominance.

- Administration—as reflected in lack of interest or feedback to students or teacher, scheduling decisions, budget allotment, goals for the music program, and quality of facilities.
- Overload—of student contact, assignment of classes, nonmusical activities, competitive events, age levels, buildings, music, and equipment.
- Disorder and management challenges—difficult or disinterested students, multiple room assignments, music equipment and materials, not enough time to keep order.
- Inadequate preparation—vocal or instrumental techniques when assigned outside of major emphasis area, class management, changing voice, special needs children … or you learn

that the pride of your new community is the school steel drum ensemble!

- Lack of balance between idealism and realism—it seems as if there are *no* students as enthusiastic about music as you were as a student, music is valued only as an activity, your hard work is never rewarded with feedback or appreciation, or nothing "beautiful" ever seems to happen.
- Isolation—you may be the only music person in the building, district, or town.

There should be a measure of consolation in recognizing that some of these challenges have been experienced by every teacher, and that periods of excessive stress are common to the job. However, when your response to these challenges becomes chronically negative, some unfortunate symptoms emerge:

- Physical and mental exhaustion—physical symptoms may include frequent headaches, backaches, or catching every virus. Fragile emotions may result in quick anger, shouting, spontaneous irritability, a cynical or critical attitude, sarcasm, or distancing oneself from students and staff.
- Uncharacteristic inefficiency—you seem to work harder and get less done, find it difficult to focus on a task and are easily distracted, or you succumb to habitual procrastination.
- Doubt with regard to your ability.
- Frequent faultfinding and complaining.
- Getting up and going to work is always a necessity—not positively anticipated.
- Dependency on favorite adult beverages or relaxants—disproportionate everyday rewards.
- Self-criticism—you don't like how you responded to incidents during the day.

Development of care and prevention themes: Music teaching is like a vigorous dance … with the tempo usually set at allegro! And on top of all that, there may be circumstances of our position that are negative. Some of these are beyond our control. A teacher must determine what those are, stop spending energy on them, and focus on the things that they can influence and that help make the job a pleasure.

1. Establish positive relationships with members of the administration, teaching and building staff, and parents and students.

- Regarding the administration: He or she is in the vulnerable position of being the "person in the middle." Treat them with care and respect. Follow procedure.

- Create informal opportunities for administration to be educated about your curriculum other than public performances.
- Don't be reluctant to seek their advice … that's part of their job.
- Avoid being so on-task that you become isolated in your own department. (This is important both for relations with the staff and with students.) Participate in some minor role, or at least be a spectator to other student activities. Eat lunch in the student lunch room at regular intervals.

2. Keep learning—outside sources.

- Attend professional workshops and conferences. Just one or two new ideas can fuel new enthusiasm.
- Maintain contact with your professional peers. Even if you can select all your new music from recordings, go to reading sessions for the personal contact. Take advantage of opportunities to talk shop with other music teachers. (The OMEA Mentor Program was established for that very purpose.)
- Discuss issues with a trusted colleague.

Keep learning—self-evaluation: Thoughtfully develop an inventory of the multitude of skills necessary for your job (arranging, improvisation, specific techniques, communication skills, housekeeping—the list is extensive). Rate yourself 1–5 in each category, identifying your professional strengths and where you need improvement. Target a few specific areas for development—personal remedial action is confidence building, energizing, and encouraging. Rejoice in your strengths.

3. Keep your focus on curricular goals, making music, and teaching. At the secondary level it is especially easy to get side-tracked into activity.

- Know what your curricular goals are—review and evaluate them regularly.
- Often, we are the author of our activity overload. Keep competitive and nonmusic events in perspective. Question whether that third festival or competition is of real value to the students or primarily for public relations and ego gratification. Be conscious of the effect of your own vocabulary—examples: winning, being the best, getting trophies.
- Evaluate: How does each day's activity relate to curricular goals and the welfare of the students; is it educational energy well spent? What did I teach today? What did we learn?

- Establish early a grading system with objective standards. Keep the students informed throughout the grading period—don't wait until the last week.
- Take time for variety in the curriculum. Include theory, history, multicultural music, and improvisation. Listen to exemplary performances—even if at the expense of more repetition and rehearsal that might be useful.

4. Celebrate the "positives." Take time to appreciate everyday accomplishments.
- Don't always be "fixing" something.
- Guide student appreciation of success—their own and that of others. You may have to point out a well-shaped phrase or a lovely combination of sounds.
- Include *all* your students. It's easy to focus attention and time on the gifted and enthusiastic students, or the difficult students, neglecting the quiet ones who just show up and cooperate. Regularly read through the class list questioning how and when you gave individual attention in some measure to each of those students.
- Schedule simple events such as "open-mike" days that give performance opportunities to students of all skill levels.
- Take time in concerts to educate the audience about the process or the music. Most of them may have no idea what your students are learning or accomplishing.

5. Discipline and order.
- In addition to a discipline plan for students, it is important to have a plan for the orderly organization of equipment, materials, and activities.
- Student discipline problems may be, in part, responses to things you can influence. Evaluate the consistency of your discipline policy application and the pacing, variety, and sequence of class activities.
- Be timely with office requests, reports, and applications.
- Deal with problems quickly. They just become aggravated with age.

6. Hang on—Plan on staying in a place for at least three years.
In that time, skills, confidence, understanding, and common goals for the role of music in education may develop. You may even gain the opportunity to influence some of those things that were at first beyond your control. If your situation is just impossible (and there are some that are), find a new job. Don't let that one experience be the measure of your entire career.

7. Take care of yourself.
- Give appropriate attention to exercise and diet.
- Pursue other interests. Personally learn something new every year. Professionally, when possible, vary your teaching assignment ... teach something new, such as a semester music survey class or guitar.
- Take time away from students ... and from sound saturated environments.
- Spend quality time with family and friends.
- Remind yourself of the good things that regularly occur. Keep a journal in which you note the high point of every day.

Coda
An affirmation of these general tenets is revealed in interviews with twenty-five experienced teachers. Uniformly, they felt they were better teachers after fifteen or more years, and they agreed on these factors:
- Their teaching became more student centered. Emphasis shifted from their career to what was best for students.
- Continued education and learning were most influential in their growth as teachers.
- There was increased emphasis on a healthy balance between professional and personal life.

This rewarding profession comes with multiple challenges and stresses. Identify those that are beyond your control and then turn your attention to other things that you can change. Don't try to fix everything at once. Focus on music making and being a joyful teacher. Most of your students and the people in your environment are eager to join with you in that pursuit.

Bibliography
Culietta and Thompson, (November 2000), "Voices of experience speak on music teaching," *Music Educators Journal*, p. 40.

Haack and M.V. Smith, "Mentoring new music teachers," ibid, p. 23.

Hamann and Gordon, "Burnout: An occupational hazard," ibid, p. 34.

Hornstein, Daniel, (October 1997) "Burnout—A danger for those who care too much," *North Dakota Music Educator*.

McManus, John, (1988) "Music teacher burnout," Workshop presentation."

Radi, Ann, (February 2000) "Burned out in only three years," *North Dakota Music Educator*.

Sandene, Brent, (unknown date) "Determinants and implications of stress among music teachers," *UPDATE:* *Applications of Research in Music Education*.

"Members speak out,"(August 2000) *Teaching Music*.

This article originally appeared in the Spring 2002 issue of the Oregon Music Educator. *Reprinted by permission.*

Burnout
Jan Morris

B–ewildered
U–nsupported
R–ejected
N–eglected
O–verworked
U–nderpaid
T–ense

It was interesting that the e-mail asking us to write about "burnout" for this issue of the *Indiana Musicator* came just days after a university student asked me how I avoided burnout. I'm sure she was wondering how anyone could be so old and still love her job!

High stress and burnout are hot topics in all of society today, and even children are facing high stress levels. Most people in jobs with high stress levels either witness or experience professional burnout. This is also true for music educators, who face stress daily and never have an off-season. For our classes, we plan and present lessons that meet the standards and proficiencies, search for new and better ways to inspire creativity and develop musicianship, and conduct before and after school rehearsals. We move from one performance to the next with little preparation time in between. We cannot forget to fill out requests for field trips and fund-raisers, to order paper and general supplies, address budget needs, attend teacher meetings, attend committee meetings ... the list goes on and on, often seeming to be unending. Is it any wonder that some music educators experience burnout?

How does the general music teacher figure in this problem? In addition to general music classes, many times the general music teacher also has one or more performing groups which add time to the work week whether they are in the competitive mode or focus on community performance. General music classes themselves are often expected to "perform " in programs throughout the year, which can detract from teaching effectiveness. To cover all the standards effectively demands hours of weekly planning. Adding in performance expectations for a general music classroom requires even more planning time that isn't included anywhere in the school day. Teaching general music is a full-time job without the added stress of performance.

Each of us can become exhausted just thinking about all the stresses in our day, week, month, and year. Music educators must be a hardy, hard-working bunch—we had to be just to get through college and survive our first few years of teaching. Music educators are known for trying to do too much and still expect perfection in each activity. What do we look for as a warning sign of burnout? According to Dorothy Largay, PhD, codirector of the Center for Professional and Personal Renewal in Los Gatos, California, "When you feel a distinct loss of energy and motivation and a sense of paralysis about what to do about it, you may be spiraling into burnout."[1] If you are feeling a loss of satisfaction in your teaching, then you definitely need to find personal and professional nourishment and replenishment. Music educators who have burned out state that they feel bewildered, unsupported, rejected, neglected, overworked, underpaid, and tense all the time. Talking with music educators who have left the field, the recurring theme seems to be a lack of support from parents and administration while always having to defend their program. Most of us are familiar with these symptoms. Now, how do we keep burn-out from happening to us?

• Attend conferences and professional development seminars. There are always sessions that will give you affirmation that you are a good teacher and what you are doing is good! There are sessions that will spark your creativity and get you moving in new directions or expanding the ideas you already have.

• Meet periodically with other music teachers in and out of your geographical area. Most of us are on an island by ourselves. We're the only music teacher in the building and no one really understands our schedule, our pressure, and the

public evaluations of every performance.
- Take a workshop or class in the summer, music or nonmusic, as long as it helps you grow personally and professionally. Read professional journals and stay current with what is happening in music and education today.
- Dr. John Henry Pfifferling, director of the Center for Professional Well-Being says, "Maintaining a powerful family and support mechanism can be one of your best anti-burnout strategies."[2]

My personal answer as to why, twenty-nine years into teaching, I still get excited about each new school year and each new challenge and haven't experienced burnout?
1. Faith and lots of prayer.
2. Family time (even when my kids are grown).
3. My love for music and wanting to share that love with the students I meet.
4. Professional contacts that encourage and challenge me.
5. Remaining active in professional organizations, attending conventions and workshops at all levels.
6. Personal assessment of my teaching and how I am meeting my goals.
7. Listening when my administration or a col-league has a suggestion or criticism. (This is the hard one!)
8. Trying to find new and better ways to teach while trying to improve what is good.
9. Realizing that I have a lot to learn and looking forward to the challenge!

Take time to reflect on your personal and professional life. Find all the wonderful things that have happened to you this year and reflect upon them. Do not let yourself be consumed by the negative situations that have happened and will happen. Move away from the negative or just go in your classroom, shut the door, and enjoy your students and making music. Then stop and ask yourself, "Do I love music? Do I want to share that love of music with my students?" If so ... keep on keepin' on!

Endnotes

1. Musick, Janine Latus. "How Close Are You to Burnout." *Family Practice Management,* April 1997.

2. Cooper Joel, R. *The Medical Reporter. 1993.*

This article first appeared in the March 2001 issue of the Indiana Musicator. *Reprinted by permission.*

Burned Out in Only Three Years?

Ann G. Radi

The same as many newly-graduated education majors, I anxiously awaited the start of my first teaching year with great anticipation, as well as a few butterflies! Believe it or not, I remember actually reviewing my music textbooks and practicing what I was going to say to my classes—really rehearsing it. I was leaving nothing to chance!

I was hired to teach elementary music in a small town in the Midwest. I had over five hundred students in my music classes, which met three times per week. My classes were twenty minutes each, except for sixth grade, which was twenty-five minutes. My day was full, with nineteen separate classes to teach in grades one through six. On top of that, I also taught music to the kindergarten classes.

My first big disappointment was on September 20 when my first payday rolled around. I will never forget the feeling as I looked at my first paycheck and thought, "I worked so hard teaching a whole month for this?" In fact, I was so disappointed, I cried. Don't get me wrong—I never planned to get rich teaching. I did think that I would be able to make a decent living after spending five years in college and earning a double major.

There were two major performances I was responsible for in that job—one at Christmas and the other in the spring. One was for K–3 and the other for 4–6. Each year, they rotated as to who had which concert (about 270 children were involved in each). Another big letdown came the night of my first program. The basketball coach couldn't begin to understand why he might consider moving his practice to another gym, so from 6 to 6:45 p.m. the janitors and I madly set up chairs. I was naturally upset, my arms ached, and I had to accompany my students in less than an hour. For each succeeding concert, it was always the same story. To say that this was discouraging is a *big* understatement.

We all know that stress can contribute to health problems. That was certainly the case for me! Chronic sore throats lead to vocal problems and Christmas vacation found me having my tonsils removed. (As an adult, I wouldn't recommend it.) A hospital nurse told me that they can easily see a difference between kids younger than five and those older. Needless to say, I was much older than 5! I didn't take the time at home to recover as I should have, and a week later I was back in school. This was a *big* mistake. Each day for several weeks was a struggle until I felt completely healed.

At the start of my second year, I felt I knew what I was in for. I saw hundreds of students each day. I remember a new boy in the sixth grade who was living in a foster home. As teachers, we had been informed about his background by the administration and social services. He had been through a lot and had a reputation for violence. This was obviously working on my mind, because one day, while we were playing a music game, I stood by his desk. As I was getting the flash cards ready, the unbidden thought came to me, "He won't know the answer and out of frustration, he'll punch me." I silently breathed a sigh of relief as I moved by his desk with my face still intact.

The Christmas program came and went. I decided to do the musical *Tom Sawyer* for the spring 4–6 grade program. Evidently, this was something that had never been done before in this community, because the public reaction was quite extraordinary. A volunteer sixth-grade choir was also added to my schedule. I was proud of this group, because we had nearly 100 percent participation. We'd sing at the nursing home or the Lions Club meeting or whatever. I now know that this was adding stress and taking time away from my personal life, but at the time I felt our choir members were "Ambassadors for Our School."

During my third year of teaching, seventh-grade general music at the high school building was added to my schedule in addition to everything else. The spring concert was bigger and better than ever because two classroom teachers and I decided to write our own musical celebrating the town's centennial. Though the other teachers were always very helpful with rehearsing, sets, or whatever else needed doing, it was still too much for me. By May, I was totally drained and resigned from my position, thinking, "I will never teach again. I just can't do this any more. I have nothing left inside me to give."

Sound familiar? In *A Nation Prepared: Teachers for the 21st Century,* a 1986 task force report on teaching as a profession, one of the conclusions drawn was that teaching is a high turnover profession (p. 98). Working conditions are awful. The typical salary schedule puts teaching at a huge disadvantage in competing with other professions for America's best students. Teachers are at the low end of the entire range of salaries for college graduates and the prospect for salary growth is dismal compared to other occupations. Teacher salaries start low and stay there. Most teachers reach the top of the pay scale within ten to twelve years and are stuck there. This is the time of life when their friends in other professions are just beginning to enter their prime earning years. It is understandable that half of all teachers leave the profession within seven years. Sadly enough, many of the teachers interviewed for the study emphatically said that they would not choose teaching if they were beginning their careers again (p. 31).

Paradoxically, the book *Take This Job and Love It! Making the Midcareer Move to Teaching* (1998) states that America badly needs talented, well-prepared, committed new teachers (p. 8). The authors estimate that over two million new teachers will be needed over the next ten years. There are not enough teachers training or high school students indicating an interest in education as a major to meet that need.

Why does this situation exist? Besides low salaries, various authorities cite different factors. Michael Huberman's book *The Lives of Teachers* (1993) states that the pupils themselves and how they react to the school and teacher are one of the major causes of teacher burnout. But personal or family events can also play a major role in teacher burnout. Evidence suggests that teacher burnout has a complex nature, with several different contributing causes (both in and out of the classroom).

In chapter 4, "Teacher Workload and Teacher Dropout" of *The Teacher Dropout* (1970), David Selden indicates that teaching does not seem like a difficult job to the average person (p. 61). To a nine-to-five production worker the hours look good and the breaks and summer vacation pretty appealing. Yet thousands of teachers are emotionally worn out by day's end, and every year many are driven from the classroom by overwork. Selden agrees with Huberman in that the causes of teacher burnout are many and include poor salaries and fringe benefits, frustration, and lack of social status. Since the workload of a teacher has a great deal to do with that teacher's success in actually teaching the students, an overloaded teacher is naturally a frustrated teacher. It is interesting to note that he points out that heavy workloads are a common indicator of "low status" in society.

In his book *Changing Teachers, Changing Times* (1994), Andy Hargreaves states that teaching can become a never-ending process of constant giving, much like the field of nursing (p. 148), which is another low-paid, heavy workload profession suffering high rates of burnout. He cites as an example the large bags of work many teachers carry home each night. But the good teacher feels obligated to take care of everything, for to leave work behind is to leave care behind, and with it the needs and interests of children. This is extremely difficult for committed, caring teachers to do. He goes on to say that in many cases, teachers' attitudes can descend into burnout, cynicism, and eventual exit from the profession.

In chapter 11, "Thinking and Teaching" from his book *To Become a Teacher* (1995), William Ayers explains that it is important for teachers to fight the isolation that is so common in teaching (p. 63). He says that teachers typically find themselves alone in a classroom with too many children and too little time—isn't that the truth? He found that when teachers do get the chance to talk to other teachers it is usually for less than a minute at a lunch break, typically not enough time to really create relationships or bolster each other's attitudes. Isolation can easily lead to disconnection, which then spirals rapidly down into burnout.

In chapter 6 of the same book, "A Teacher's Awesome Power," Mary Ann Raywid states that teachers don't see themselves as powerful figures (p. 78). She says that within school systems, teachers occupy the sub-basement of the pyramid, with everybody else in the system occupying a higher level. Department chairs, grade-level chairs, principals, supervisors, superintendents, test makers, textbook authors and publishers, state agencies, parents, and other community members as well as legislators, governors, school boards, and city council members all influence teacher behavior. So from the teacher's perspective, he or she is quite vulnerable and on the bottom rung of the power ladder. There were many times I felt that I was not treated as a professional, but as some low-level uneducated employee.

And yet the teacher is all-powerful in the life of a child. Raywid further states that teaching power is awesome with regard to the classroom environment. It is the teacher who decides whether students will be treated with respect or as a group to be controlled so they don't get out of hand.

For John Godar, an English teacher, 1985 was a bad year. First his father died. Two months later, his girlfriend left. Around the same time, he got a new principal who thought he was the greatest thing since apple pie and God's gift to the principal world. As a result, he became another burned out teacher. After teaching for twelve years, he felt he just wasn't accomplishing anything and left the profession. Yet he was still vitally interested in education. He decided to travel the country to listen to other teachers' views on education. His 1990 book, *Teachers Talk,* was the result of interviewing 282 teachers in ten different states working in over thirty different school districts. It is real life—his interviews are quoted word-for-word from teaching professionals and express their views of today's public education.

He states that every teacher is a tired teacher . . . every good teacher, that is (p. 41). He decided to keep track once of how many extra hours (in addition to and outside the regular paid school hours) he put in. One year he spent 565 hours on school work outside the regular school day. So much for those three months off during the summer.

Godar also states that the first reason teachers who had quit gave for leaving education wasn't the pay (that was in second place); the major reason they cited for walking away from the blackboard was administrators and "not being treated as professionals" (p. 96). His view is that many administrators treat teachers as if they're dealing with kids and are overly concerned with rules and paperwork. He tells the story of a teacher who he had planned to interview the following day. She was so afraid of administrative repercussions that she anxiously phoned and canceled her interview the night before. Naturally, he was disappointed. Think of the tales she might have been able to tell!

Another common complaint found by Godar is that working teachers are rarely listened to or asked for possible solutions to school problems (p.198). Obviously this is an ignored resource for America. As Godar says, "Who would know best?" Lack of input often leads to lack of control, which was another of the reasons he found for teachers becoming ex-teachers (p. 199).

Godar concludes that "our changing society," a less-caring society than past times, is one of the most obvious negative influences in our schools today (p. 144). He states that schools do not exist in a vacuum. Not only do schools reflect the society in which they exist, but also they have to deal with those very same problems of which they are a part. It is not enough, according to Godar, to say that it is a different world today than it was twenty years ago; it is a different universe!

Two books, David Hansen's *The Call to Teach* (1995) and *Schoolteachers in Twentieth-Century America* (1994) discuss similar problems. Hansen says that teachers cannot really know what their influence on students has been (p. 117). A teacher's words can influence a student fifty years later. No wonder some find teaching intimidating and quite overwhelming. William Ayers' essay in the latter book, "A Teacher Ain't Nothin' But a Hero:

Teachers and Teaching in Film," states that becoming an outstanding teacher, who may sometimes break the rules to go the extra mile if need be, for and with the kids, is quite difficult (p. 155).

What can be done about this situation? How do we deal with the constant hemorrhaging of gifted, dedicated, caring individuals from the profession? What can be done about the shortage of teachers in our own specialty (MENC reports that California was short three hundred music teachers and Texas four hundred for the 1998–99 school year), and in our own state (North Dakota was one hundred teachers, in all fields, short as of the second week of the 1999–2000 school year)? How about dealing with the issues of the lack of respect, poor pay, very little esteem, and family issues? How can a teacher help the students and society's problems that they bring in the school door with them? Of course, many of these problems are beyond the scope of an individual to fix.

However, for those that can be dealt with, Huberman recommends making a change in your life, searching for support within your own school, participating in new activities outside of school, taking a leave of absence, or just "hanging in there" (p. 258).

Hargreaves states that "teacher guilt" could be eased by reducing the restrictions and demands on them (p. 157). To do this, he suggests reconstructing the culture of teaching as well as stressing the need for working relationships to provide teachers with guidance and support. He also advises professional learning to involve teachers in setting goals while establishing "realistic limits" on what they can do.

Ayers tells about a new network of teachers in Chicago called "Teacher Talks" (p. 63). Some groups are based at a particular school, and others are cross-city, involving teachers who share common views. Each network is small, focused, and teacher-built. These networks are promising because they are built on the needs, experiences, and cumulative wisdom of the teachers themselves.

Hansen points out that even if we do not have much control over the events of our teaching lives, we have a great deal of control over how those events effect us. How you see yourself and your situation makes all the difference (p. 127). You can picture the cup as half empty or half full. This perspective will shape your life.

Finally, Godar believes that one of the most inexpensive ways to improve education would be to give the teachers a lot more control of it (p. 199). In this country, we have a lot of untrained amateurs who have never worked with kids in charge of our educational system—the local school boards. And education is often shaped by "ivory tower" university philosophers and theorizers who may have never been in an elementary classroom. It seems logical to have those people who really know be put in charge; this would certainly change the "fad of the month" model of education that we have been living with for the past thirty years.

To conclude my personal story: Within a year, the school where I had started my career hired two people for the position I had previously done all by myself. After taking a year off for further schooling (in a different field), I did resume teaching, but in the elementary classroom and not music. I enjoyed seven happy years there. Situations again drew me to music, and I taught another five as a music teacher. But it began to happen again; an added assignment here, an additional school building there, some major vocal problems building: I began to feel that burn-out feeling beginning to creep closer. Rather than crash and burn, I resigned to accept a classroom position in another school system hundreds of miles away.

Personal considerations and circumstances prevented me from actually completing the move, and I spent last year substitute teaching. I do plan to return to the field of education because I just can't imagine being anywhere else than with children. I believe our nation's greatest natural resource is our children. I want to be part of nurturing that resource in the most important vocation there is . . . teaching. After everything, I still want to be the teacher they'll always remember.

Sources and Recommended Reading

A Nation Prepared: Teachers for the 21st Century. The Report of the Task Force on Teaching as a Profession. Fourth Printing. The Carnegie Forum on Education and the Economy, 1986.

Ayers, W. (ed.) *To Become a Teacher.* New York: Teachers College Press, 1995.

Godar, J. *Teachers Talk.* Macomb, IL: Glenbridge Publishing, 1990.

Joseph P., and Burnaford, G., (eds.) *Images of Schoolteachers in Twentieth-Century America: Paragons, Polarities, Complexities.* New York: St. Martin's Press, 1994.

Hargreaves, A. *Changing Teachers, Changing Times.* New York: Teachers College Press, 1994.

Hansen, D. *The Call to Teach.* New York: Teachers College Press, 1995.

Huberman, M. *The Lives of Teachers.* New York: Teachers College Press, 1993.

Nathan, R., Staats, T., and Rosch, P. *The Doctor's Guide to Instant Stress Relief.* New York: Ballantine Books, 1987.

McQuade, W., and Aikman, A. *Stress.* New York: Bantam Books, 1974.

Rosenblum-Lowden, R. *You Have to Go to School ... You're the Teacher!* Thousand Oaks, CA: Corwin Press, 1997.

Stinnett, T. M. (ed.) *The Teacher Dropout.* Itasca, IL: F. E. Peacock Publishers, 1970.

Take This Job and Love It! Making the Midcareer Move to Teaching. Recruiting New Teachers, 1998.

This article first appeared in the February 2000 issue of the North Dakota Music Educator. *Reprinted by permission.*

Section 11

 Do you need encouragement?

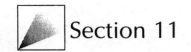

Section 11

Do you need encouragement?

Why I Teach, or What Else Is There to Do?

Eric Engebretson

When I first started teaching in Wolf Point several years ago, our school was going through an accreditation, and I remember the inquiry into my philosophy of music education. To tell you the truth, I don't have a clue what I spewed forth. Even though it was "flowery" and highly philosophical, I don't remember what I said! If asked that question today, I would probably threaten my school's accreditation by saying, "I teach because … well, … what *else* is there to do!"

There were some other alternatives, but I never pursued them to completion. My gracious wife and I traveled all the way to Champaign-Urbana, Illinois, so I might pursue a career in trumpet playing. I had all my trumpets: B flat, piccolo, C with a Herseth lead pipe, a gig bag, mutes, and stacks of solos and method books, ready to conquer the graduate world of trumpet playing.

I sat in a tiny little practice room for hours playing Marcel Bitsch (yes, that was his name and his exercises were, er … difficult) and orchestral excerpts, which lost a lot of entertainment value without an orchestra playing. On trumpet you play wildly and frenetically for five measures then you count. At least when the orchestra plays you can listen; in the practice room, it's not the same. Yes, I needed to practice my counting. That was one of my biggest weaknesses, especially when playing the *Magic Flute*, for which the music requires 250 measures of rest, then dominant and tonic—and you're done.

But what really sent me back to the students was when my best friend talked about trumpet articulation for forty-five minutes without stopping. He loved every minute of that one-sided conversation, while I would have much preferred to watch the Packers on TV.

Ranching could be in my future, though my in-laws haven't suggested it. I don't think they want to file bankruptcy. I have the idea: you need to think like a cow, but the problem is, I don't know how to think like a cow, much less get them to do anything I want them to do. Swathing was an interesting experience: I thought it was just like mowing your backyard with a giant mower. The levers, so many levers: one for the header, one to turn right, and one to turn left, one to start the cutting bar … there was so much to keep track of, I forgot about the alfalfa.

Fly-fishing is one occupation that has interested me. It is peaceful and calming, and I enjoy the challenge of catching a fish (sometimes more than one). Yet, my portable CD player is always getting caught in the brush, and it's just not the same without music to fish to—or did I fish just so I could listen to music?

Directing bands is what I'm hopelessly attached to. Like putting pants on in the morning, I don't really think about it, I just live it. I live for the moment the fifth-grade band plays "Big Rock Candy Mountain" the first time and they *love* it, even though it sounds like Arnold Schoenberg. Eventually the fifth-grade band plays "Big Rock Candy Mountain" all the way through and, of course, they want to do it again and again. I live for that.

I also live for the feel of a fresh full score, even though the beautiful sounds I imagine unfolding in my mind are shattered when the band sight-reads the piece for the first time. But gradually those pages of notes come to life after many hours of rehearsal; stopping and starting over and over again, checking this and that, sectional work, tuning this chord and correcting that note, all the while the baton communicates wordlessly, full of feeling and intent. I live for the moment the concert band tunes a chord just right or expresses the emotions that flowed from the baton and we all get goose bumps. Yes, I love goose bumps when music communicates emotion at a deeper level.

I remember when I was student teaching at a consolidated school in northeastern Iowa and my adviser asked me what I wanted to do as a teacher. I told him I was going to attempt to build great band programs to play great music and, in my arrogance (since I knew *everything* as surely as only a college senior can), I asked him, "Why do you suppose he (my supervising teacher) stayed so long is his position (a high school with about 160 students) when there was no potential for growth?" My college supervisor answered, "I believe he enjoys watching and being part of those individual students' lives. He likes kids, no matter how well or poorly they play." There weren't many more questions after that—even though true understanding hadn't occurred.

I still don't have words for why I teach, I just teach. There certainly aren't enough goose bumps, if I were in it strictly for the thrill of the goose bumps. And even my favorite fifth-grade bands love to play songs until I become overdosed with them. Yet, maybe I'm just like them—they just love to play over and over again, and I just love to teach over and over again because each time I become a little better and something inside of me gains a bit more fulfillment.

Why do *you* teach? That's a great Question!

This article first appeared in the January 1997 issue of Montana's Cadenza. *Reprinted by permission.*

How Do We Go from Competent to Good to Great?
Walter Kaweski

Music teachers tend to form themselves into the pyramid we see in all areas of human talent and human creativity. At the bottom are the bad ones. Most of them don't last too long. They learn that the profession was not meant for them and seek other work. Above them is where most of us dwell. These are the competent teachers. They are found at every level and discipline.

The next level is smaller. These are the really good teachers. These are the people we look up to. The excellence of their programs has little to do with the socioeconomic status of their school and community, and a lot to do with them. They know the tools of the trade and how to use the tools to bring out the best in their groups.

The next level is much smaller. These are the great teachers. Most of us have one or two of these in our lives. They are unforgettable. They are special. They changed us for the better. The lessons we learned from them transcended the subjects they taught.

Above them, above almost all of us, are the Leonard Bernsteins, Fredrick Fennells, Eugene Corporans, and John Rutters. They are the geniuses, gifted beyond our ability to grasp, let alone attain. They possess natural gifts of creation and divine insight. We are in awe of them and their work transcends the time they worked into the future where they influence generations of students and teachers.

I now come to the three points I most want you to gain from this article: The first is that good teaching consists of mastering the fundamentals of musicianship and acquiring the techniques that deliver your ideas to your performing group.

The second is that while it may be impossible to make a Bernstein out of a competent music teacher, it is possible, with lots of hard work, dedication, and timely help, to make a good teacher, perhaps even a great teacher, out of a competent one.

Third, teachers, regardless of their professional strengths and weaknesses, must possess integrity, passion, commitment, dedication, and love. A teacher who has a toolbox full of techniques to bring out the best musical result but lacks basic human love and respect is not a very good teacher. Great teachers love music and children. They have a toolbox full of techniques, yet they are driven by a love and concern for children.

What follows is what I have learned about good and great teachers from my twenty-seven years in music education. The advice I give to you comes from dozens of people I have learned from over the years. Some are famous: Eugene Corporan, Tim Lautzenheiser, Fredrick Fennell, Stephen Covey. Others are equally distinguished: Ron Jones, Tim Smith, Mallory Thompson, Robert Halseth, Craig Kirchoff, Gary Hill. If an idea I offer helps you, great! If not, forgetaboutit!

I love teaching and learning because of the potential for growth. Personal growth, ensemble growth, program growth. Every year we get to start over. Every year we have another opportunity to grow and learn from our successes and failures. Every year we have a chance to connect with our students in a way that impacts our lives and their's for the good.

I hope you love it, too. But if you're not willing to work hard, you have no business guiding young people. Find a new line of work. Music education has no room for slackers.

"Successful people do the things unsuccessful people are unwilling to do." If you want to be a good music teacher read, study, observe, listen, ask for advice, attend conferences, and enroll in courses. Broaden your life perspective by traveling and reading great literature. Dr. Robert Halseth, director of bands at CSU Sacramento, taught me the importance of reading beyond methodology. He turned me on to a great book that every music teacher should read: *What to Listen for in the World* by Bruce Adophe. Here's one of my favorite excerpts from this book:

Who is a true musician?
A true musician hears before doing. A true musician loves ideas better than systems.
A true musician feels before analyzing. A true musician discovers patterns everywhere.
A true musician connects anything to anything else.
A true musician enjoys the feeling of sound and the sounds of feeling.
A true musician plays through silences.
A true musician can find pulse in a single tone.
A true musician listens to lilt, accent, vowels, and consonants, not just words.
A true musician listens to the still, inner voice.

Students need more from you than course content and a grading system. They need to learn life's lessons. Music is your medium to teach them the lessons of life. Develop a breadth of knowledge to draw from to impact meaning.

If you teach a performing group, learn about the composition, the history surrounding the work and the composer's life and times. Music is a composer's response to his/her world. Inhabit that world and share what you discover with your students. Every musical work has its own lesson or lessons. Even bad compositions can teach, but don't waste too much time on musical junk food.

Good music teaches just like great literature does. Style, line, texture, thematic development, and nuance are available to you with great music literature. Being swept away by great musicianship is part of every music teacher's formation. You can't hope to impress someone by the force of your teaching and musicianship until it has been done to you.

Attend quality concerts, purchase quality recordings, and listen until the music becomes a part of you. I remember the love affair I had with the music of Richard Strauss. I listened to his tone poems for months without hearing any other recordings. I can hear in my inner ear that great horn solo in *Don Juan* as I write this article. Listen to the mediocre as well as the downright rotten, too. Such experiences help us recognize those qualities when they begin to creep into our own work and caution us to steer clear of them.

Spend a Saturday at a music festival on a day when you're not bringing a performing group. Sit with a note pad and jot down impressions of each group, the good and the bad. What contributes to the problems you hear? What could have been done differently? How would you improve the sound if the conductor handed over the group to you? What makes the next group so much better? Look for as many reasons as possible. What are the tangible things you can point to that contribute to the excellence of the group?

Attend honor-group rehearsals. Sit in the back and take notes. Some of the best techniques I've learned were picked up watching great teachers teach. Mallory Thompson, director of bands at Northwestern, was rehearsing the California All-State Honor Band. She needed a big sound from the low brass and wasn't getting it. She stopped the group and said: "A good day for my tuba player is when he loses all feeling in his fingers due to lack of oxygen from blowing so hard. If you're not there yet, best blow more air through the horn." What came out after that comment amazed me. From that point on, my groups played with a bigger, fuller sound.

Get your head out of the score and look at your group. I'm amazed at how many school music directors look down instead of up. The kids stare at their music and the director stares at his or her score. There's no chance for you to give expression and nuance to the music when no one is watching. The kids don't need a human metronome. They need you for entrances, tempo changes, and defining the musical structure through phrasing gestures. Try this. Give the group a downbeat and then stop conducting. Chances are they will stay close to tempo. Your job is to bring out the expressive qualities of the music, help with attacks and releases, and balance the texture … among other things!

Score study helps, and so do conducting clinics. After taking my first one, I realized that what I do at the podium does matter. My bands and choirs improved when I learned what to do beyond beating time and pointing. Your face can be a tool to coax expression out of your musicians. Start the year insisting that they watch you, but be prepared to give them more than the beat. If they look up and see you staring at your score beating time, chances are they won't look up again. Offer them something new and they will look up for direction.

Practice your conducting in front of a mirror. Videotape yourself during rehearsals and analyze your strengths and weaknesses. This can be very painful at first but do it anyway. The height of hypocrisy is the director who expects students to practice their parts before rehearsal but spends no time in score analysis, rehearsal planning, or conducting practice.

Buy this book: *The Modern Conductor* by Elizabeth Green. The book offers established and innovative techniques that will help you improve your conducting. I promise you, if you work through the conducting exercises in this book, you will be a better conductor and teacher.

Most of your teaching time should be spent making music, not talking or lecturing. Studies have shown that student attitude improves proportionately to the amount of talking the director does. The less talk, the more students enjoy the rehearsal.

If you must stop to correct, make it brief and succinct. Never, never, never put a student down in front of the group. Praise publicly, criticize privately. If you want to correct someone, refer to the section instead of the individual. Keep the rehearsal moving on a high note. Leave them wanting more.

Let the group hear professional recordings of the pieces they are working on. You've heard the saying "A picture is worth a thousand words." This also applies to music. There's nothing like hearing the development of a beautiful phrase. You'll accomplish a lot more in one listening than a dozen run-throughs.

Record your rehearsals and listen back. Students are more aware of their musical shortcomings than we think they are. Musical discrimination is a higher order learning objective. Start developing your students' ability to discriminate between good music making and bad music making. "A picture is worth a thousand words." Let them compare and contrast their recording to the professional version. Then work to reach that next level.

Remember to carefully criticize. When commenting, use what I call the "compliment sandwich." Start with a comment that is positive: "I'm really proud of how we made it all the way through without stopping." Then carefully interject the criticism where improvement is needed. "We could make it sound even better if we were softer during the pianissimo passages." Then finish with another compliment: "But wow were we expressive!"

Good teachers know their limitations. Whenever possible, bring in guest conductors and clinicians that can add to the student's knowledge. A fresh voice can help reinforce skills you have introduced.

If you teach instrumental music, all the best teaching in the world can be sabotaged by bad equipment. Insist that your woodwind students use good quality reeds, ligatures, and mouthpieces. I attended a clinic by Lorin Levee, principal first clarinet for the Los Angeles Philharmonic. He placed two clarinets on the table in front of us. One was his professional model. The other was a student model plastic clarinet with a standard mouthpiece, ligature, and reed. He played each in turn and obviously his professional model sounded far better. But now catch this. He switched mouthpieces, placing his professional mouthpiece on the plastic student clarinet with his special ligature and quality reed and placed the student mouthpiece on his clarinet. When he played his clarinet, it sounded more like the student model. But even more amazing was the sound that came out of the plastic student clarinet. By just placing his professional mouthpiece, ligature and reed on the plastic clarinet he was able to transform the sound into a vastly improved clarinet sound, near in quality to his professional model.

Do you want your students to sound great? Of course you do! Insist on using quality equipment. Treat reeds with respect. Insist that your students store them in a reed holder. Leaving the reed on the mouthpiece causes the reed to warp. When you blow across a poorly maintained reed, the sound becomes thin and fuzzy. Learn about the equipment and keep it in optimal shape.

Good technique and vast knowledge of music education is not enough. As a teacher you must be a person of integrity. Live by a code of behavior that reflects the best that humans can be. I know this sounds preachy but it's true.

I remember a lesson I was taught by one of my students that has always stuck with me. I was rehearsing my band and things were not going well. I was not in the best of moods. My personal life wasn't going that well, and I wasn't very respectful of my position on the podium. I blurted out "Damn it! You all need to listen!" The room got silent. The kids were stunned. I was out of character. My first flutist leaned back in her chair, looked up at me, and said "Mr. Kaweski (with emphasis) you are a teacher!" She made me realize the importance of dignity. I needed to be more than Walt Kaweski with all his human inadequacies.

"Mr. Kaweski you are a teacher!" Whenever I feel a bad mood coming on, I hear those words. Teachers are role models. No matter how tough it gets, remain dignified and professional.

Be responsible and set a professional tone in your classroom. Don't waste your students' time. If you expect the kids to be punctual, start class on time. Be prepared and ready to teach before the bell rings and, if possible, start early. Have everything you need ready and in place. Be enthusiastic and interested in them. Learn their names as soon as possible. Attend their nonmusical events whenever possible. They really love seeing you there! Remember birthdays and special occasions. If you learn of an accomplishment by one of your students, announce it in front of their class.

Clearly define your objectives and grading. Don't make exceptions unless you can defend your reasoning. Be available after school and at lunch. Contact their parents when they do something good. Return phone calls within twenty-four hours. If you make a promise, keep it. Never say "I forgot" or "Sorry about that." Every sorry you give lessens the respect they have for you. Say, "I'll try" less and "I will" more. Students, especially teenagers, are very perceptive. They pick out insincerity sooner then most.

Keep your life in balance. Make time for yourself! Line out days and evenings during the month that are family time or personal time. When you get the inevitable extra request, tell them you are already committed. And lastly, do what you do best and leave the rest for others. If you run a large program, delegate responsibility to your students and parents. There's no reason why you should sort music and stuff folders when a student librarian could do it just as well.

In addition to the books mentioned previously in this article, I recommend reading the following books. They offer insight beyond the limitations of this article. They will impact your personal and professional life. They are worth far more than the time you will invest reading them:
Tuesdays with Morrie, an old man, a young man, and life's greatest lesson by Mitch Albom
The Seven Habits of Highly Effective People—Powerful Lessons in Personal Change by Stephen Covey
The Joy of Inspired Teaching by Tim Lautzenheiser
The Art of Successful Teaching: A Blend of Content and Context by Tim Lautzenheiser

I leave you with this excerpt from *What to Listen for in the World* by Bruce Adophe:

- Best wishes for a successful year!
- To be musical is to love your work.
- Enjoyment is an aspect of learning.
- Enjoyment is an aspect of technique.
- Musicians never want to stop learning.
- Teach through music and your students will learn.

This article first appeared in the Fall 2002 issue of California's CMEA *Magazine. Reprinted by permission.*

I Can Perform, Therefore, I Teach!

Penny Meitz

To perform? Or to teach? That is a choice that many young musicians perceive they must make when choosing music as a career. Those of us who have chosen to combine these two paths have learned that a musician can be successful in both fields, and that experience and success as a performer enhance one's experience and success as a teacher. The old adage, "Those who can, do: those who cannot do, teach," is a myth, disproved time and again by teachers who perform regularly.

A performer must set high standards for him- or herself and work to meet them consistently. Likewise, a teacher must set high standards for students, challenging them to live up to their potential. Good teachers know how vital modeling is; what better way to walk the walk than by being active as a performer! Additionally, our own performance level is often impacted by our involvement in teaching in ways that are not always obvious.

Teachers who perform model many aspects of musicianship for their students. Reaching for high standards of performance and continually raising that bar is one of the most obvious. Another vital extension of this is communicating these standards and expectations in a supportive and positive way.

Several weeks after beginning a new solo piece, my high school violin teacher, Emily Austin, would usually say to me, "You are going to play this so very well!" She was a member of the first violin section in the Detroit Symphony (one of the few women in the orchestra in the 1960s), which only added to the import of her comments. This sincere, supportive expectation expressed by my teacher inspired me to live up to her standards, not out of fear, but from deep respect and the desire to not let her down. When I was performing as her student, I consciously wanted to be an illustration of her love of teaching and her success as a performer.

While I was still in high school, Mrs. Austin invited me to begin playing with the Detroit Women's Symphony. As concert master of that orchestra, she recommended several of her students to the conductor for membership. I was honored by the invitation to join DWS, with its roster made up of professional women musicians and community members. The experience of playing in an orchestra that my teacher played in was awe inspiring! For teachers, depending on our students to practice is a basic expectation for their success as young musicians. Most of us realize that many of our charges are also involved in a variety of other activities, from achieving high grades scholastically and participating in after school clubs and athletics to working part-time jobs in afternoons and on weekends. Practice is not always a high priority on a student's to-do list. Practicing what we preach is a terrific way to inspire students to redefine their priorities.

When teaching orchestra at a middle school, I required the students to turn in weekly practice reports as part of their grade. I posted my practice report every week as well. The students could see evidence of my commitment to personal performance skills, as well as an example of prioritizing and time management. They also were witness to those hectic periods when my practicing hit a slump and learned that the important thing is to resume your practice routine just as soon as possible.

For a full-time teacher, personal practice time is at a premium. While combining teaching and performance decreases the free time for practicing, it forces us to find more efficient ways to maintain technical skills and learn new music. How many of us play warm-up exercises with our students to warm-up ourselves? While doing this, we focus on the same details in our own playing that we ask our students to address. Practice time is precious! Remember when it seemed an endless chore?

The analysis skills that most good teachers develop are often forged as we work on our own musicianship. These skills mature and become second nature as we apply them to our students. The same idea applies to aural skills. I know I am not alone in experiencing the honing of my ear as I listen more and more critically to my students and myself. The more I listen, the more I am able to discern, and visa versa.

One important aspect of musicianship that our students grapple with is dealing with performance anxiety. As an active performer, a teacher is often better equipped to help prepare students for the stress of auditioning and performing. Counseling and consoling those students who feel they fall short of sometimes unrealistic self-imposed standards is perhaps even more important. Teachers who perform put it on the line every time they are in front of an audience. Students know their teacher is speaking from experience, and that can be comforting to many young people.

This article first appeared in the Fall 2001 issue of Texas's TMEC Connections. *Reprinted by permission.*

Ten Tips for Greater Job Satisfaction
Karen A. Miyamoto

There are many of us who at times wished for greater job satisfaction, a better boss or principal, better peers to work with, better students, an easier job load, more preparation time, fewer meetings, and an overall feeling of loving your job day in and day out. Here are ten tips that may lead to greater job satisfaction if any of the above apply to you.

1. Have an attitude of thankfulness.
A thankful heart is a happy heart. There is an old saying: The glass is either half empty or half full. You may think you are in an unpleasant job situation (which may very well be), but seeing the good side of it can change your perspective. Instead of saying, "I have to go to work," you might say, "I get to go to work. I am thankful to have a job." Instead of saying, "I have to work with those students," you might say "I get to work with those students and make a difference in their lives." Instead of saying, "I have to go to the rehearsal," one might say "I get to go to the rehearsal, and I am thankful that I have the skills to do it."

2. Learn to be content in whatever state you are in.
Be satisfied to the point where you are not disturbed or disquieted. It is human nature to always want more—more pay, more funds, more students in your program, etc. While it is good to strive for the better, we should also learn to be content even if we do not get it. Most of us will never get all that we want, so we might as well learn to be content when we live in abundance as well as when we live with the minimum.

3. Enter into a state of rest.
When something goes wrong, instead of getting upset, enter into a state of rest. Finding rest, relief, ease, refreshment, recreation, and quiet for your soul means finding freedom from mental activity. It means not having to constantly try to figure out what you should do about everything in your life. We can overcome many of the obstacles in our lives by simply refusing to become upset over them.

4. Do not rely on others.
When we expect things from people who are not able to give them to us, we always end up disappointed and hurt.

5. Keep balance in your life.
Take time for recreation, work, hobbies, family, etc. It will make us all better people.

6. Remember that this too shall pass.
If we are ever going to have stability in our lives, we must quit looking for one thing that will be "it." We must recall that life is a continual process in which everything is constantly changing—including ourselves. Adversity makes us stronger people.

7. Do not depend on what others think of you.
It does not matter what people think of us. Our weaknesses and inabilities do not matter. We will never be happy if we are always trying to impress others. There will always be someone who is critical of you. Remember that each one of us has a special talent, gift, and ability.

8. Learn to be humble.
Be free from pride and arrogance. Pride and arrogance prohibit us from improving ourselves.

9. Continue to learn.
Fresh ideas will produce fresh results in our teaching and student learning. Some teachers may go through their entire careers without ever learning something new. Let's face it, no one will ever know all that there is to know about teaching music and student learning. The fact is, the more you know, the more you realize how much you don't know. Take some classes, go to the HMEA State Conference, and exchange ideas with your peers.

10. Know why you teach.
It is easy to become sidetracked from your original purpose for teaching, whatever it may have been. Stick to your purpose. If you went into teaching to help foster music learning, remember that when your students don't always perform or behave the way you want them to. You may have to reevaluate why you are teaching to prevent burnout.

This article first appeared in the July 2002 issue of Hawaii's Leka Nu Hou. *Reprinted by permission.*

Essential Parts of Musical Training

1. illuminating teachers; 2. motivated students 3. involved parents; 4. administrative support; 5. legislative action; 6. adequate funding; 7. love of music; 8. public appreciation; 9. performance opportunities; 10. industry support; 11. early childhood music programs; 12. up-to-date textbooks; 13. well-attended concerts; 14. strong secondary school music; 15. challenging curriculum; 16. extraordinary college and university education; 17. well-tuned instruments; 18. musical scholarships; 19. multicultural traditions; 20. ear training; 21. educational research; 22. jazz studies; 23. marching bands; 24. sound and recording equipment; 25. community bands; 26. civic symphonies; 27. choir groups; 28. interactive software; 29. vibrant elementary school music; 30. well-maintained facilities 31. practice rooms; 32. creativity; 33. good embouchure; 34. guest artists; 35. awards and recognition; 36. financial compensation; 37. musical theatre productions; 38. folk traditions; 39. sight reading; 40. recruiting great teachers; 41. chamber groups; 42. wind ensembles; 43. historical perspective; 44. modern innovations; 45. good posture; 46. time management; 47. band uniforms; 48. opera; 49. digital music technologies; 50. extensive music library; 51. internet resources; 52. music for special learners; 53. music theory; 54. basic piano; 55. solfeggio; 56. scales and modes; 57. instrument repair; 58. musical mentors; 59. patience; 60. passion.

This illustration first appeared as the cover of the February/March 2000 issue of California's CMEA *Magazine. Reprinted by permission.*

Planting for the Present and Future
Vicki Portis

I was enjoying a moment of quiet reverie before the opening bars of the concert when my friend Jane nudged me and said, "Turn to page 44 in the program. There is something you can use in your newsletter article." This is what I read:

An old man was planting a carob tree by the side of the road when a young man passed by. "Why do you plant a carob tree, old man? Don't you know carob trees take years to bear fruit and you will be surely gone by then," said the young man scornfully. The old man smiled thoughtfully and said, "Ah, but you see, I don't plant for myself, I plant for those who come after me."

Have you ever been asked why you teach elementary music? More importantly, have you asked yourself this question lately? Each child has tremendous potential for musical growth. No, they may not all be able to sing the best or play the best, but we can plant the seeds to help them creatively express themselves musically. We elementary music teachers have the privilege of bringing out and developing the latent musical abilities in our young students.

What a joy to see the wonder in their eye when "the light clicks on." Not only do we help them develop skills, but also we help them develop an appreciation of music of different cultures and styles. We help them develop critical thinking skills as they analyze and create their own music. The world of music becomes filled with endless possibilities.

Planting is followed by nurturing. Children need to be encouraged, guided, and challenged to develop their musical potential. The more success they have in their musical experiences, the more they apply themselves and the more they want to learn. Truly, success breeds success.

What you do does make a difference. In addition to the research which shows that music benefits cognitive brain development, you are touching the life of each child with knowledge and experiences that can enrich the rest of his life. The results of the seeds you planted probably will not manifest its fullness in the present, but your influence will be lasting.

Is your labor of planting, watering and nurturing worth it? Absolutely!!!

This article first appeared in the October 1998 issue of Alabama's Ala Breve. *Reprinted by permission.*

The Teacher-Musician
Steven Sudduth

Teaching instrumental or vocal music requires the utmost dedication to the craft of one's applied area. Only serious musicians are able to increase a community's musical environment. Within this environment lies the creative aspect that compels others to learn and mature musically. A musician will not learn essential musical values from text materials, but rather from the experience of performance etiquette. It is not what one knows, but what one demonstrates. Teaching is showcased, and learning takes place, at this level.

The teacher-musician's life is absorbed in music. Anything less is hypocritical. Students learning to teach music must absorb all aspects of the music profession. Future directors study their trade and continually develop a music curriculum tailored to their own individual teaching philosophies. Anything less welcomes failure—anything more welcomes success.

A teacher-musician is aware of their surroundings and has the capacity to alter a musical environment toward effective learning. This capacity lies within a person's depth of knowledge in performance. A strong teacher-musician has a greater ability to recognize the necessity of change and the ability to offer higher expectations to other musicians than an instructor who is weak musically.

A person must remain vigorous toward performance and therefore must continually practice in order to achieve a higher standard. Ignorance is no excuse. A strong student-musician seeks answers. A strong teacher-musician expects answers. Little is learned when an answer is given without discovery on the part of the student. Little can be taught to those who do not seek it. A strong musician is an advocate toward the unknown and, therefore, offers questions toward discovery. The teacher-musician is this kind of person. Performing music is for those who wish to do so. Teaching music is for those who love to do so.

This article first appeared in the December 2001 issue of the North Dakota Music Educator. *Reprinted by permission.*

Reflections

Jerry Ulrich

Reflect for a moment on your teaching. Ask yourself the following questions:

- How many cultures have my students experienced through the music they have heard and sung?
- How many texts have they studied?
- What are the sources of the texts? Have they studied the authors and learned the translations?
- Have I asked them how the music and/or text of what they are singing speaks to them?
- Have they studied both sacred and secular texts?
- How much modern music have they experienced?
- Have they created music and sung/played their own compositions?
- Do they sight-read at every rehearsal?
- Do they listen to recordings?
- Do I assist them with "guided listening"?
- Are they developing critical listening skills?
- Have I recorded a rehearsal, played the tape, and asked for the students' critical assessment?
- Do I stop upon occasion in rehearsal and ask the students "What is wrong with that?" "How do you fix it?"
- Have I asked what music they listen to?
- Have I asked them to bring in copies (both written and audio recordings) of "their music" for me to hear?
- Have we laughed together in rehearsal?
- Have we cried together in rehearsal?
- Have I told them what they do well?
- Have I asked them to listen to the sounds they are making?
- Have I listened?
- Do I speak to the chorus in a musical language?
- Have I worked at building "community" in my classes and ensembles?
- Have I attended a professional concert lately?
- Have I offered my students the opportunity to attend a professional concert?
- Have I attended an NYSSMA, MENC, ACDA, or similar professional conference lately?
- Have I developed professional colleagues with whom I may exchange ideas and find solutions to common pedagogical problems?
- Have I sought out a mentor?
- Have I been a mentor to new teachers?
- Have I incorporated life lessons within the music and rehearsal?
- Do I embrace and encourage disagreement and differing opinions?
- Do I encourage questions from the students?
- Must I have all the answers?
- Am I comfortable with the notion that sometimes "there is no answer?"
- Do I foster critical thinking?
- Am I a role model in the way I write, act, talk, dress, respond, and behave?
- Am I concerned more about product or process?
- How much time and thought do I give to selecting repertoire and curriculum?
- Do I realize that my students' musical world and pedagogical training may be only as large and as well crafted as the literature and training I offer them?
- What will they remember about my classes/rehearsals ten years from now?
- Am I able and willing to teach "in the moment"?
- Do I encourage cooperation or confrontation?
- Have I asked how many cultural backgrounds are represented in my classroom?
- Have we, as a class, openly embraced and explored the music of those cultures?
- Have I as a composer/performer created in the past year?
- Have I shared those creations with my students so they see me as a living, practicing artist, and not simply a repository of factual information?
- Do I remind my students (daily) that they each possess a talent/gift which is unique to them as individuals, and that it is their life's purpose to discover that gift and bring it to fruition?
- Do I convey a genuine concern for my students as individuals beyond their musical and academic contribution?

We can teach our students either:
- Our answers to our questions, or how to question for themselves.
- How to memorize and regurgitate, or how to think creatively.
- That discipline is imposed from without, or developed within.
- For the moment, or for life.

We can either allow our students to become our disciples or become themselves.

This article first appeared in the March 2002 issue of New York's The School Music News. *Reprinted by permission.*

Appendix

MENC Position Statement: Alternative Certification

MENC Position Statement: Alternative Certification

Position Statement: Alternative Certification
June 5, 2003

Concerns

MENC: The National Association for Music Education has observed that alternative routes to teacher certification vary significantly from state to state and in quality and rigor. Alternative certification programs that take advantage of the unique strengths of prospective teachers from nontraditional educational backgrounds can be an important path for individuals to gain entry into the teaching profession and for schools to recruit motivated, talented individuals for teaching positions that would otherwise go unfilled.

However, alternative certification programs must prepare prospective teachers to meet the same rigorous standards established for college and university trained music educators. Regardless of the certification that music educators receive, MENC believes that knowledge and skills in music are absolutely essential and that without them, music teachers will not be successful and the musical education of the students they teach will be impaired.

The rationale behind alternative certification was to provide a short-term and immediate solution to the teacher shortages that are occurring in many states and in many curricular areas. The intent was to make it easier for people without teaching degrees to become teachers and to do it more quickly, without going through a four or five year college or university education program. This "quick-fix" approach, however, has the potential of being detrimental to overall teacher quality, depriving children of the right to be taught by competent, qualified, and caring music teachers.

Mentoring programs are often part of an alternative certification program. This is consistent with the "No Child Left Behind" Act of 2001.

MENC believes that for the mentoring experience to be meaningful and of value, the mentor must be an experienced music teacher with proven successes in the same music specialty area, i.e., band, choir, general music, or orchestra, as the teacher being mentored. In small school districts where there is only one music teacher, mentoring programs may require cooperation with a neighboring school district. However, when the quality of students' education is at stake, no cooperative effort is too great.

Mentoring is a professional obligation and responsibility of experienced music educators, similar to serving as a cooperating teacher in the traditional student-teaching experience. Mentoring is a professional service vital to the success of the prospective teacher receiving the assistance and to the continued growth of the music education profession. Furthermore, MENC believes mentors should be adequately compensated either in release time or in the form of a supplemental stipend for this service. Release time can be provided by the mentor's school district. Supplemental stipends can be provided either by the state's certification or licensing agency that determines the rules and regulations for alternative certification or by the school or district in which the prospective teacher is being served by the mentor.

The Music Educator's Role

The "No Child Left Behind" (NCLB) Act of 2001 mandated that public schools have highly qualified educators teaching every class in core academic subjects by the end of the 2005–06 school year. Because music is identified in NCLB as one of the core academic subjects and there is already a shortage of music teachers, legislators, higher education officials, and local school district officials have expressed an increased interest in, as well as concerns about, alternative certification.

This interest is shared by individuals from non-music-education backgrounds, such as people from other careers or the military, liberal arts graduates, and early retirees, who may wish to become music educators. Concerns are shared by practicing music educators and professors in higher education who teach music education courses.

The roles of the established music educator—and the music educator trainee—include those of interested observer and concerned participant. The first role calls for being informed and aware of alternative certification developments in their state. The second role involves a willingness to participate in the preparation of alternatively trained teachers that meets the standards of knowledge, performance, and quality expected of college and university-trained members of the profession. The third role is related to the second in that the established music educator should be willing to serve as a mentor to the alternatively trained music teacher. Serving as a mentor can be challenging and rewarding. It is seen as a professional obligation similar to serving as a cooperating teacher to student teachers.

NCLB regulations require that teachers hired through alternative certification must receive "high quality professional development that is sustained, intensive, and classroom-focused in order to have a positive and lasting impact on classroom instruction, before and while teaching; participate in a program of intensive supervision that consists of structured guidance and regular ongoing support for teachers or a teacher mentoring program; assume functions as a teacher only for a specified period of time not to exceed three years; and demonstrate satisfactory progress toward full certification as prescribed by the state." The regulations also clarify that the final end of teacher certification should be to "enable all students ... to meet the State's academic standards."

The tenor of these regulations is that professional development, supervision, and structured guidance should be delivered in a way that is consistent with reaching the teaching goals set out in the states' standards. This strongly implies, and MENC strongly recommends, that most of this mentoring must be delivered by individuals with acknowledged expertise in the field of study—most logically by colleagues. For prospective music teachers, this means another music teacher who is experienced and acknowledged by peers as outstanding. During their first three years those with an alternative certificate should be observed a minimum of three times in the first year and two times in each of the next two years. These observations and the post-observation feedback conferences should be done by an outstanding experienced music educator colleague.

Guidelines for Music Educators

- Exemplify for all music students your own respect for teaching and for future teachers.
- Encourage graduates who are already teaching to continue and encourage those who have left to return.
- Support your colleagues in their individual professional development activities.
- Insist upon comprehensive—and comprehensible—standards for alternative certification.
- Regardless of their certification, volunteer to mentor new music teachers.
- Hold alternatively certified teachers to the same standards of teaching excellence to which traditionally certified teachers are held.
- Accept alternatively certified music educators who become competent, quality, caring teachers as fellow professionals and colleagues.
- If you see flaws or oversights in the music teacher certification process, speak up through your state MEA, to your state's board of education, and to the state or local legislative body that determines alternative certification regulations.

For Music Supervisors and Administrators

- Contribute to the development of regulations for alternative certification using research-based information whenever possible.
- Endorse quality programs that have been specifically designed to recruit, prepare, and license talented potential teachers.
- Look for alternative certification candidates who have undergone rigorous screening that includes tests, interviews, demonstrated mastery of content, and actual classroom teaching experiences.
- Provide individualized support and mentoring by outstanding experienced music educators to alternatively certified candidates in music education positions.
- Match hiring policies and practices with community expectations and district goals.

For Prospective Music Educators

- Look for programs that are field-based. These programs should offer course work or equivalent experiences in professional education studies before and while you are teaching and offer intensive experience with trained mentor music teachers in their classrooms.

- Look for selective admissions standards—a baccalaureate degree in music, and assessment of your subject matter competency, personal characteristics, and communication skills.
- Seek a curriculum that provides you with the knowledge and skills you will need to help students reach the state's music education standards. Of particular importance are comprehensive music pedagogy courses.
- Expect to learn a wide variety of approaches to student learning and to use a wide variety of instructional strategies that will positively affect student learning, especially in the areas of critical-thinking, problem-solving, and performance skills.
- Look for a supervised internship under the direction of an experienced, outstanding music educator.
- Expect that your teaching competency will grow and be assessed using an array of techniques, including observations of you teaching in your classroom.
- Expect to meet high performance standards for completion of your program.
- Do not let any "shortcuts" compromise your training experiences and jeopardize the quality and effectiveness of your teaching.
- Expect to be held to the same competency standards as traditionally certified music educators.
- Know the difference between alternative certification and emergency certification.
- Seek the support and assistance of college and university music faculty, experienced music teachers, building administrators, and your peers.

For All
- Regardless of your certification, invest in self-evaluation and continuous professional development, growth, and improvement.
- Regardless of the program followed to obtain music certification, the education and training of prospective music educators should involve the cooperative efforts of the prospective teacher, current music educators and supervisors, school administrators, and music education professors in higher education.
- Become involved in establishing music teacher preparation and evaluation standards, designing and delivering preparation programs, recruiting and selecting music teachers, and developing criteria for assessing music teacher qualifications, content area knowledge, and teaching effectiveness.
- Focus on student learning and achievement. Regardless of how a person has qualified to become a music educator, his or her role is to help students achieve the knowledge and skills included in the national, state, and local standards for music education.

Other MENC resources for new teachers and those that encourage, train, and support them

Teacher Success Kit: How to Succeed in Music Education (CD-ROM). Updated 2002. #3101.

Promoting the Profession: Recruiting and Retaining Music Teachers (brochure). Set of 20. 2000. 4 pages. #4009.

TIPS: Discipline in the Music Classroom. Compiled by R. Louis Rossman. 1989. 32 pages. #1095.

Syllabi for Music Methods Courses, 2nd ed. Edited by Barbara Lewis. 2002. 262 pages. #1052.

Exploring Careers in Music, 2nd ed. 2000. 148 pages. #1051.

How to Nail a College Entrance Audition (brochure). Set of 20. 2002. #4025.

Great Beginnings for Music Teachers: Mentoring and Supporting New Teachers. Edited by Coleen M. Conway. 2003. 220 pages. #1674.

Strategies for Teaching Series. Each volume focuses on a specific curricular area and a particular level with teaching strategies based on the National Standards.

The Grandmaster Series: Collected Thoughts of Leaders in Twentieth-Century Music Education. Edited by Mark Fonder. 2003. 92 pages. #1681.

Classroom Management in General, Choral, and Instrumental Programs. Marvelene C. Moore with Angela L. Batey and David M. Royse. 2002. 52 pages. #1027.

Online resources
www.menc.org

A host of music education experts are contributing to MENC's online network communities for band, orchestra, chorus, and general music throughout the year. MENC members can post questions and review responses.

"Careers in Music" is a collection of online resources designed to help students, parents, teachers, and all those curious in discovering the many possibilities of this field. (Click on Jobs, then Career Information.)

For complete ordering information on these and other publications, contact:

MENC
Publications Sales
1806 Robert Fulton Drive
Reston, VA 20191-4348

Credit card holders may call 1-800-828-0229